What Pric

Memoir of Eugene E Adams

Dorothy A Adams

© 2017 by Dorothy A. Adams

All rights reserved.
Published in the United States by

Bone It Publishing
Donna, TX

www.boneitpublishing.com

ISBN: 1519411758
ISBN-13: 978-1519411754

Library of Congress Control Number: 2017905204
Create Space Independent Publishing Platform
North Charleston, SC

First Edition

What Price Honor, Memoir of Eugene Adams

INCREDIBLE picture was taken in <u>1918</u>.

It is <u>18,000 men</u> preparing for war in a training camp at Camp Dodge, Iowa.

STANDING TALL Titled "Human Statue of Liberty," this image was taken at Camp Dodge in Iowa and used eighteen thousand men.

Dorothy A Adams

DEDICATION

My father, Eugene E. Adams, gave me a direct order to get this memoir in order and published. This occurred less than a week before his death. It is his first-hand account which was recorded in a manuscript he had prepared in the early 1970s. I had read it and discussed it with him multiple times, and though it has been lost, I remember it well. As a child I had listened to him and my uncles, Wallace S. Patterson (Scott) and Joel Parrott, discuss WWII, and later the Korean Conflict, when they would sit around the kitchen table at my maternal grandmother's home. Uncle Scott was in the USAAF, and would continue service in the Korean Conflict, ultimately retiring with over 20 years of service. Uncle Joel served in an artillery unit, but did not continue with the Army after his discharge. Sometimes my Great Aunt May, also a WWII veteran, would join them. She retired after 20 years of service. In addition to those early influences, my father talked with me all my life about his lifelong experiences, beginning those discussions when I was a toddler. It was said then that if he stopped quickly, I would run into him. I learned about events leading up to, percolating through, and after all these conflicts, because his knowledge of history and geopolitics was encyclopedic. He died while I was in Japan on maneuvers, and a Japanese General gave the most beautiful eulogy in honor of a fellow warrior that I had ever heard.

This book is a serious discussion of events leading up to WW I, WW II, the Korean Conflict, Viet Nam, Cambodia, Laos, and conditions that will lead inevitably to WW III, for war has traditionally been an extension of geopolitical ambitions of power structures throughout the habitation of this planet since the beginning of time. The Bible is a documentary of conflict, starting with Adam and Eve, their sons, and literally eons before the birth of Jesus Christ.

Part I – Everything has a Beginning

Chapter One – In the Beginning

<u>What Price Honor</u> is written in commemoration of warriors, in memory of my father, and is largely taken from a manuscript that he wrote just prior to his death. It began with the birth of Eugene Edward Adams on 18 December 1918 to Fred Dewey Adams and Edna Ellen Crouch, and their simultaneous marriage on that date. Dorothy A. Adams, MD, Ph.D., MS V

I am Eugene Edward Adams, born on the 18th of December 1918, in Elkhart, Indiana, to young parents on the simultaneous date of their marriage. I am a WW II veteran, and part of the Occupation Forces following that conflict. During the Korean Conflict, I served briefly until I was forcibly retired from US Army Active Duty as a Captain, due to injuries previously received. I walk with a limp, and am blind in one eye, but still fail to understand why I cannot serve still, for my knowledge base might help save young soldiers when the next World War breaks out, and it will. I was allowed to remain in the US Army Reserves for that purpose. My chosen field of expertise is world political geography, and I still remain current to the extent that is possible. A quotation from Plato is appropriate at this juncture:

"Only the dead have seen the end of War." - - Plato

The conflicts throughout history have not often recorded the effects of conflicts on those who support those who go forward to prosecute the conflict. Their thoughts and worries, along with privation from war change them significantly. When the loved one comes home, it is not the same place they departed from. Those at home have served, too, and the changes they have undergone are significant and often disruptive to previous relationships. I am told that my father went into the Navy during WW I, but since our family was what was called a "broken home," I had little contact with him in the post war years, after he returned from war. But I shall content myself with relating the conditions leading up to, and following that bloodiest of all wars. Then, I shall relate my own experiences in the aftermath of it which, 20 years later was called WW II.

In my thoughts and deliberations, I have concluded that Plato was right. For centuries, societies have arisen, and when the question of when the Hand of God will strike them down, I believe there is no need for Him to do that. Man has invented the very thing that will destroy him, again and again. It is called government. The only reason for defeats we have suffered or may suffer will come from that invention of our own. Wars, as we all know, are simply extensions of politics, when their convoluted methodology has been unsuccessful in meeting their goals. Conflicts are prolonged by political interference in the execution of military strategic objectives. Harnessing of General Patton by those with political agendas is a prime example of the interference in military operations. The Germans actually feared the unleashing of Patton, but he was held back for purely political reasons. Then he was mysteriously murdered at the end of WW II. I have always believed that it was done by agents of Joe Stalin, so his excellence could not be again unleashed.

But what was the world like prior to WW I, which resulted in trenches being dug literally across the entire European Continent? It has been nearly 100 years since the outbreak of what was called the War to End All Wars, or the Great War. Most of the veterans of that conflict have died, but many thousands died during it. In the outbreak of WW I, the entire continent was wrenched and the fabric of what had been a time when people of most of the world enjoyed and increasingly similar culture was ripped to shreds. What went on in the pre-WW1 years? The arts flourished. Operas and symphonies were written, and enjoyed, and literature, with authors like Zola, Hugo, Dickens, Tolstoy and the classics, was revered. In essence, Christian Europe was a coherent cultural entity among the educated classes. One could say it was essentially international, with the last significant ground war having been concluded in 1871 (Franco-Prussian War), and the Ottoman Empire had virtually collapsed from within. However, since that time, the European countries had remained heavily armed and all countries had and maintained armed forces.

And what do armies and navies do while "peace has broken out?" Well, they think up new and better ways to kill an enemy, should they have one. Smaller conflicts had to suffice in the interim, and those did occasionally occur. The improvements in and the mechanization of industry offered magnificent new options. The minds of soldiers everywhere, including the United States, teemed with new ideas. Arsenals and weaponry were modernized, and often motorized. Tanks were literally invented then. Ammunition and even artillery pieces were significantly modernized. It would be the end of warfare as previously conducted. The planners were busy, too, and wasted no time developing things like the Schlieffen Plan, which would be implemented during WW I. The British were quite active with expanding and improving their navy, which was at the time superior to all others in the world. There were also shifts in leadership among the 'great powers,' which would impact the interlude of peace. New alliances were being formed, and the greed for more territory and power still percolated in the capitals of nations. Britain was jealous of her enormous empire and powerful navy. France was humiliated because of her defeat in 1871. Franz Josef had assumed leadership in Austria, but was no longer a young man. He ultimately was to finish his 67 year reign at age 86. His heir had been designated, Archduke Franz Ferdinand, a nephew. Kaiser Wilhelm II had replaced Frederick III as emperor of Germany. King George V was king of England, having taken over in 1910 from his father. Tzar Nicholas was the young leader of Russia. Oddly enough those last three were first cousins and grandsons of Queen Victoria. Poincare and Clemenceau had come into power in France. President Wilson was the Commander in Chief in the United States. The kettle of war was bubbling, and would erupt on 28 July 1914 and the era of trench warfare began. As many of us old enough to have benefitted from good educations know, the trigger was the murder of Archduke Ferdinand and his wife, Sophie, in Sarajevo by a Serbian national.

Dorothy A Adams

There are many 'laundry lists' of the battles, but the Germans under Kaiser Wilhelm were initially implementing the Schlieffen Plan, which had been formulated by retired Count von Schlieffen, who headed the German General Staff in 1905, as a possible foil against war with France and Russia, should that occur. It involved crossing Belgium, then France, and finally heading east to Russia. It had never been actually fleshed out. It was a thought plan, and it is rumored that Otto von Bismarck, whom the Kaiser had fired as Chancellor, advised against it, primarily because it would be a two-front war if implemented under the modifications of von Moltke, who followed von Schlieffen in office. Besides, it was a thought plan and not a deployment plan. The biggest flaw the Kaiser would face was the fact that Belgium refused crossage. On top of that, the Belgians had a treaty with Great Britain to protect their sovereignty, and France also had one with Russia. But Kaiser Wilhelm was undaunted by facts, and proceeded to march into Belgium anyhow, though the new head of the General Staff (von Moltke) recommended fewer troops than the original plan called for. The Kaiser definitely had excellent military assets, but fewer troops were utilized than called for in the original tactical plan. He also didn't consider that his action would trigger something that would ultimately involve about 100 nations. Nor did he pay close enough attention to logistics of how to feed and keep ammunition available to troops. When the Germans marched into Belgium, Belgium called for help from Britain. With France in the German cross hairs, they called on Russia. That allied group became known as the Triple Entente, or simply The Allies. And what happens when soldiers who have had no war to fight have been given a war to fight? They are eager to do it. Britain immediately sent the British Expeditionary Force to confront the Germans, but that was a catastrophe.

The order of events cascaded rapidly, and after Austria had declared war on Serbia on the 28th of July, Germany followed suit on the 1st of August according to some sources, and on 30 July by others. They declared war on France by the 31st of July, and with a flanking movement swept through Luxembourg and into Belgium by the 1st of August. By mid-August, they were already in Brussels, having destroyed the fortifications in Liege and set fire to a village, where civilians were murdered. This was actually a shocking event to young German soldiers, but they soon got over the abhorrence of the brutality of war. Great Britain declared war on the 4th of August, at almost midnight. There was a German minelaying ship caught at the mouth of the Thames the next day, which shocked the country. In Europe, there was the Eastern Front and the Western Front, just as there was to be later in WW II. The French were unprepared because they lacked barbed wire, ammunition, or machine guns, and were convinced that the antiquated methodology of fighting in the open was the only way Frenchmen could fight. Trenches were an anathema to them, but that was where they were to wind up, because otherwise the death toll was simply too great. There were many battles, but the quick, decisive defeat of the French as described in the original German plan did not occur due to the modifications made in German troop strength, and the diversion of forces to protect the region of Alsace and Lorraine, which Germany had reacquired in 1871. The French mounted an offensive there, but were to suffer the greatest casualties they had ever had in their history in a single day, totaling about 27,000. They were pounded by heavy German artillery and machine gun fire. By the time they retreated toward Paris, more than 300,000 French soldiers had died. But to sum it up, armed peace ended in 1914, which was propagated by imperialism giving way to nationalism in both England and Germany, who had a very aggressive, almost megalomaniacal form of it. That usually finds its strongest supporters in the military, governmental sectors, and big business. At the end of the first week of August, 120,000 soldiers of the British Expeditionary Force landed to face the Germans, and simultaneously, the Russians were mobilizing.

Russia had the largest standing army forces, of all countries at the outset of WWI, approximately 6 million, and they entered eastern Prussia with a whole army, which resulted in the Battle of Tannenberg. The Eastern Front then erupted, but the German troops under Generals von Hindenburg and Ludendorff had both aerial reconnaissance and a couple of decoded Russian radio messages, so they repositioned their troops. They countered the advance of the Russian 2nd Army, surrounded them, and captured over 125,000 Russians. That victory was successful in driving

Russians out of East Prussia, and the Russians suffered heavy casualties. At home, Russia was experiencing other significant problems with the growth of socialistic and communistic ideas throughout the country, but they did manage to complete mobilization, begun at the end of July when Austria attacked Serbia. It was possibly accelerated after their defeat at Tannenberg, and approximately doubled.

Back in early 1902, Japan had made a naval alliance with Great Britain, so the German possessions in the far East were at risk. Toward the end of August 1914, Japan declared war on Germany, and began to invade and occupy those vulnerable islands along with the German naval base at Qingdao on the coast of China. But the German navy had Graf von Spee, who with his naval squadron, cut the British communication cable to the Pacific in early September. By November, Admiral Graf von Spee would hand the British the worst naval defeat they had ever experienced, in a battle in the Pacific, where his squadron sank two of their ships, with no survivors.

While the German navy was successful in the far-East, the Battle of the Marne was taking place on the Western Front. The combined British and French forces were able to save Paris from German invasion by mounting a coordinated counteroffensive. Aerial reconnaissance was becoming extremely important in this new technologically improved warfare, and with it, the French had found some gaps in the German lines. Those were exploited, and even the Parisian taxi cab companies participated by moving French troops to the front in their vehicles. The German forces kept withdrawing from the onslaught of British and French attacks, toward the English Channel, and the Allies kept following them. That was later called the Race to the Sea, and it played an important strategic part, since by controlling the ports, the Germans could cut the supply lines of the Allies to great military advantage. Each side kept trying to outmaneuver the other. Finally, Germany stopped along the Aisne River and dug themselves in. France was temporarily saved, but Germany still had superior numbers, military skill, and equipment. The Allies didn't yet have the heavy artillery with high explosive shells, or tanks to smash the entrenchment. Casualties were mounting for all combatants, and ultimately, more and more trenches would be dug. In both France and Britain, wartime control of the economy, national security, and civil liberties was instituted. On the Western Front, Austrian forces were retreating before the Russians, and the Germans had to send reinforcements to the Austrians. The original Schlieffen Plan, as implemented by von Moltke wasn't working, and the rains were coming.

In September, the British gave birth to a new tool of warfare. Their air raid resulted in bombing of Zeppelin facilities in Koln (Cologne) and Dusseldorf. The value of air strikes and reconnaissance was being recognized, and pilots were being recruited and trained in each of the embattled nations. But the ground war was going on in increasingly inclement weather. The first battle of Ypres in Belgium began in October, 1914, and continued through most of November. The Germans massed a major attack on Ypres, and though suffering incredibly massive casualties, the British, French, and Belgians were able to hold the line. The Germans, stretched for manpower, had been sending in troops as young as 17, advancing in the old way, shoulder to shoulder, where they were gunned down. Although the Germans had superior guns and equipment, they couldn't break through. Nearly half of the British Army was killed, and the total casualties for the entire battle was a quarter of a million. Inventiveness could have come into play for the Allies, because Britain had a model of a tank, but it was not yet fielded. It could have broken through the entrenchment, had it been used. At about the same time, the Germans invented the flame thrower, but it was as much danger to the user as to his enemy; but they had gas capability, and for the first time ever, it was used on the Canadian and Algerian participants in their own trenches at the second battle of Ypres. They had no defense against it, and the result was devastating, but still the line held. Shortly thereafter, the British ingenuity in chemistry resulted in the fielding of protective gear against gas attacks, though for the first victims, it was too little too late.

As if enough countries weren't already involved, in October, the Ottoman Empire joined in as part of the Central Powers.

Russia then declared war on Turkey, where Constantinople was the capital of the Ottoman Empire. They each lined up on either side of the border between the Russian Caucasus and the Ottoman Empire. The Austrians were still embroiled, but unable to achieve anything but indecisive results. Germany kept having to divert troops to support them, which drained power from other points in the melee. Kaiser Wilhelm fired von Moltke, and hoped that things would get better. The slaughter continued, and in Britain, Lord Kitchner, a soldier who gained his reputation in the Boer Wars, and the Secretary of State in Britain for war, recruited volunteers from 1914-1915. He was the only active military man in the cabinet, and his the recruitment was enhanced by creation of a poster, seen below, of him in a Field Marshall uniform staring intently forward with stern, demanding eyes. He had also announced that "men, materiel and money are the immediate necessities" on a second poster that also threatened conscription. Both of these are shown below. It is impossible to ignore the fact that the first inspired the later recruiting poster in the US, and secondly, that with the heavy moustache and strong visage, Kitchner actually resembled Kaiser Wilhelm II. These posters were very effective, as was the subsequent conscription. Kitchner was able to swell the ranks of the British Army from about 145,000 to about 4.3 million men. He actually would visit the battlefields, which was also of great benefit to morale. Conscription was instituted not because volunteers were not plentiful enough, because the recruitment stations were overwhelmed with them, and various townships and communities competed to see who could give the most and best champions of the British cause. Patriotism hit an almost fever pitch, and the recruits eagerly partook of their rigorous training. They were even impatient to get to France. They were supposed to train for at least a year, but replacement demands were too critical to allow this time frame, so they went forward in droves, many never to return again. But they were determined to prove that the Germans were **not** superior beings; they were determined to drive the Germans back to Germany where they belonged. Thousands upon thousands would die over the next two years, with the bloodletting on all fronts accelerating.

What Price Honor, Memoir of Eugene Adams

But trench warfare had truly begun and the Western Front remained embattled along two continuous lines of trenches from the North Sea to Switzerland, until 1916. Serving the Allies were the entire populations of her far-flung empire, and the Central Powers consisted of Austria-Hungary, the Ottoman Empire, and Germany. The military of millions of men on both sides roiled about in the trenches, slogging about in mud and misery, between getting a new disease called Trench Foot, bouts of dysentery, and bloody offensives. However, none of these seemed to incapacitate the combatants sufficiently to bring a cessation on either side. The Germans did possess many siege guns with high explosives, developed originally to smash fortresses. These worked well to smash trenches, as well. The Allies did not have large guns, so their losses continued to be higher than Germany's. Survival of this bloodbath was more a matter of chance than of anything else, and the term "over the top" meant give your soul to God, because only He will decide. You went over the top of the trench to advance in "No man's land" toward the enemy. Within the trenches, danger also lurked, for the Germans had excellent snipers to accompany their large guns, along with machine guns, and fierce determination. But the determination wasn't unilateral, which is why trench warfare went on so long.

What, you may ask, was going on in America? I was not born yet, but my ancestors certainly were emotionally, and sometimes physically involved before the conflagration finally was doused, temporarily. But at the time, Thomas Woodrow Wilson was the 28th President (1913-1921) of the United States, and was the world leader of what was (and is) called the Progressive Movement. His Democrat Party controlled both the White House and both houses of Congress. At the outbreak of WW I, the attitude in the US was essentially Isolationist, and he was re-elected for his second term in 1916 with the slogan "He kept us out of war." That was to be short lived, though, and his second term was virtually consumed, by a Declaration of War on 6 April 1917. Restraint of the US up to that point had probably been as much from a difference in foreign policy overall, as it was to the anti-war attitude of the citizens. The US, when it acquired new territories, whether on the North American Continent or elsewhere, had a very different method of dealing with them, which was completely different from colonialism. Only the interference with world shipping and the perceived threat of German U-boats shifted the willingness of the nation to enter WW I. The sinking of the Lusitania on 7 May 1915, which carried some American passengers, and goods, touted as the fastest ocean liner on the seas, broke the straw with the US. Despite the fact that Germany claimed she had struck it because it carried ammo and war materiel for the Allies, which its huge explosion at impact of German fire gave credence to, the media inflamed the US public with anti-German sentiment. The mindset of the US public shifted from isolationism to defeating the perceived wicked aggressor in Europe...Germany. The US military had been small at the time in 1917, but grew rapidly. Doughboys were enlisted and trained. Even the music in the country changed, and the two most popular songs were "The Grand Old Flag," and "The Yanks Are Coming," written by George M. Cohan, were sung across the nation. Cohan eventually was awarded the Congressional Medal of Honor for that contribution, but was rejected as a soldier because he was too old to enlist.

What Price Honor, Memoir of Eugene Adams

The US took her best and went at preparation to join the Allies with vim and vigor. My grandmother was later to talk about the support given by non-combatants in making bandages, shaving kits, blankets, and many other items for the soldiers. That actually continued after I was born, because I can vaguely remember the piles of things being made for the returning wounded, and vets of that war. My mother entered nurses training in 1917 so that she could possibly go to France to treat the injured Allies, so she studied, and helped her mother with the preparations for assistance to the effort. The infusion of another powerful ally definitely helped turn the tide for the Allies, and the war ended on 11/11/1918 at 11 PM. That was the cessation of hostilities, but the Treaty of Versailles had yet to be signed. Many of the surviving vets from that War to End All Wars would serve again in WWII, and their expertise would be valued, but sometimes attenuated by political interference.

Chapter Two – Education

Education begins at home, around the kitchen table, practically, intellectually, attitudinally.

The root cause of WWI, I finally concluded, was imperialism. My maternal grandmother said so, and grandmothers are wise. She dominated the discussion around the kitchen table on Rice Street, Elkhart, Indiana, because to defy her might result in a thump on the skull for the more vociferous of the dissenters. She could thump hard enough to raise a knot on the head of the offender. Then, my grandfather Crouch would tap his cane on the floor, but he held his tongue judiciously.

When I learned to read, I read voraciously about WW I, and about what might have caused it, particularly focusing on the bits and pieces I had heard in the animated discussions. Grandpa John had said, in his quiet but commanding sonorous voice that the start of it all was the Treaty of San Stefano after the Berlin Conference. He didn't offer any details, except that the peace that settled over Europe after that was very uneasy, particularly since the Balkan States had been rearranged. When I looked that up, I found that the 1878 Treaty of San Stefano, signed in a little village close to Constantinople, ended the Russo-Turkish War. It granted Bulgaria controlled autonomy, after 500 years of rule by the Ottoman Empire and a great deal of territory. Then, the Berlin Conference revised that treaty. That was what my grandmother called "the fly in the ointment."

The Berlin Conference revised the Treaty of San Stefano three months later, and as a result, the Balkan states were rearranged again. That was done to appease the "Great Powers." The Balkan states are geographically located as a land bridge from Europe, leading to the nations that border the Mediterranean and Aegean Seas. The "Great Powers" attended this conference, which included the Russian Empire, the Ottoman Empire, Kingdom of Italy, United Kingdom, German Empire, Romania, Greece, Serbia, and Austria-Hungary. Bosnia-Herzogovina was to be occupied

What Price Honor, Memoir of Eugene Adams

and administered by Austria-Hungary. When I found out who had been there, and that Bulgaria would stay as an independent principality, under the umbrella of the Ottoman Empire, I could understand why Bulgaria still celebrates their "independence day" as March 3rd, under the San Stefano Treaty, as modified by the Berlin Congress. I still couldn't quite understand why Great Britain was given Cyprus, but their representatives, led by Disraeli called it "peace with honour." It probably did more to plant the coals to be fanned into a raging fire in 1914-1918. The Ottoman Empire had less influence in Europe after that, but disgruntlement of several other nations, including Germany under Otto von Bismarck, continued to fester, and Russia retained Georgia and Armenia as per the Treaty of San Stefano. That meant that when Joseph Stalin (Dzhugashvilli) was born to a cobbler in Gori, Georgia on the 18th of December in 1878, he was Russian. It wasn't important to me to share a birthday with him until I was an invited participant in WW II. His citizenship was.

This was the tag end of the Industrial Revolution, and by the 1870s, there had been rapid innovation in weapons, transport, and communication, altering forever the possibility to wage war without complete dislocation and disruption of normal civilian life. Even the governments became cautious and fearful of war, although no federal or economic control systems were initiated to prevent the drift to war. Also, the British Empire had the world's greatest navy, and had grown so large that it literally covered the world. They were the greatest colonial power of the world until the end of WW I. But Tzar Nicholas II (1894-1917) was idealistic enough to think that the slow shifts in power and imperial designs of nations could be attenuated. He called the "Great Powers" to a conference, hoping to engineer a universal peace. He was idealistic in his view that, like Alexander I and the Holy Alliance, discord could be displaced and peace could be established by sovereign governments. He failed entirely to consider that this could not be, without regard to the mindset, needs, and rights of the populations of all nations. The people of all nations would have to be taught to consider themselves citizens of the world instead of citizens of nations, states, or municipalities in order for peace to be universal. But imperialism and lack of integration of peoples of differing ancestry was alive and well.

There were two conferences held at The Hague. The first was in 1899, and the second in 1907, with nearly all of the sovereign states represented. Though they deliberated diplomatically, the common man/woman often didn't even know anything of the sort was taking place. The bottom line is that after the cunning haggling and discussions, there was a general unwillingness of the Great Powers to merge sovereign power into a coherent, effective entity. Competiveness actually won the days of intensive deliberation. The media didn't report accurately the deliberations of the conferences, except in small clips on non-descript pages. Grandpa John, though, managed to get some information on it, which evidently had been roundly debated by the family, prior to the overthrow of the Romanovs and the Bolshevik Revolution. In the interim, Kaiser Wilhelm II had come to power in Germany. Although he was a grandson of Queen Victoria, he was of a whole different mindset, and competition with the other sovereign nations was almost an obsession of his. He sincerely disliked that the British claimed, accurately, that the sun never set on the British Empire, and that their navy was the greatest in the world.
The Great Powers, according to the familial debates, were only attending the conferences to be polite to Nicholas II, and had no intention whatsoever of entering a global sovereignty. They simply wanted to make war, which would rare its head over the frequent disputes among nations, cheaper, and minimize the waste of resources on minor disputes. War was becoming too costly, so they favored some international laws which could embarrass more formidable opponents in war time in their favor, without giving anything up in overall power. The attendees to the Holy Alliance also had mostly done so to be polite to Alexander I, where the monarchs of Europe had proscribed to the evangelical propositions, within limits.

Grandpa John was convinced that no such merging of national sovereignty would ever happen, peacefully or otherwise. He was actually rather pleased at first with the rise of Kaiser Wilhelm, which embattled him with his wife. She was of Irish American heritage, and was a counterbalance to his Hessian ancestry. She often referred to the Hessian soldiers as "the best soldiers money can buy." There was probably a great deal of truth to that, particularly back in the 1700s, when John F. Crouch's ancestor, John F. Crouch, came to "the colonies" from Germany as a Hessian soldier. They also discussed the invention of the name "Anglo-Saxon," sometimes late into the night. It made me aware that not only are Americans a mixture of blood lines, but so are Europeans, to include the British Isles. The Irish are a particularly mixed race, but at the end of the discussions, the grandparents would both acknowledge that there was a definite Teutonic strain in Ireland. The English and Irish are still separated by a different temperament, exacerbated by the existence of a separate language, which is still preserved. The English rule of Ireland has been for centuries an intermittent civil war, and probably will remain so. But, despite the ill treatment of the Irish by the English for hundreds of years, the Irish dutifully rose to put aside their animosity to fight with the British forces at the outbreak of WW I, from August 1914 until well into 1915, when the efforts at reconciliation between Ireland and Britain were sabotaged. They talked about the Dublin Revolt, of which I don't really remember much. However, she did point out that my last name was Adams, which is common in Ireland. He countered with the fact that the Adams name has been common in what became the United States since before the Revolutionary War.

They had some tea after their discussion(s), and some wonderful pastry with it. Young people who had been listening were treated to milk and pastry and dispatched to bed.

    I remembered that night well, because it made me wonder if nations are like families, but without the treat at the end of discussions. I told Grandpa Crouch what I thought about it, and his blue eyes twinkled as he laughed and patted me on the head, saying "I expect so, little owl. I expect so!"

Chapter Three – Wisdom of the Elders

In my peregrinations to learn more about conditions existing which ultimately led the Great War, the bloodiest of all wars in recorded history, I turned to historical accounts, which had terms like "Pan-Slavism," and the Balkan War of 1912. The name of the German Chancellor, Otto von Bismarck also entered the discussions, along with Kaiser Wilhelm II of Germany and what they called the unpronounceable Hohenzollernization of the country.

Early one morning, in about December, 1925, I approached my grandfather Crouch, while he was finishing his coffee. I sat opposite him, and had brought a pencil and piece of paper. I didn't say anything, but kept looking at him expectantly, as a child will do.

"And what is it, young man, that brings you to fix me with those questioning eyes?" he asked.

"I was wondering," I stammered, "well there is a big word I don't understand, and there is a war that I don't know about. Could you help me?"

"You've been a little pesky since you learned to read," he chuckled. "What is the word?"

"Sir, I can't say it, but it was so long that I only wrote down the first part of it. Here is what I have." I handed him the paper on which I had printed Hohohenz. It wasn't all the letters, but it was all I had.

He took the paper, looked at it quizzically, rubbed his brow, then looked at me with amazement. "What in the name of Zeus have you been reading, young man? That is pronounced Hohohenzollern," he said, with a uvular sound in the long word. "It's a family that once ruled Prussia, Brandenburg, and some of Germany, or maybe all of it. I don't remember. You have one too many 'oh's' in it. It's Hohenzollern." Then he shook his head. "What war was it?"

"The Balkan War of 1912," I said, as I held out my hand for the paper. I almost swallowed the eraser of the pencil when my Grandma Crouch came up behind me, and I reflexively ducked.

"What are you ducking for," she demanded. "What have you done wrong, and what are you doing in here at this hour, Eugene Edward Adams?"

I couldn't even let out a pitiful squeak, because the use of my entire name with that tone of voice meant real trouble, so I am sure there were tears in my eyes, and a look of pathetic pleading when I looked up at her. Then she saw the paper being handed back. She gave my grandfather the "eagle look," which could pierce the heart of the most fearless opponent.

He smiled, and then waved his hand, saying "Oh, no, Mother. I didn't write the word. The poor lad was just asking how it is spoken, and then had another question from his reading. Did you know how much he reads, and how well he understands most of it? The boy's questions should be answered, you know."

She softened a little, and a little smile seemed to try to escape at the corners of her mouth. "And what were you wondering about, you little curmudgeon? What books have you been reading now? You know that curiosity killed the cat, but since you are not a cat, just say what you want to know."

I knew that could be dangerous, but I really did want to know. I told her that I had been trying to understand what caused the Great War, and why everyone is still talking about it all the time. That seemed to please her very much, so it wasn't hard to tell her that I had been reading her big fat book that she had by her chair in the sitting room. I also swore on my honor that I hadn't made any marks in it or wrinkled any pages, and that I had placed it precisely as I found it, on her little table next to the pretty lamp. Then I dared hand her the paper, and tell her that I had Grandpa say the whole thing for me, and that it sounded almost like spitting. She laughed so hard that she put her apron up to her face with one hand and patted me on the shoulder with the other one. When she could catch her breath, she asked about the other question. While she poured herself a cup of coffee, I said something about not understanding what the Balkan War of 1912 was, and asked why people didn't just stop fighting.

"Only God knows the answer to that one," Grandma said, as she settled herself into a chair. "Go get that book for me, please."

Happy to be free, even for a few minutes, I almost tripped over my "uncle," Clifford, who is only a few years older than I am. He had been sitting on the floor behind me, listening. He laughed and rolled out of my way, saying "See, I told you it would stir things up!"

I dutifully brought the book, and Grandma patted the chair beside her and waved for Cliff to take a chair, too. She quickly turned to the page she had bookmarked, and noticed that it actually had the information I wanted. Then she asked "What part of this didn't you understand, my little fellow who is only 7 and thinks he is 70?"

"I just didn't know where those countries were, and why the people would fight like that. Were there many people killed?"

Without even looking at the book, she said that the countries involved were Greece, Serbia, Montenegro, and Bulgaria on one side, and the Ottoman Empire on the other. The first one lasted from October 1912 to May 1913. I don't know to this day how she could remember all those things, but she did. Then she explained that there were thousands upon thousands of people either killed or wounded on both sides, but the Ottoman Empire was beaten. But people being people, one of the countries wasn't happy with the division of the spoils, which triggered another war. Grandpa made a "Harrumph" sound, and looked out the window.

"Greed and imperialism," he grunted to himself.

What Price Honor, Memoir of Eugene Adams

"How about your favorite Kaiser," Grandma retorted. Then to me, she said "Why don't you ask your other grandparents about it. Alva is coming to get you pretty soon."

"Can Cliff go with me, please, please, please?" Then I got the standard, mumble about how we will see, and we will ask, and we were dismissed.

Cliff and I hovered just beyond the door, and could make out the occasional comment, but I still wanted to know more about that very big word. I gathered it had a great deal of meaning, but I only could hear that it was something that the Kaiser did to the whole German people to make them prouder of themselves. Then my other grandfather came to the door. Those older folks talked for a while, and it was decided that we both could go to his farm in the Champaign area of Illinois. Grandma scurried about getting some food and drinks packed for us, because it was going to be a long trip. We were shooed up to get some clothing and not to "dawdle." It was another of those words that all grownups understood, but little boys don't. It wasn't long before a call in that flat Midwestern twang came up the stairs.

"Get a move on! Shake a leg! We don't have all day, and daylight is burning."

We were herded to a black machine outside, and told to get in the side away from the steering wheel, or in the "boot." We didn't know what a boot was, so we both got into the seat away from the steering wheel. Then Grandpa Alva got in, and Grandpa John did something with a big handle to get the thing to growl and make a constant noise. It was our first ride in a motor car, and we were so totally intrigued that we were still and quiet as statues. It didn't take too long for us to be hypnotized by the vibration, and the scenery flashing by, so our eyelids traitorously closed. We must have slept for most of the trip, because it was pretty dark when we got there. We woke up immediately when the car stopped, and just sat there in a daze. Grandpa Alva came over and picked us up, one in one arm, one in the other, and headed to a house, dimly outlined in the gloaming. We were placed on what he called a "pallet" made of quilts, and there was a pillow for each one. Then he stopped.

"Do either of you need to relieve yourself?" he asked as a kind of afterthought.

"I don't know what that means," Cliff said, "but I need to pee."

"Good. Both of you up, follow me, we are going outside," came that calm voice.

We did our business, and washed our hands under the pump spigot, and even took a drink of the cool water. We were told to go back in and go to sleep, because morning comes earlier on the farm than anywhere else. And it did. At about 0400, we woke to the delicious smell of bacon frying, fresh biscuits baking, eggs sputtering, and someone humming a happy song. Then we heard clumping footsteps, and Grandpa Alva appeared in the doorway.

"Git up, git outside, wash faces and hands, and git to the table. Breakfast is almost ready!" Then he pointed the way. "We got work to do today, so shake a leg."

We both marveled at the strange expressions the "old" people used, but we definitely did move quickly. There wasn't much in the world that could keep us from those wonderful smells. We went into a bright kitchen with a table covered with a red and white checkered table cloth. A lady with a very big, beautiful smile on her face put a plate in front of each of us, followed by a glass full of frothy milk. The utensils were already there, but we were too busy to notice much else, because we were busy stuffing our mouths with the delicious food. I began to feel like that other expression the other grandmother had. I felt "full as a tick." When we started to leave the table after saying our thank yous, she smiled again and pointed at the napkins. They were pure white, and I was reluctant to wipe my face very thoroughly with mine.

What Price Honor, Memoir of Eugene Adams

"Don't worry, young-un. They wash. Use it quick. Grandpa is waiting," she said with another one of her lovely smiles.

And he was waiting. He didn't talk much, except to give short instructions. We learned about feeding and watering the livestock, how milking was done, and why it was critically important that the buckets and jars for the milk were absolutely clean. We learned about how to harness and hook up Old Bob to the plough, and how to talk to him softly and gently. We were a little startled when Grandpa Alva set the plough, then smartly smacked the long leather tethers against Old Bob's back. Then he started to plough a field, telling us as we walked along to go get some cans from the barn, fill them halfway with dirt, and pick up the earthworms, put them in the cans, because we would go fishing in the early evening. Neither of us had ever touched an earthworm before, and we choked back the squeals when they wiggled and squirmed in our fingers. We only had to follow for about two rows, and he said to go set the cans in the shade, just inside the barn. Then we were to wash our hands and go ask if there were any chores Grandma had for us to do. Neither of us had ever been fishing before, either, and we discussed how on earth we were supposed to use those squirmy worms to fish with.

Grandma asked if we were hungry or thirsty. We weren't hungry yet, but a cool drink of water was gratefully accepted. Then she handed us a big bucket and asked if we had ever slopped hogs. We didn't know what that meant, so she took us out to show us. That revolting mixture was poured into a trough, and the pigs squealed and nudged each other to gobble it up. Then she put feed in another trough, where the losers over the slops went to gratefully eat. We helped pump water, with the windmill hooked up to a contraption with a hose. That didn't take much work. It was just a curiosity, and we were told that it certainly was better than having to carry the water in buckets to the watering trough. When I tried to reach over later to pet the pigs, she stopped me with a stern warning that it was extremely dangerous. That under no circumstances was I to do that, or to try picking up a piglet from the pen, because an angry sow can actually kill a human. Ever curious, I asked about the calves, and how their mothers would react, and she laughed. It was OK to pet the calves and the cows, but not OK to try to pet the bull. We learned how to feed the chickens, but she collected the eggs herself. Then we had lunch and went to the garden to learn how to pick beans, pull beets, and so forth. It was a lot to learn in one day. We were tired, but we noticed that she kept working away inside the house. She sent us to wash up, and then gave us a book to read out on the front porch, which had a wonderful porch swing, big enough for us to sit side by side and swing gently back and forth. Then an old hound dog wandered up, looking up at us mournfully. It reminded us of Bill, Grandpa John's beautiful hunting dog, except that it wasn't white with black spots. It was brown, black with some white, it had great floppy ears, and big brown eyes. We had to abandon reading for a little while to pet it, and it was grateful for the attention. But then we went back to the book. It was full of short stories, many of which were about the American Revolution.

Evening began to fall, and Grandpa Alva came into the barnyard with Old Bob. He rubbed the old horse's neck, checked his hooves, set down a bucket of water for him, and then called for us. Each one of us was handed a brush, and shown how to brush Old Bob's coat. He was a little damp, but we could tell he appreciated the brushing. Grandpa Alva combed his mane, and talked to him in a soft voice, and after inspecting and making sure we had done a good job, we were each handed a carrot and shown how to feed it to the horse without getting a finger bitten. Then we went to the barn, and Old Bob went straight into his stall and began to have his supper. Next, the plough was checked and put away. After that, he went to the house for a few minutes. When he came back he was smiling, and said if we weren't too tired or hungry, we could go get in an hour or so of fishing. We weren't, and we did. Another new adventure, and one I would use often in my lifetime, because it has a distinctly calming effect. My first experience with baiting a hook with a worm was not pleasant, but luckily, I caught a fish with that first worm, and was extremely pleased with myself. Cliff and I caught three fish each, and were taught how to put them on a stringer. The only fish I didn't like was a catfish, because they are ugly and can sting you, but later I found out that they taste better and are less boney than the sunfish or bass. We didn't learn how to fillet the fish that night, because mercifully, we could smell supper cooking as we went back to the house. We were sent to wash up, and handed clean shirts to change into. The prayer we said at the table was a little different than the one we knew from the Crouch house. There was a crossing of ourselves, and a prayer recited, then a thanks for our presence at that table. It reminded me of a church Grandma Crouch sometimes took me to. The word Catholic came up into my mind. At 7 years of age, I didn't really understand what it meant, but I intended to find out.

I waited expectantly for the discussions to begin, but they didn't seem to be about anything but the farm. As I sat at the table, twiddling a little crumb of bread, I was asked if I would shake the cloth. I wasn't sure what that meant, and the puzzlement was obvious, but Cliff said he would do it, and was happy as a clam to have some special thing to do. Then Grandma asked what I was thinking about. I didn't tell her that it was about the Balkan War. I looked straight at Grampa Alva and said that I was wondering about what started WW I. The look of shock on his face was amazing, and the tension became palpable. Grandma intervened and said that she wished she knew, so it wouldn't happen again. Their sons had been sent to fight in it, and some of them didn't come home. Then Alva rubbed his forehead clasped his hands and stared into space for a minute or two.

"Your father, Fred Dewey Adams, went into the Navy, and he did come home. He didn't exactly volunteer, but at least he came home. But I guess he didn't come home to you and your sister. He is alive, though."

"Your father is a very smart, handsome man, Gene. You resemble him a great deal in many ways. He lives in Chicago now," Grandma interjected. "I got to meet your sister, and Alva says she looks like me."

"She does," Alva said, "but she always looks so very unhappy."

Cliff had come in by then and facing Grandma said "Yes, it would be wonderful if she smiled like you. You have a pretty smile."

Grandma smiled, and reached out to Cliff and hugged him, then he smiled almost all over himself.

Grandpa Alva gave me a very serious look and seemed to be thinking about something heavy enough to pull a man down. "We'll talk about the causes of the war tomorrow. Walk by me while I plough. It helps me think. I'm glad you've come to visit. You can always come visit, any time. You both can."

It was good to know that we were welcome, and as I drifted off to sleep, I was both ashamed that I had caused the sorrow to bubble up in this very strong ancestor of mine, but very happy that we had learned so much in just one day. Then Cliff told me that I was so very lucky, because he didn't have any grandparents, and I had four of them, his mother and father, and Alva and Ida. He was so happy that he was welcome to share these grandparents with me, and was also glad to share his parents, too. Cliff never had a mean bone in his body, and we were closer than most brothers even are.

As I was drifting off to sleep, I saw a bookshelf that went from the floor all the way to the ceiling, and it was full of books. Absolutely full. I sat up and pulled one off the shelf, and it fell open to the flyleaf. It had been published in 1919. Another one on the shelf had been published in 1865. That was a long time ago. There was some spidery writing on that flyleaf, and I couldn't quite make it out. I was always full of questions, but this one would have to wait until morning.

Chapter Four – To Predict the Future, Know the Past

History is always repeating itself, though within a few years of an event, the story is often changed by those with a hidden agenda. However, these people are part of history, too. They follow every major event. Even the Bible speaks of wars and rumors of wars, for they have been with us always.

    The next morning, we went out to plough with Grandpa Alva. He asked who wanted to go pick apples with Grandma. Cliff practically danced, and said that he did, so he was given a bushel basket and sent to her. I was given a hat to put on in case I was sensitive to the sun, and I walked. Grandpa Alva ploughed about half a row, while chewing on a grass stem. Then he began. It was very much like a recitation, and he started with something I had been afraid to ask about…the Balkan Wars, because he said there were two of them, and they set the stage for continuing deterioration of geopolitical conditions in Europe. That was a big word for me then, 'geopolitical,' but he continued. I made a mental note to remember to find out exactly what it meant.

    Then he began his explanation of the conditions in Europe at the end of the last century, and the continual competition among nations to gobble up every last acre of land they could claim as their own, particularly since the Ottoman Empire was falling apart. I stopped him and asked him about the Ottoman Empire, and he explained in rather terse terms that it had been what is called a Caliphate, and that their religion was radically different from Christianity, upon which this nation had been founded. It was quick, direct, and to the point. The Caliphate had existed for hundreds of years, but he said that was a discussion for a different time. At the time of interest, the early 1900s, it had lost significant military, political and economic power. That seemed a mouthful to me, but as he ploughed, he was a veritable fount of information, and I contented myself with listening, and saving up questions for later. According to his narrative, a disgruntlement of the Slavic peoples over the fact that Russia and Austria-Hungary were taking pieces of that pie for themselves, without regard to the desires of the people who lived in a place called the Balkans, and it gave rise to conflict. In a way, it was the collision of predominantly Christian people with something called Muslims and people of Slavic heritage. Just as he said that the two things you never discuss with people you want to have as friends are politics and religion, the plough hit a large rock.

He stopped Old Bob from straining against the rock, and then got down to wrestle with it. He grumbled and mumbled, and had me get some grass and weeds to feed Old Bob while he freed the plough. After a few minutes, he managed to get it loose both from the ground and the plough, and rolled it off to the side of the field, where there was a hedge row. Once he was underway again, he said that the history of the world has large rocks in it from time to time, and for centuries, the way countries had dealt with it was through war. In October of 1912, the Slavic coalition fought against several nations which they thought were drawing new lines that divided the Slavs who lived in what was called the Balkans. He said the same thing my other grandparents had said about the Balkans, that it was a large land bridge that connected the major European nations from the ones that lay to the south. Conflicting tensions brought war, which included Greece, Montenegro, Bulgaria, and Serbia, known as the Balkan League, against the Ottoman Empire, but initiated by the Pan-Slavic union. It lasted until May of 1913, and continued to simmer. Artificial division of peoples of similar heritage and religion will always initiate tensions, which can erupt into violence. He reckoned that around a million people were either killed or wounded in that conflict, but the Ottomans were numerically inferior by that time, so they lost. But the Slavs were still dissatisfied, so there was a second Balkan War.

The second Balkan War started at the end of June in 1913, and lasted only about a month. It was because the winners of the first one were not happy with the division of territory at the end of the first conflict. Bulgaria thought it should get the lion's share, and when it didn't, it attacked Greece and Serbia. So Greece and Serbia beat the literal tarnation out of Bulgaria, and when they entered that nation, Romania joined in. The Ottomans thought it was a good time to get back some of the territory it had lost, so it entered the fray against Bulgaria. In August, that war ended, with about a 100,000 people, total, either killed or wounded, and there was yet another treaty. Alva mopped his brow, and was silent for a little while. I kicked clods, and wondered if I would remember all of this, but the lesson was that wars in Europe just went on and on, the seeds of the last one planting the foul harvest of the next. But I seized the moment to ask a question.

"Grandfather, did you ever teach school?"

"No, son, I never taught school. I came up in the school of hard knocks, but found that reading and learning can be done on your own, to feed your soul, while other work can and must be done to feed your body."

"But you know so much. You think so much, and you tell all these things like a story."

"It is one of the many stories of mankind's journey on this earth. Not all of them are beautiful, but not all are horrific, either. The best way to learn the stories is to read the histories written right after the events happen, because nobody with ulterior motives has had the time to change the facts. I read a lot of very old history books. Many people will not agree with me, but I am closer to the truth than they will ever be." Then he turned and looked at me. "Yes," he said. "I will answer the question spinning around in your head."

I looked down at the toe of my shoe, and wondered if he really could see into my mind and know what I wanted to ask. Then he answered that very question, with a little bit of laughter twinkling from his very blue, very beautiful eyes. He continued the tale as he ploughed.

"This ties into the beginning of WW I, which was the bloodiest war that ever was, and it was supposed to be the War that Ends all War. It spun out of the constant conflicts that preceded it, and while politicians, leaders, and people thought to be wise concoct things called treaties, these are only small bandages on massive wounds. They don't last, and never have. There were many new lines drawn, erased, and redrawn as things called alliances formed. What was really happening was that every country wanted an empire, and they kept carving up the world to gain more territory, which meant some other country lost territory, which kept the coals of upheaval alive. The slide into war was precipitated when an angry Serbian shot and killed Archduke Franz Ferdinand, heir to the Austria-Hungarian Empire, and his wife, Sophie, in Sarajevo while the Archduke was there on official business. But it was a mere tremor in an already shaky geopolitical world. Yes, even an old farmer like me knows a word like that, and the world as we knew it was shattered because it was so fragile from the hunger for power and possessions that it was smashed into hundreds of pieces."

It was a more detailed and yet indefinite answer to my question, which indeed I had been thinking about. I still wasn't sure just how the world of supposed adults could have gotten that far out of control, but it surely had done it. He continued the tale, and even remembered the date that the Archduke was assassinated. He said it was 28 June 1914. Then there was only about a month left until war was being declared hither and thither amongst the European nations, according to their existing alliances. Everywhere there were conflicts, and there were five big empires at the time. They were Germany, Austria-Hungary, France, Britain, and Russia. The Ottoman Empire was to the south and in decline. After the murder of Franz Ferdinand, his father, Franz Josef, contacted Kaiser Wilhelm II, requesting help to discipline the Serbs for the atrocity. Germany agreed. Britain, France, and Russia became allied to stop them from gaining too much power and absorbing too much territory. That whole web of alliances ultimately wound up in a war starting in 1914 on July 28th, which would involve at least 100 nations, and cost over a million casualties. A nationalist fervor seemed to run rampant like an infection in all the countries, but was greatest in Germany and Great Britain.

What Price Honor, Memoir of Eugene Adams

My head was spinning by then, so I wanted to take a break. As I walked away I tossed back over my shoulder a question about why the Kaiser and Great Britain were so jealous of each other. And I asked if I could bring him a drink of water. He nodded, and continued to laugh. The walk did me good, and let my brain rest for a few minutes. Grandma gave me a jug of cool water from the ice box to carry back to him, but she sat me down first for a glass of my own. Cliff was out under the shade tree playing with the dog and having a wonderful time. I toyed with the idea of joining him for a while, but then remembered I had promised to bring Grandpa Alva a drink of water. Grandma gave me a straw hat to wear because she said my dark hair absorbed too much heat. I thought about that, and wondered at the time if she was right, but stored the thought away for later deliberation, took the jug, and caught the plough coming back toward me. I started to run, because I didn't want to be accused of dawdling. I petted Old Bob while Grandpa had a drink of water, and realized that I should have brought some paper and a pencil to write down all the facts. I promised myself that I would do that next time.

We started up again, and I found it harder to listen, but caught the word 'nationalism' which ran around between my ears for a while. All the nations had become "nationalistic. I stored it away for later consideration. But he went on for a time about which countries had competed to be the best in all things. Kaiser Wilhelm II had told his countrymen when he took the helm of Germany that they were the best, but that he didn't value the politicians or diplomats nearly as much as he did the army. He also planned to expand the navy, which was a challenge to Great Britain's superiority on the seas. That was a curious thought but Grandpa went on to say that the Kaiser pushed excellence in everything from science to art, to music, to education, and convinced the German people that they were the best in everything. He pushed them to _be_ the best. He made them intensely proud of their nation and convinced them of their invincibility, particularly militarily. Of course, the British took issue with this, because they had the world's greatest navy, and believed that they were the best at everything, including colonization of much of the world. One of their alliances was with

Belgium, whose sovereignty they had pledged to protect in case of invasion. It seems that pride is one of the original sins, and France's pride had been wounded in a previous war (Franco-Prussian) that they didn't win. Russia was largely disorganized, and underdeveloped in many ways, but it had an alliance with France, so when hostilities arose, they stood ready to stand with France, although the days of the Romanov dynasty were definitely numbered.

The two sides were called the Triple Entente or Allies, and the Central Powers. The Triple Entente was composed of Great Britain, France, and Russia. The Central Powers at the beginning of the war was composed of Austria-Hungary, Germany, Ottoman Empire and Bulgaria. The shooting started when Austria-Hungary attacked Serbia in retribution for the murder of Archduke Ferdinand on 28 July 1914. Germany entered on 1 August 1914, followed by the Ottoman Empire on 2 August 1914, and then by Bulgaria in October 1914. Kaiser Wilhelm II decided that the best strategic move, to conserve military superiority and prevent other forces from joining the allies was to swing down through Belgium and Luxembourg, then through France and come up between Russia and some of the smaller nations. Belgium declined passage through their country, and since they had an alliance with Great Britain, they faced off against Germany. So the dominoes started to fall. The Germans marched into Belgium, personally led by the Kaiser, and mounted a determined offensive to march through to Paris, under what was called the Schlieffen Plan. Britain immediately declared war on Germany, and since they were so sure of their military superiority, they sent in their British Expeditionary Force. It was a disastrous move on their part, because the British fell like kernels off a corn cob.

At that point, I just had to ask what the Schlieffen Plan was. Grandpa Alva said that it was made up in about 1905 by a famous German Field Marshal, whose name was von Schlieffen. He also said that it would have to wait until we finished with the battle we were talking about. He mopped his brow, and made a clicking sound with his tongue. Old Bob perked up a bit, but it was clear that he was getting very tired. So was I, and surely Grandpa Alva was, too. I could tell he wasn't young, either, so I asked the last question of that expedition,

"Grandpa, how old are you?"

"Old enough," he chuckled.

"Well, then, when were you born?" I persisted.

"You're a nosey little fellow, aren't you? I was born in 1858, or so I'm told. So how old does that make me?"

"I think you'd be 67, and that is very old," I responded, scratching my ear.

He laughed and said "I guess I must have that birthdate wrong, because I am not that old. It's time to call it a day, because it's getting ready to rain. No more questions for today, especially not nosey ones."

I kicked a stone, and waited while he finished that row. The raindrops began to fall, big fat ones, and we went to put the equipment and the horse away. Old Bob was grateful, and so was I. I needed some quiet time to think through all I had learned that day. Listening to him was almost like having a book read to you, and then I remembered all those books where our pallets were. We really didn't have to wash up, because the rain had done a good job of that. We went to the back door, and just inside there was what was called a mud porch. Grandma stepped out the door and handed us towels. We sat on a bench, and looked quizzically at my feet. She came back about then with dry clothes, which she hung on hooks, and told me to leave the shoes on the mud porch…and that was the end of it for that day.

There would be many visits to the farm over the years, but I used this one to examine the content of the library. There were many volumes of note, and it was plain to see that they had all been read. There was one that would be given to me later for my 10th birthday, on the life, speeches, and public service of Abraham

Lincoln, written mostly during his lifetime, and finalized after he was murdered. It was leather bound, and smelled wonderful. It was written by J.H. Barrett and published in 1865, and Grandpa Alva gave it to me. It was the finest gift he could have given, and I carried it with me for a large part of my life. I gave it to my oldest daughter, Dorothy, when she was 16 years old, because I knew she would treasure it, too

Chapter Five – What Happened in the German Empire under Kaiser Wilhelm II

Following the Franco-Prussian War. Germany was essentially Prussianized, and the mental growth of generations educated after the 1871 victories soared under the Hohenzollern dynasty.

During the time following the Franco-Prussian War, France was humiliated, and Germany was exhilarated, because the shame she experienced during and after the Napoleonic Wars was expiated. Kaiser Wilhelm II was a devotee to the measures instituted by the Hohenzollern dynasty. Any teacher or professor who failed to impart to his/her student the innate superiority of Germans over all other peoples was doomed to either obscurity, death, or both. Lessons in history became a deliberate and skillful, systematic falsification of the history of humanity, and a promising view of the German future.

By representing all other populations and nations as ignorant, incompetent, stupid and decadent, the Prussians were seen clearly as superior and the natural regenerators of human kind.

Through the education of the youth, both in schools and churches, as well as in an overweening societal attitude, superiority became a passionate conviction. It was poured into each child by his teachers of literature, biology, chemistry, physics, mathematics, art, music, or any other formal imparting of knowledge. It calls to mind some of the ancient Talmudic writing, which are as true today as when it was penned.

Dorothy A Adams

"A scholar is greater than a prophet"
"You should revere the teacher even more than your father. The latter only brought you into the world. The former indicates the way to the next."
"Jerusalem was destroyed because the instruction of the young was neglected."
"The world is saved by the breath of the school children."
"Even for the rebuilding of the Temple, the schools must not be neglected."
"Study is more meritorious than sacrifice."

These were written before the birth of Christianity, and the truth of them is clear. But what is truth? The answer is that truth is ALL. All else passes into nothingness as the ages in their inexorable journey turn relentlessly onward. Truth never does. But with constant repetition, a lie can be perceived as truth, and repetition is simply synonymous with reputation. The German efficiency continually improved under the dynastic demand for excellence, and there was great attention given to education of the masses, because it was correctly believed that an educated worker is a better worker, and good work, even in industrial skills and production, was rewarded. This was especially true of the military, because Kaiser Wilhelm even stated during his accession in 1888 to the throne, in an address to his navy and army: "The soldier and the army, not parliamentary majorities, have welded together the German Empire. My trust is placed in the army." Two years later, he dismissed Chancellor Otto von Bismarck, who my Grandfather Crouch claimed had actually built the German Empire. The outgoing Chancellor wasn't vitriolic about it, and he simply that he thought the new Emperor intended to be his own Chancellor. The Kaiser's opening salvo was a predictor of a very active, aggressive, and militaristic career. He always appeared in impressive military uniforms, with his thick, ink black moustache carefully turned up on the ends, and a fierce look on his young, strong face. It didn't seem to matter that the regalia cleverly concealed his withered left arm, so few even knew of the deformity. None ever spoke of it openly. He was theatrical, restless, and fearless of what his and the Empire's manifest destiny would be. He travelled frequently to Rome, Vienna, London, Athens, Constantinople, and was the very first Christian sovereign to ever be welcomed by the Sultan. When he went to Palestine, they even knocked a passage through a very special, ancient wall, so he could enter on horseback, because he considered inappropriate for him to enter on foot.

By 1895, the eager young and ambitious Kaiser made the announcement to the world that Germany was definitely a world power, and they were going to expand, modernize and equip their navy to challenge the British superiority on the sea. The hostility of many nations against the British because of the Boer War was effectively used against them while Germany built its navy to new standards of excellence. Simultaneously, the Kaiser proselytized the Pan-German brotherhood by claiming the Dutch, Scandinavians, Flemish, and German Swiss as part of that extended family. The colonial extension of the Empire in Africa and in the Far East likewise became a significant burr under the British saddle because they wanted to retain their colonial and naval superiority. The Kaiser claimed loudly that he would work tirelessly until his navy was as large and as excellent as his army. That meant the British government made more and more expenditures to attenuate this threat, to the exasperation of the tax paying citizens.

As I have mentioned before, in this time frame, the world was at the end of the Industrial Revolution, and things were still moving extremely rapidly in communications, transport, weapon development, aircraft design and production, and all manner of industrial products. Factories could turn out literally hundreds of products that had previously been made more slowly by hand, due to mechanized production. A significant advantage accrued to the German Empire, because the workers were valued, educated, and rewarded for excellence, which equated to a higher quality product at less expense to the manufacturer. To them, the laborer was valued as an asset. The British, on the other hand, saw labor as just a tool, which didn't actually exist outside the factory or business, therefore illiteracy and job insecurity were commonplace. Job insecurity and lack of humanizing treatment created a baseness in laborers, accustomed to unpredictable employment practices, lack of respect, and perpetual poverty. The whole birth of the chemical industry was the brainchild of an Englishman (Sir William Perkins), but he couldn't get any backers in his own country. He took it to Germany where it grew and prospered. Meanwhile, Germany was educating, organizing, and improving scientific endeavors at an amazing rate. The series of books created by Beilstein as systematic reference for organic chemistry in 1881 categorized that field of chemistry from 1771 forward, and according to my daughter, they are still updated and used today.

It is amazing how many regions of the world were involved by 1915. The war had been considered in the USA as primarily a European war, but it was global. The cauldron bubbled on, and the names of the great leaders of that long past time have been buried in the ever deepening sands of time. No one remembers them, or even the corridors of time that they walked. The cycle continues, immutable in many respects, and unending.

The Balkan War lasted from October 1912 to May 1913, comprised actions of the Balkan League (Serbia, Greece, Montenegro and Bulgaria) against the Ottoman Empire. The combined armies of the Balkan states overcame the numerically inferior and strategically disadvantaged Ottoman armies and achieved rapid success.

But who was in charge, and who even remembers their names?

What Price Honor, Memoir of Eugene Adams

United Kingdom

- Benjamin Disraeli Earl of Beaconsfield (Prime Minister 1874-1880)
- Marquess of Salisbury (Foreign Secretary, Future Prime Minister)
- Baron Ampthill

Russian Empire

- Prince Gorchakov
- Count Shuvalov
- Baron d'Oubril

German Empire

- Otto von Bismarck
- Prince Hohenlohe
- Bernhard Ernst von Bülow

Austria-Hungary

- Count Andrássy
- Count Károlyi
- Baron Heinrich Karl von Haymerle

French Third Republic

- Monsieur Waddington
- Comte de Saint-Vallier
- Monsieur Desprey

Kingdom of Italy

- Count Corti
- Count De Launay

Ottoman Empire

- Karatheodori Pasha
- Sadoullah Bey
- Mehmed Ali Pasha
- Catholicos Mkrtich Khrimian (representing Armenian population)

Romania

- Ion C. Brătianu
- Mihail Kogălniceanu

Greece

- Theodoros Deligiannis

Serbia

- Jovan Ristić

Montenegro

- Božo Petrović
- Stanko Radonjić

Chapter Six - Warfare

The historical existence of warfare predates the existence of such things as the state, diplomacy, and nationalism by thousands of years. It is as old as humankind, itself, possibly because the seeds of it are deep within the human heart. The advent of what is called civilization, the proliferation of what we call society, and the rise of politics causes these seeds not only to sprout but to flourish.

Aristotle said that man is a political animal, and Clausewitz elaborated on that thought by saying that a political animal is a war-making animal. Perhaps it is simpler than that. As an animal that can think, and born with a natural urge to hunt and kill, war lies dormant within us. In learning more and more about warfare throughout my lifetime, I have concluded that the savage in all of us is just beneath the skin. I was able to witness this in myself, and in others when my time came to be a warrior. But that didn't happen until 20 years after the close of WW I. Back in 1915, three years before I was born, the USA was watching closely the events occurring around the globe, and trying to assimilate the meanings of the new central bank known as the "Federal Reserve", and terminology like The League of Nations being discussed by Wilson. These issues were widely discussed later on at that kitchen table in Elkhart, Indiana, and the one in Champaign-Urbana in the years following the formal closing of the war by the Treaty of Versailles.

There were 28 different gases utilized in WWI, with an estimated total 10,000,000 casualties. The first use was in Ypres with chlorine gas in April of 2015. Later, Adolf Hitler, a young German soldier, was temporarily blinded by British mustard gas. It affects the skin and mucous membranes of the victim, which includes eyes, and throat. By 1915, the Western Front was essentially deadlocked, and both sides were trying to find new and different ways to defeat their opponents. The trenches in some places weren't very far apart, but between the two lines of misery, there was a place called "no man's land," where following an offensive, there would be the grim reaper collecting the souls of the fallen. Then reinforcements would arrive, to replace those who would never fight again.

    In February of 1915, the British mounted an offensive in the Artois region of France and were able to break through at Neuve Chapelle in March, but as had happened with the Allies before, they could not take advantage of their success. Their intent was to interrupt German logistics by breaking through German lines. The French were also to attack at a place called Vilmy Ridge, which would insure cutting off German access to roads, railroads, and canals, which was essential to their ability to wage war at that point. Logistics is critical to all warfare, and between 1870 and 1913, the Germans had paid particular attention to it. They had created a separate department for railroads, where their efficiency shone through. Even today, in Germany, if the train is to leave at 0600, you had best be on board and seated at precisely that moment, or you either get left behind, or if barely on board, you'll hit your seat roughly. Germany had constructed railroads throughout the country, and then down to the Belgian border, where most had boarding platforms were long enough to disgorge over a thousand troops and their equipment within minutes. The French, aware of their poor logistics in the Franco-Prussian war, had also improved their own transportation system to avoid that pitfall in WWI. Therefore, if German logistics, which required transport not only of troops, but supplies, materiel, and even horses, could be severed, they could be driven back and Reims would be under Allied control. The concept was good, but required close orchestration of French and British troops to accomplish it.

    Although the French 10th was supposed to capture Vilmy Ridge, they elected to reinforce their 9th Army in the Ypres region, and contributed only artillery support to the British. The British had detailed aerial reconnaissance, which contributed to the tactical success and allowed a surprise attack on the Germans. However, their failure, due to disorganized interaction with the French allowed the Germans to regroup, receive reinforcements, and dig a new line. The Germans counterattacked with infantry battalions, numbering over 15,000 soldiers. Losses to the British of both British and Indian troops were 11,200; the Germans lost 10,000 men. The second battle of Artois took place shortly thereafter, from 9 May to 18 June, according to records. It was more successful, but took place along a 70 mile front. The losses were stupendous on both sides. Gains by the Allies were miniscule, but the combined Allied death toll was 130, 409 and the expenditure of over two million artillery rounds by the allies against the Germans. The Germans didn't escape unscathed, either. They lost over 73,000 troops there and continued to stack up casualties at the 2nd Battle of Ypres. They ended their offensive at Ypres, which had begun on 12 April, and concluded on 25 May 1915, in order to divert forces to Artois. But French General Foch maintained that failure to achieve more than a very modest advantage at Artois was clearly due to placement and utilization of British Forces and an inadequate reinforcement plan. Foch was prolific in his criticisms, but ineffective in accomplishing the mission. The Germans dug in deeply enough to resist most artillery from June 1915 onward. Their tactic with defensive positions was to make the enemy artillery move in closer and thereby exposing it to destruction by German fire. This made the French methods of attack by shoulder to shoulder advance of infantry completely obsolete.

These things were roundly discussed by my grandparents, and I had to keep a pencil and paper to try to keep up with the discussions. Grandpa John and Grandpa Alva most definitely disliked the French, and Grandma Crouch found it increasingly difficult to interject anything positive about them. As for the British, whose far flung members of their Empire, included the Irish for a time, sent troops to participate in the slaughter, she could muster a few kind words. All agreed that supply and logistics were absolutely critical on either side, and they marveled at the hideous loss of life due to mechanization of production of weapons, and the failure to actually find better ways than horse drawn lorries to deliver supplies to the combatants. Untold millions of horses were used, and thousands upon thousands of them died as a result. That put farmers in dire straits, because often their horses were simply requisitioned by the governments on either side, so fields didn't get ploughed efficiently, and it was far more difficult to harvest fields and get the crops in without their horses. And then the governments would simply requisition the crops, too, so there were food shortages everywhere. Also, the horses had to be fed, and literally tons of fodder had to be sent. They all agreed on one point. It was a waste of literally everything that had made countries in the prewar era both productive and prosperous. Grandma Ida would be silent through most of this discussion, and a look of profound sadness would replace that warm, sunny smile of hers. Then shooting of horses came up…horses stuck in the mud, mired sometimes even to their knees, due to the thick, slippery earth often along canals after the heavy rains. This was accomplished by British officers after wagons and harnesses had been removed. It was thought that the freeing of them could not be done, and they didn't want to slow down the movement of supplies and materiel – or leave horses that might survive to be taken by the enemy. Grandpa Alva had tears in his eyes when he told about it, and Grandma, who was openly weeping, hurriedly left the room. I was teary, too, thinking about gentle Old Bob, who despite his obvious age, diligently pulled the heavy plough each day. Grandpa Alva slammed his fist on the table and said that it didn't speed up the delivery of shells, ammo, food, water, impedimenta, or anything. Without the horses, who the Hell was going to pull the wagons? They had no motorized assets at the time. They only had soldiers. Besides, he reckoned that some poor civilian farmers whose livestock had been taken could possibly have come and saved those animals.

Blood, waste, cruelty, and horror spun through my mind, pushing out any romantic notion of how glorious war was. Grandpa sat back, looked at the ceiling for a while, and to reassure me, commented that later in the war, motorized vehicles would be used instead of horses and mules. That helped, but it didn't take away the sour taste in the mouth of a small boy. I was to give Old Bob special attention and love after that, which he returned by snuffing at my hands and neck, and whinnying when he heard my voice.

There were plenty more discussions at both of those kitchen tables over the years, and I was glad to hear about such faraway places as Gallipoli, the location of which I was shown on the globe. It was at the straits known as the Dardanelles, and sat near Russia's access to the Black Sea. Therefore, it was an avenue to mount an attack against the Turks and open up a sea channel for the Russians. It also was considered a way to divert German attention from the bogged down Western Front, and cause her to divide her forces further. Described by Sir Winston Churchill, then the First Lord of the Admiralty in Great Britain, as the "soft underbelly of Europe," the 1915 Battle of Gallipoli was a magnificent failure. Exquisitely planned by Churchill and Lord Kitchner, it potentially could have ended the war, but execution was completely botched. An inappropriate and unexplained airstrike in February forewarned the Turks, and they dug in in the high ground, implanted their guns, and mined the straits. Amphibious operations at the time were certainly an inexact, poorly developed tactical science. With the Turks dug in, particularly at an angle along the slopes, where they couldn't easily be observed or detected, the reliance on ship armament for British artillery support for the landing was a disaster when the Allies attacked in April. The Allied flotilla retreated because of the Turkish guns, which were in the high ground firing down on the Allies and out at the ships. The Allies dug in, too, so combatants peeped at each other from trenches similar to the situation on the Western Front, except it was a lot drier in the Dardanelles, and the Turks definitely had the advantage. The British finally withdrew by the end of 1915. Churchill was fired.

It was clear in the later discussions that Grandma Lovina Alice Shaw Crouch approved of the disengagement of the troops provided to the British effort by Ireland. Below is the only picture I have of her and the rest of the Shaw daughters. Their mother and grandmother (seated) are shown too, and Lovina, nicknamed "Lovey," is seated, at the far right. As far as I know, there were no sons, and she said she was born in "Brown County," which was as foreign to me as Gallipoli when I was a child.

What Price Honor, Memoir of Eugene Adams

Since she was born in 1874, and at the time of the photograph, she was probably about 18 years old, therefore this was taken circa 1892. I do not know the names of the others, but the mother, dressed in the dark clothes, upper left, was named Ellen. She always looked daintier than her daughters to me. According to my grandmother, all of them were well schooled, well read, and industrious. I can certainly vouch for the last two of those, because she worked all the time, and when she wasn't working at something, she was reading. Although she brooked no nonsense, she loved deeply, and always had time to answer those innumerable questions that children are bound to ask. When she was annoyed, she made bread, punching that dough into obedience and smacking it into perfect loaves, or she would sew. She had what was called a treadle machine, and she could make it hum along to make almost anything, or patch up holes in clothing that "still had a lot of wear left in it." Grandpa John said that she was so thrifty that she could even save the squeal of a hog when they had one butchered. Though they were town folks by the time I came along, they had lived in the country when they were a young married couple, but moved into Elkhart because John was a butcher by trade, and his shop was in town. They had six children, but one died in infancy when they had decided to take a Conestoga wagon westward through Illinois. My mother was the older of their two daughters. Their younger daughter, Arvilla, died young, either of consumption or from exposure to hydrochloric acid fumes as a result of working at metal plating processes. She was quite young when she died in 1933, and Grandmother was buried beside her in Rice Cemetery after her death in 1955. In the picture below, Mary, wife of Clifford Crouch, my youngest uncle, is standing beside their tombstones. Clifford has died, too, as has my mother. My father was murdered in 1941, and is buried in the same cemetery, but has no headstone.

I don't have many pictures to share, but the one below is of the whole Crouch family, taken when I was about ten years of age, which would make it about 1928. I am in the front row, with the funny stockings, and my sister, Mary Ellen is to my immediate right. Families tended to stay together.

What Price Honor, Memoir of Eugene Adams

Crouch extended family circa 1928

Fourth from the left in the first row of adults is Lovina Alice Crouch, and John F. Crouch is fourth from the left on the second row of adults. Fred Adams is the third from the left on that row, and directly behind him on the upper row is Clifford Crouch, with my mother, Edna Ellen Crouch immediately to his right. To her right is Paul Crouch, whom you will meet later on, because he was a pilot during WW II.

I don't have any pictures of Grandpa and Grandma Adams, but I have fond memories of all of these ancestors. I was told family legends about their ancestry, and it is fascinating. Evidently, I had an ancestor in every conflict the United States was ever involved in, and that is believable. My forbearers all arrived before the American Revolution, so I have concluded that anything is possible. But every family has those tales that are passed on from generation to generation. According to what I have been told, an Adams in a room by himself/herself is an argument, and Grandpa Adams assured me that President John Adams retired to a farm after his Presidency, telling everyone that if you scratch an Adams, you will find a farmer. But we must now get back to WWI in 1916, still before I was born. I benefitted tremendously by the interaction with the grandparents to know their version of the history, for subsequent accounts are neither as colorful, and probably not as accurate as the one I absorbed as a boy.

Chapter Seven – World War I

The Grim Reaper works overtime when war raises its head, opens its greedy mouth, and devours states, nations, continents, and the world. It is a serpent that sleeps, but does not die, for it lives in the heart of man.

    Deaths kept mounting up, and in a place called Champagne, from the 25th of September to the end of November of 1915, the French fielded 20 divisions against 6 German divisions. This was to grow on both sides. That translates into approximately 450,000 French soldiers (27 divisions) against 220,000 (19 divisions) German soldiers. This can be found in historical records, and is mind boggling to say the least. A division equates to 11,600 to 17,500 soldiers at full strength. It depends on the configuration of the individual nation fielding them. But with all these men, equipment, and impedimenta in the field, it began to rain. Cold, miserable rain turned the earth again into a treacherous ocean of mud and misery. While the name of the geographical location brings up pleasant enough thoughts, the battle fought there was so bloody that the ground could scarce swallow it up or wash it away.

    The French made inroads on the first two days, but despite the reports written later by French General Joffre, no real tactical advantage was gained, and the French were again unable to take advantage of superior numbers. In short, the Germans ultimately won, and the French troops fell into chaos, bordering on mutiny, so after losing over 145,000 troops, to losses of about 73,000 for the Germans, Joffre terminated the offensive. The Allies had fired over three million shells, and the French were simply out of ammunition. The British decided for the first time to use chlorine gas, and it was effective, but the lines were close enough that there were times that the poison gas would blow back on the Allied troops. Soldiers would, as they were to do later in my time of war, remove their gas masks when firing, because the visibility was poor when the lenses on the mask fogged up. The number of British troops injured or killed from their own gas attack couldn't be found when I asked that question.

There was a positive "first" for the Allies. The advent of air warfare came into play, bringing some better news and improvement in future operations. The British were also short of ammo, so the Royal Flying Corps provided aerial ID of German targets to economize on artillery assets. These squadrons were equipped with better communication than previously due to wireless transmitters, so information gathered could be quickly sent, and operations could be closely coordinated. Artillery rounds could be more accurately placed on German targets. Another "first" occurred, as well. The pilots of two Air Wings from the RFC flew over and dropped 100 pound bombs on German troops and their logistical assets, to include rail lines, staging areas, stockpiled ammunition, and alternate supply lines. Still, the result was another hard won victory for the Germans, despite what the "official" reports of the French would transmit to their populance. But something of great significance had happened. The use of tactical air warfare by the Allies was a significant advancement…and the German citizens were growing weary of the bloodletting. Socialism was beginning to creep through both there and in other nations, most remarkably in Russia. This war would ultimately end the days of the monarch, in all practicality, and introduce serious air warfare into the picture.

A second offensive was mounted. Losses were again stupendous on both sides, but many of the 60,000 Allied losses were due to lack of adequate ammunition, even down to hand grenades and failure of coordinated troop mobility. A shake-up of military leadership ensued, and at home, production of ammunition was kicked into high gear. It was a war where in one day, of 10,000 troops going forward, 8,000 would be lost. The Germans lost another 26,000 troops, and suffered significantly from the effects of both chlorine gas and the bombs, but in the bloodbath, they were considered to have won, but the war was not over. There was pressure on the Kaiser to use his navy.

The Battle of Jutland, in the North Sea off the coast of Denmark took place on the 31st of May in 1916. The British had deployed their battleships in the area to both pen in the German

Navy, and cut supply lines to the Wehrmacht in the field. It also prevented food and supplies to get to the German civilian population. The Kaiser had been reluctant to risk his precious naval assets, which he had begun to build up since before the war, perhaps as early as 1905. But the British interdiction of the movement of badly needed supplies into Germany by sea had caused critical shortages. The Navy, held hostage in their ports because of the Kaiser's reluctance to let them attack, was eager to be released, and an attack against the British Grand Fleet was planned and authorized for 31 May. Unfortunately for the Germans, the British had received intelligence about the imminent attack, so Germans in the impending battle lost the element of surprise. 250 ships collided in battle, one steel ring against another, on that fateful day. The British lost fourteen ships and over 6,000 men and the Germans lost eleven ships and 2,500 sailors. For all practical purposes, it could be called a draw, but those losses to the Germans were a higher percentage of their total assets in battle ships. At the end of the day, the German Navy slipped away and holed up back its ports, and their naval strength, except for the omnipresent U-boats, was effectively neutralized. It is difficult to assess how political support for Kaiser Wilhelm II was negatively impacted by this monumental disaster, but it was definitely waning. The Germans were suffering at home, because they had inadequate food or medical supplies to continually treat the wounded returning in such massive numbers, or even to care for the general population. But more importantly, the continued news of soldiers who would never again come home was devastating. Morale was plummeting; superiority in the field mattered less and less to the civilian population. Back home, there was something called "socialism" moving like a new wartime disease through Germany. It was infecting other nations, too, with a virulent strain in Russia.

Other battles were raging simultaneously, and the Americans were becoming more aware of the responsibility of being a "great power." In January of that year, President Wilson had tried to get a peace conference started, but that was a failure. Perhaps that effort was spurred by advice from a former President, Theodore Roosevelt, who had commented about the futile effort of nonintervention and avoidance of entangling alliances in 1912. Roosevelt said "We have no choice, we people of the United States, as to whether we shall play a great part in the affairs of the world. That has been decided for us by Fate, by the march of events." But Wilson's platform had been almost devoid of attention to foreign affairs. It became apparent even to Americans, and to their President, by 1916 that the policy of political isolationism from Europe could no longer continue. The nations of the world, since the turn of the century, had been drawn closer and closer due to international trade relations, exchange of ideas through the many social, scientific, economic, educational and financial societies. A greater degree of cooperation than ever before had been developing since the revolutionary industrial and economic progress worldwide. The entire face of finance had begun to change since the re-establishment of a central bank under Wilson in 1913, after having been abolished by President Jackson in the 1830s. Peace organizations had proliferated worldwide, during the decade before the outbreak of war, and the question of peace and outlawing war had been widely discussed. Many of the agencies, due to her geographical and the US history of political isolation made her a hospitable place for the "peace agencies" to discuss their views and present their teachings. Wilson was a leader in the worldwide Progressive Movement, but even he could see that America, despite her advantageous geographical location, could no longer remain uninvolved, so he sought to become an international arbitrator. The US government had issued a declaration of neutrality, but even so, was benefitting greatly from international trade with both sides of the European conflagration. Wilson possibly believed that when it was all over, the US might be the only "great power" able to negotiate a healing peace.

    The down side of international trade was the fact that the United States didn't have a Merchant Marine of its own, and the bulk of its goods were shipped by foreign carriers. According to international law, neutrality was supposed to be respected by all of the belligerents. Great Britain was still clearly the greatest sea power, and her trade ships were the most numerous of any on the sea. International law was still a vague and contradictory set of rules regarding commerce among nations neutral and embattled.

As a major power within the Allies, Britain turned to their 1909 Declaration of London, and began placing a great number of items which could not be shipped to countries with whom they were at war. However, this boomeranged into also stopping any vessel bound for neutral countries like Sweden, Holland, Denmark, or Norway, bringing them into a British port, searching them, and seizing any cargo they had placed on their contraband list. They included many things like cotton, which was used in making munitions, all munitions, or products intended for military use, and at last, even foodstuffs and medicines, which they deigned a military asset as well. Most of the items on the contraband list had not been on the original schedule of the Declaration. The list of products was so extensive that for all practical purposes, it curtailed American trade, which had up to that time been very lucrative. Although this alone placed a strain on what had been very profitable to both industry and agriculture of the United States, the British seizure, opening and preventing delivery of mail from American citizens to European friends or relatives, and mail coming to America from Europe raised an outcry in the United States, which kept increasing in volume. What had become closer and closer ties to an international community in prewar times were precious to the citizens with British ancestry and to many Midwestern citizens with ties to the Germanic nations were severed by what was considered criminal interference, and the US government was doing nothing to stop it. The avowed purpose of Britain was to obtain any military intelligence which could be used by the Allies, but it did not recognize the neutrality of the United States, which should have guaranteed the sanctity of their right to trade, even with other neutral countries.

  Prior to the outbreak of war in Europe, the United States did not have a sizeable standing Army. They had not participated in the arms races prevalent in Europe prior to 1914, and of the approximately 92,000 man Army, almost 20,000 were not trained as combatants, but were in logistical or administrative occupations. Wilson's federalization of the National Guard, and claims that the civilian militias could be called up to make up for the deficit were at best ludicrous. The Navy was in an even worse state of readiness. Although the technology for building sturdy steel-hulled ships had long been known, and had been adopted because iron was much harder to work than steel, and required significant amounts of time plus very skilled workmen to accomplish making a hull from it. The manufacture of a steel hull could be mechanized, and the product could be turned out much faster. Naval experts had long been trying to get sufficient ships to even protect the coastal waters, but their input had been studiously ignored. The Navy was severely under strength. There were about enough ships to protect for a day the long east and west coasts, and the Gulf of Mexico to the south, and some naval experts doubted even that.

  Though the US made many protests against the British extension of the contraband list and claimed something called "the continuous voyage"[1] right, which the US had invoked against Britain during the Civil War, the US protests, claims for seized cargo and seizure and examination of personal mail were ignored. Not only did Britain ignore the protests, she refused to alter her drastic, often illegal policy, which was unnecessarily arbitrary and in opposition to the rights of neutrals on the high seas. Bringing ships thought to be carrying products for the Central Powers caused a great deal of delay and financial loss to the shippers. Germany watched with intense interest, because she could not understand why the US would continue to allow Great Britain to abridge the right of neutral nations. Germany depended somewhat on accessibility of the neutral markets of the world for a successful outcome of the war. But German use of U-boats to disrupt trade not only among combatants, but neutrals as well, was viewed askance by the US. A serious conflict between the US and Germany then arose over the brutal, ruthless destruction of shipments of munitions to the Allies by sinking of cargo ships with great regularity. The outcry by businesses over these losses were answered by Germany asking that the US stop shipping munitions only to Germany's enemies, for that was not true neutrality, which

---

[1] "continuous voyage" was invoked by the US during the Civil War to stop British goods from being shipped to Havana, Nassau, or Mexico, and then onto the Confederacy. Confederate Union naval vessels seized goods before the English cargo reached their ports.

certainly made a credible point. The Wilson Administration brushed that complaint aside, so Germany tried to arouse pro-German sentiment in the US to get them to sell to the Central Powers, too. That ultimately failed, but the details are too complex to outline here. The end result was anti-German and anti-Austrian sentiment and Wilson issued a demand for recall of the Austrian ambassador and all German military and naval attachés because of "improper activities." He later dubbed the American citizens with German heritage "hyphenates," and denounced their efforts to influence American foreign policy. It actually spurred him to give serious consideration to US military preparedness.

Another factor was that only 10% American foreign trade was carried on in American vessels, because there were so few of them. In 1913, the US had only six cargo ships, but at the outbreak of WWI, shipbuilding underwent a significant revival. A Ship Registry Act was passed in 1914, which allowed foreign-built ships to be registered as American, if owned by an American, or by a corporation with American officers. Still, 66% of American trade was carried on British ships. Revenues from customs bottomed out in 1915 so the government raised excise and general taxes in 1914-1916 for what was supposedly required to increase "preparedness." Republicans called it "war taxes."

The President and his Secretary of State (Bryan) kept saying they could raise a million men between sunrise and sunset, should they be needed for defense. Conscription was ruled out. Wilson had maintained that an all-volunteer army was the best and was quoted in responding to pressure for conscription with "We shall not ask our young men to spend the best years of their lives making soldiers of themselves." But by 1916, it was becoming more and more apparent that noninvolvement was an unreasonable expectation and volunteers were not flooding the recruiting offices. General Leonard Wood made some public addresses, literally begging for better preparedness. He said in one of his public appearances "The Regular Army is just about equal to the police forces of Boston, New York, and Philadelphia," and that the militia might be worse than useless in war against any of the European "great powers" due to disorganization and lack of training. Two new organizations sprang up (National Security League, and Navy League) to increase pressure on the Administration about military preparedness, and to educate the public about the danger of failing to prepare. In May of 1916, a parade of 125,000 citizens marched up 5th Avenue in New York City in support of military preparedness in case of war. The central states were not as adamant about it. The peace organizations and Socialists kicked into high gear to counter this "warlike" sentiment. It was a contest to win the hearts and minds of the people. Roosevelt recommended declaring war on Germany because of their "ruthlessness." Wilson waffled, but began to change his anti-military stance, saying the US might be the sole champions of liberty and human dignity at the end of the war. But after a trip through the US, on June 14, Wilson led a preparedness parade of 60,000 in Washington, D.C.

The measures that Wilson wanted to take, though, were far below what the military deemed necessary, so his Secretary of War disgustedly resigned. He was quickly replaced by a pacifist. The National Defense Act was passed on June 3, 1916, and it allowed an increase of the Army to 186,000 over a five year period, and up to 220,000 by executive order. Suffice it to say, more than that many soldiers were often lost in ONE battle in Europe, but the plan was to also federalize the National Guard and manpower was to be limited to not more than 425,000 officers and men. More government offices were set up and manned to administer the program. Secretary of the Navy, Daniels, had set up a similar organization in 1915 and it was working. However, he hadn't met as much resistance as the Army, because American citizens seemed to understand that the necessity for a stronger Navy. Money was quickly appropriated for building and commissioning of 10 dreadnoughts, six battle cruisers, and 140 smaller vessels, as well as for naval munitions. But the final movement to get prepared came within months of America's entry into the war, and another election was at hand.

But back to the conflagration in Europe. Further to the east of Champagne in the European Theater was Verdun. Both small cities were near Reims, and very close to Paris. The Battle of

Verdun was taking place as the United States was still deliberating the best posture to take, to enter or not to enter that bloodiest of all wars. The Battle of Verdun began in February of 1916 and raged until the 18th of December, exactly two years before I was born. Joseph Stalin would have been 38 years old then. Verdun was chosen as the point of German attack on the Western Front because of its historical value to the French, and the Germans bombarded it with artillery fire for hours, hoping to cripple them into retreating to save the city. The very first round fired demonstrated the result of German intensive improvements in artillery guns. That first round was fired into a treasured cathedral in Verdun with a long barreled gun located twenty miles away. The 1000 year old cathedral was demolished. The German commanders issued orders to bombard in saturation form so that no supply line would be left open, and no enemy could feel safe. Verdun was a small, picturesque city which had previously been remote from the ravages of war, but since it was a treasured place to the French, the Germans decided to obliterate it. It is situated along the Meuse River and was protected by a fort, which was taken by the Germans quickly without firing a shot. But this time, the French were able to bring in reinforcements, and Petain had taken command of them himself. Many of the French trenches had been destroyed by the earlier German bombardment, but nature conspired to make conditions worse. There was mud, freezing rain, and ferocious fighting, which stalled the German offensive into March, but the casualties were becoming massive to both sides. The French asked the Russians to attack in order to divert German troops to the Eastern Front, but already the Russians were having trouble with, as Lenin called it, Russian people voting with their feet over the extended warfare. However, their numbers were significantly greater than those of the Germans, and the Germans clearly won; the Russians lost over 70,000 men. This had significant negative impact on Russian morale and boosted support of the already strong Socialist movement against the Romanovs. In April of 1916, the Germans attacked again on the Western Front against Verdun, with a long front along the Meuse River. This was met with stiff French resistance, who declared that Verdun would not be taken. Germany's attack only made minimal gains, but casualties were again high on both sides. Sentiment in

What Price Honor, Memoir of Eugene Adams

Germany for the war was waning, as it was among all the countries deadlocked in war, and civilian losses were also mounting.

The first Battle of the Marne had probably been the most important battle of the war, because German forces at the battlefront had been weakened by redirecting troops to prevent the mobilizing Russians from attacking Berlin. That saved France from immediate defeat and capture of Paris, which had been an integral part of the Schlieffen plan. The Battle of the Marne ended in the deadlock of trenches, and the Battle of Verdun was waged to continue the advance to Paris. Both sides had in 1914 anticipated a brief, decisive war lasting perhaps only a few months. Lord Kitchener of Britain actually predicted a 3 year campaign and was ridiculed, but in 1916, there was still no end in sight. Although the German occupied part of France at the time was small, it was strategically very important, because it contained France's iron and coal mines, and almost of all of the iron and steel manufacturing. As a result, France had to rely on Britain and America for munitions, putting additional strain on Britain. However, the next attack at Verdun saw the Germans attempt to maintain an over 25 mile front on both sides of the Meuse River. The tremendous advantage rail had given in the war to move thousands of men, horses and materiel from peacetime garrisons to the battlefield was lost once they disembarked. That the Germans had built some of their platforms a mile long, so that large units, up to a division, could unload in moments of arrival simply didn't override the conditions Mother Nature had made of the terrain. The soldiers on both sides had to move with the same rapidity as had the ancient Biblical armies, once they were deposited at the rail head. So the battle raged on for Verdun, and the Germans only made modest advances in early April, but on 18 April, the US had severed diplomatic relations with Germany altogether, after the U-boat sinking of the passenger ferry Sussex in the English Channel.

The Germans did, at that point, at the request of President Wilson, call off the U-boats, but through the rest of the Spring and Summer, the Germans took objectives at great cost, but failed to advance further than the bridges over the Meuse, where they briefly used phosgene gas. They took one small town, then settled into an attrition struggle for both sides until November. They had to send at first 4 divisions to support the foundering Austro-Hungarian Army on the Eastern Front, to be followed by another 20 divisions. The residual Austro-Hungarian soldiers were absorbed into the German Army. This rescue continual operations to support the Austrians had been a steady manpower drain and organizational impediment to the usual German military efficiency. Disengagement finally occurred in the Battle of Verdun on 18 December 1916, but only after repeated offenses and counteroffensives, when the Germans finally withdrew. I could remember the date because it was exactly two years before I was born, and my grandparents said that there was a total of over a half million combined casualties. Other sources placed it at a full million, but either way, it was an almost unimaginable loss of life. The Germans never captured Verdun. In addition to the front at Verdun, they had been fighting on multiple other fronts, had lost one of their only colonies, Cameroon, and though the Russians under Gen Brusilov were defeated, the victory was costly, as was the one in the Middle East. On the Eastern Front, the Russians had initially captured 350,000 Austro-Hungarians, but ultimately lost the campaign and a million casualties, so the morale of the Russian troops sank to new lows. The Battle of the Somme had begun for Germany against the Allies, and Wilson had won the 1916 election in November, with his slogan "He kept us out of War."

All across the military spectrum during the timespan of the Battle of Verdun, leaders were being replaced. Nivelle replaced Joffre for France; Britain had a new Prime Minister, Lloyd George, and the war cabinet was reorganized; Emperor Franz Joseph of Austro-Hungary died and was replaced by Archduke Charles; Gen Falkenhayn was replaced as German Chief of General Staff by Gen von Hindenberg; Blackjack Pershing would take command of the US troops. The military and political landscape was definitely different, but more importantly than that, a young corporal, Adolf Hitler, had been wounded in the trenches at the Battle of the Somme. Also, the British had finally released the new tank, which would impact the outcome of future trench warfare.

What Price Honor, Memoir of Eugene Adams

Time would be spent in the Post War Era, trying to fix blame for the outbreak of WWI, but that is irrelevant, except for the impact it would have had on the Treaty of Versailles, which set the stage for the inevitable outbreak of WWII.

Chapter Eight – Down in the Trenches

In a war, a single battlefield cannot define the scope of the conflict, just as a single stone does not reveal the design in a kaleidoscope, and like the kaleidoscope, the designs continually change in response to movement.

While battles raged in both the Eastern Front, where Austria faced Brusilov, and the Western Fronts, such as Verdun, in late June another conflict was erupting along the Somme River in Northern France. The British, under General Sir Douglas Haig initiated artillery bombardment against German positions. Several French divisions had been diverted to Verdun, so the British were the primary contenders at the Somme. As a part of his carefully designed battle plan, artillery was to shell the German lines for a full week, and on the 24th of June, this was initiated against German positions to soften the objective for a major Allied offensive. Still, in the heart of the fire zone, mobility of the infantry was severely limited at nearly catastrophic cost in "No Man's Land," the 900 yards between trenches. The artillery bombardment continued, though in that first week before the offensive, more than a million and a half shells were fired in the hopes of destroying the integrity of the barbed wire and German trenches. Haig had believed that this maneuver would allow the infantry to rapidly advance to push back and subdue German resistance. Though it was a grand plan, it was recorded shortly thereafter that a significant number of the British shells didn't detonate, and the wire that was struck became a Gordian knot of tangles, with only some gaps along it. Logistically, use of such a large amount of ammunition and guns placed a strain on resources and resupply, which was still done by horse cart from rail to the front. Supply of horse fodder also became critical. Though motor transport was in its infancy, it was vastly insufficient to reduce the need for thousands upon thousands of horses.

On 1 July, the British, advancing their infantry through rough terrain, pockmarked by shell craters, smoke and debris, weighted down by bulky packs that weighed between 60 to 70 pounds, were faced with a wall of death from the highly mobile German machine gun crews. The packs were carried over the top because it was believed that the German trenches would be quickly penetrated, and the advancing infantrymen would need them to clean out the enemy trenches for their own use. Given the rough ground and stiff resistance, it was not possible for them to move at anything but a fast walk. The machine guns could fire 600 rounds per minute on continuous feed, and there was no need to aim, because of the virtual wall of Allied infantry, advancing shoulder to shoulder, as fast as they could under prohibitive conditions. On top of that, the 12 to 13 divisions were sent forward in broad daylight, in successive waves, under what was called a "creeping barrage" of artillery fire. As soon as they got within 100 yards of the German lines, they would have to find gaps in the tangled barbed wire, which made them even better targets. The ground was soon covered with dead and dying, and the air was split with the agonized screams of the dead and dying. Finally some of the German crews even stopped firing because of the gargantuan horror of it. The British Army had never before in its history lost as many men in one day as they did on the first offensive at the Somme River. Of 100,000 men, they lost 20,000 killed and 40,000 wounded. Some observers even noted that some of the artillery duds had struck deeply into the soft earth, providing concealment for German riflemen, and the covering artillery bombardment wasn't effectively coordinated with the infantry advance, which left them exposed. But the German machine gunners were amazed at the persistence of the British, and that is where they began to refer to them as bulldogs. The German line held that day, with 6,000 casualties, as it held on a subsequent attack in mid-July.

   As mentioned earlier, the million and a half artillery rounds were fired during the first offensive and weighed about 20 tons of metal and explosive, which had to be transported to the front, and then replaced upon expenditure. These resupply needs caused the French and British factories to increase both quantity and quality. The British introduced 36 of their new tanks in September, terrifying the Germans with their size and potential capability. The tanks had two small side cannons, four machine guns, made a horrendous noise, and could advance ahead of the infantry to provide them some much needed cover for their advance. Inside, the eight man crew was protected by the shielding on the outside of these large, lumbering, noisy, tracked behemoths. It was the first utilization of tanks, and they all broke down mechanically or were destroyed by German artillery fire after having gained about one half of the 900 yards between trenches (approximately 3,500 yards), and clearly, if perfected, would be useful against trenches. They would be used again later in the battle, which dragged on for four more months, with greater success. But with the arrival of winter snowstorms and rain, the terrain was turned into a mud bath. The Allies, mostly British, lost 600,000 total for a gain of 7 miles; the Germans lost 450,000, and the front deteriorated into attrition on both sides.

There was a serious change in key leaderships in the opposing forces, as often happens when the desired result is not attained. In late August, before the end of the Battle of Somme, Kaiser Wilhelm II placed von Hindenberg in the office of Chief of General staff. Some others had estimated the total German losses at 600,000, which was equal to those lost by the Allies. I was the first time German losses had been virtually equivalent to those lost by the Allies. The battle ended along the 15 to 25 mile front along the Somme River at the end of November, and one of the injured was Corporal Adolf Hitler. Emperor Franz Joseph of Austria died at the end of November at the age of 86, after a 67 year reign and was succeeded by Archduke Charles, who wanted out of the war. In early December, Lloyd George became Prime Minister of Britain, and he reorganized the war cabinet. On 12 December, Gen Joffre was pressured into resigning as Commander in Chief of the French Army, and Gen Nivelle was promoted. However, the French morale was very low, they were not being properly provisioned or even fed, the effects of typhus, dysentery, trench foot, and chaotic offensives that ended in high casualties, so they were on the verge of mutiny. After the change of command of the French Army, the Germans withdrew from Verdun, and the combined losses for both sides in that long struggle was over a million. The government in Russia was becoming unstable, despite the success of General Alexei Brusilov in the humiliating defeat the Austro-Hungarians, who lost over 350,000 men, but the

What Price Honor, Memoir of Eugene Adams

Russians were unable to sustain and capitalize on the victory. The Germans sent in reinforcements, and the Russians could not obtain either supplies or reinforcements, so the withdrawal with the loss of a million men broke the Russian troop morale, further inflaming the political chaos on their home front. Italy had declared war on Germany in August because of the end of a power struggle within that nation. Wilson had tried to organize a peace conference, but that was not well received. At home, pressure was rising to enter the fray, and the troop strength was not yet adequate, nor completely trained. To say that things were in a tsunami-like flux is perhaps an understatement.

There were many other war zones where assets were taken and lost; allies and enemies came and went. The other events that were to influence the further prosecution of the war were going on in other parts of the world, as they had been since the beginning. In December 1916, the Romanian capital Bucharest fell to the Austrians, which gave the Central Powers the Ploesti Oil Fields, and access to their natural resources, as well as agricultural and industrial assets. Romania simply ceased to resist along the border with Austria. In the beginning, Russia had been able to mobilize much more rapidly than the Germans expected, and had invaded East Prussia and Austrian Galicia. Although von Hindenburg was successful in the Battle of Tannenberg, the Russian steamroller overran the bulk of Galicia and was stopped only by the Carpathian Mountains from descending into Hungary. Under Gen von Mackensen, a German-Austrian force broke the Russian lines, took back Galicia, and caused a general retreat along the whole Russian front. The Central Powers then had the extensive grain fields of Poland and Lithuania. It is possible that if the Russians had not been able to field forces all along the Eastern Front at the beginning of WW I, the Central Powers might have been able to concentrate on the Western front and take Paris within the first few months. That, however, is speculation. The bottom line is that Russian logistics might have been significantly improved if the Allied attempt at Galipoli had opened her sea access for supplies. It failed, and she had to rely on trickles of supplies from the Artic or Pacific. The Turks had effectively shut off the Black Sea to Russia; she could not reach the Mediterranean; the German fleet had sealed the Baltic. Perhaps if this had not happened, Russia might not have collapsed in 1917. Turkey had entered the war, allied with the Central Powers, and Russia failed to conquer Turkish Armenia, which later resulted in the extremely cruel, inhumane torture of the Armenians by the Turks. But by entering the war as part of the Central Powers, Turkey lost her 'overlordship' of Egypt and Cyprus (which had been previously given to the British). By 1917, the British forces occupied Bagdad and Jerusalem, and General T. E. Lawrence (Lawrence of Arabia) stirred up the Arabs against the Turks so that they didn't even have support among the Mohammedans of the Ottoman Empire.

Meanwhile, the naval superiority of the British component of the Allies allowed the easy capture of German colonies in Africa and the Pacific. The Germans were able to only hold on to one colony, which was in East Africa, until the end of the war. Japan took the colony on the Chinese coast, and the German islands north of the Equator; Australia and New Zealand occupied German islands in the South Pacific; the Union of South Africa conquered German South-West Africa; Germany's southern African colonies were divided between Britain and France. So before the end of the war, Germany's colonial status had in all practicality ceased to exist. Germany had concerns other than the deadlocked war in Europe, and so did the rest of the world. When Italy had joined the war in 1915, America was the only Great Power in the world remaining neutral. At the end of 1916, that was about to change. After his failure after a year to get a Peace Conference arranged, President Wilson asked the combatants to submit a list of their "proposed peace options." The response was less than encouraging. Through his confidential advisor, COL House, he had gotten word to the Allies that if they would submit their options, and Germany wouldn't, that the US might enter the war on their side. Nothing substantive happened. Germany offered a peace conference, but refused to submit options. The Entente Allies simply refused to participate in a peace conference, but sent Wilson a laundry list of their terms through an unofficial channel. Their terms were (1) restoration of all invaded nations, Belgium, Serbia, Montenegro, France, Russia and Rumania, with reparations for all damage done, (2) restoration to France of Alsace-Lorraine (not specifically named, but immistakably implied), (3) liberation of all subject nations of Austria-Hungary, Turkey, and expulsion of Turkish rule from Europe, (4) union of an autonomous Poland under the Russian Tsar. This so infuriated Germany that she went back to unrestricted U-boat blockade and even offered Mexico, in return for an alliance, all of the territory lost in the war of Texas Independence in 1836. That would have included New Mexico, Arizona, and Texas. If the US declared war on Germany, Mexico was to support Germany by initiation of supporting conflicts at the US southern border, to include German troops on the ground. Unfortunately for Germany, that telecommunication was intercepted by the US, and Mexico dared not accept the alliance. Wilson tried for a while to avoid outright declaration of war by arming merchant ships so they could defend themselves, but that was insufficient without an adequate merchant marine force. Wilson asked Congress to declare war on Germany on April 2, 1917, which they did unanimously. On 6 April 1917, America was at war with Germany, and shortly thereafter, Congress enacted a mandatory selective service law.

My mother had entered nurse's training in early 1917, so that she could go to France to help tend the wounded, sick, and dying. My grandmother, and her mother, was not particularly supportive, and my grandfather was positive about seeking a trade, but not about a trip to France. Neither was enthused about her serving the Allies. They were also displeased about her relationship with my father, whom she called her fiancé. She dutifully continued her studies, even after she discovered she was pregnant in 1918, but she did not go to France. She did, however, both marry my father, and she became a surgical nurse, in which profession she was to work until shortly before her death in the late 1970s.

Russia was collapsing, and German casualties were mounting faster than they had previously. The Germans withdrew to what the Allies called the Hindenberg line, but known as the Siegfried Line in Germany. Russia's revolt was primarily caused by the reverses in war, exacerbated by the privation at home. While the Tsar, Nicholas II, was honest, kind and patriotic, he was also an extremely weak leader who depended entirely too much on his advisors. Intriguers, like Rasputin, had too much influence in court, and were convinced that the way to avoid revolution was to refuse to concede to the demands of the public. There was a virtually explosive situation in the army, due in part to the arrogance, cruelty, inefficiency, and downright insolence of the officers. Whole regiments were ready to mutiny. There was a lack of food, ammo, guns, supplies, and support. While plagued with hunger, filth and relentless insistence that they mount futile offensives, resulting in massive losses and failure of the leadership to capitalize on any successes had destroyed the morale. There were also many Poles, Finns, Lithuanians, Jews, Ukrainians, and many others who did not consider themselves Russians, therefore there was no patriotic drive to fight under the flag they were required to serve. When the "bread riots" broke out in the capital of St. Petersburg, soldiers would often fight the police with the rioters. In February of 1917, a revolution broke out, and in March, the Tsar abdicated from the constitutional monarchy. For a short while, there was a provisional government, which tried to restore the war effort, but the people were chanting "bread, peace, and freedom." A brief attempt was made by a General to take control under a military dictatorship, but by November, the Bolsheviki Red Guards took over. They preferred to be called 'Communists,' and though various shades of liberals tried to forestall it, they failed, because they hadn't understood that the mutinous soldiers and hungry civilians weren't interested in more war or privation. The Bolsheviks were a radical faction of Socialists, who demanded peace, under the leadership of Vladimir Ulianov (Nikolai Lenin). This single faction of a single party established a dictatorship, for Lenin had returned to Russia from Scandinavia by way of Germany, having studied the teachings of Karl Marx. He understood that socialism could be permanently established by a dictatorial party called the "dictatorship of the proletariat." Next, as part of the new dictatorship, Leiba Bronstein, (Leon Trotsky), a well-travelled, cultivated Jew, became Commissar for Foreign Affairs. This new government quickly began peace negotiations with Germany and Austria-Hungary. The Treaty of Brest Litovsk was finally agreed upon in March of 1918, and Russia gave up many of her holdings. That closed the Eastern Front, providing Germany with increased foodstuffs, oil, and resources, rendering the impact of naval blockade by the Allies on the Central Powers less critical. It also left Germany to concentrate on conquest of Paris and defeat of the Allies. Lenin and Trotsky saw to the elimination of the threat of the return to Romanov rule by executing the Tsar and his entire family on 7 July 1918. So ended the protection of Orthodox Christians in Russia. According to Trotsky's diary, Lenin issued the order.

Chapter Nine – Isolation to Intervention

Dazed, stumbling, weary and hungry, the nations of Europe looked despairingly for any hope of an end to war, but clouds were forming within the nations, and Russia's collapse would be followed by the downfall of other nations if the terrible sound of bombs and gunfire did not cease.

America made very rapid transition from isolationist to interventionalist mindset with the declaration of war against Germany on that fateful day, 6 April of 1917. In Wilson's speech to request that declaration of war from Congress, he had stated that the United States had to make the world "safe for democracy." This followed on the heels of the increased German U-boat campaigns, which were taking out approximately one ship per day, and the sinking of an American grain ship, the Housitonic on 3 February 1917. He failed to mention that the resumption of U-boat assault on the blockade against Germany had begun after he had sent messages to the Allies hinting that if they would submit their terms for peace, and Germany didn't, America might enter the war on their side. Congressional passage of a mandatory selective service requirement, implemented on 18 May, resulted in rapid swelling of US military manpower. In the War Department, Douglas MacArthur, a recently promoted Major, was on detail as the Bureau of Information Officer of the War Department. There would be many more names of warriors involved in WWI that would later reappear during WWII. MacArthur, First Captain of his 1903 West Point Class, was a protégé of Gen Leonard Wood, and son of Gen Arthur MacArthur. Ted Roosevelt, son of Theodore Roosevelt, would also be involved in the prosecution of WWI as American involvement unfolded. His father, President Theodore Roosevelt had long been a supporter of both preparedness and the entry of the US into WWI. General J.J. Pershing, who was leading the Punitive Expedition, US Army after the 1916 attack on Columbus, New Mexico by Pancho Villa, (where LT George S. Patton had mounted a Gatling gun on a vehicle and killed many of the banditos) was recalled by Wilson. At that time, it became obvious that the US would have to enter

What Price Honor, Memoir of Eugene Adams

WWI, and Gen "Blackjack" Pershing would at the helm of the American troops in the Expeditionary Force. His name was put forward to Secretary Baker and President Wilson by then MAJ Douglas MacArthur, when Gen Funston, who had been selected for that post suddenly died on 19 February 1917. When the Rainbow Division of National Guardsmen was created, with units from all across the nation, it literally covered the United States like a rainbow, drawing the states together through the citizen soldiers they had contributed. Brigadier General Mann was chosen as Division Commander, and MacArthur was instantaneously promoted to Colonel and became his Chief of Staff.

Congress had rescued thousands of American citizens who found themselves stranded in Europe at the outbreak of WWI by immediate dispatch of warships to transport them to the US, and funds were appropriated for their ordinary expenses. To assist with the unwieldy numbers of refugees who fled across the Channel to England during the war, frightened, penniless, and homeless, an American Relief Committee under Chairman Herbert Hoover was formed. Hoover, a distinguished mining engineer, had been, by happenstance, in London at the time. He was also put in charge of the Commission for the Relief of Belgium. Hundreds of Americans, still in Europe in the early days of the war, volunteered for this agency and others like it. More came later to augment the effort.

The effects of the war had been felt in the US economy, such as trade, industry and revenue, in the extended effort to remain neutral. The illusions of isolation were dispelled initially by the loss of the thriving trade with the nations that became the Central Powers. Actually, many of the products previously shipped to England and the Allies were also no longer in demand. The large German Merchant Marine was withdrawn from the seas, so although there were many requisitions for England and France for war materiel, the only way to ship them was on British carriers. Since the Europeans had to sacrifice much of their agriculture and industry for the war effort, a brief depression in the US was soon countered by voluminous exportation increases. Not only had the war made the US the breadbasket and greatest exporter of the world, she also became a great financier. But the lack of shipping capability needed to be addressed. Dependence on Great Britain for sea transport became a serious problem, also their interference with and violation of our neutrality meant that shipments actually were possible only to the Allies. Since there was money to be made to build a merchant marine, there was capital attracted. Eventually, the government created a Shipping Board to foster the growth of a merchant marine and naval auxiliary. Before the Shipping Board could actually do more than get started, the US entered the war, and it had to assume enormous responsibility in connection with carrying out the governmental war package. There were also the Emergency War Revenue Legislations to meet the requirement for increased appropriations in conjunction with the financial impact of preparation prior to and later in execution of a war effort. Hithertofore, revenue going into the government was based primarily upon duties collected on imports, and it was insufficient, primarily because of disorganization of international trade. In 1915, customs revenue had yielded less than any year since 1899, and the Treasury had a deficit. In successive years, beginning in 1914, the entire tax system of the United States was revamped. The excise taxes were put on things like liquors and stamp taxes on virtually everything like brokerage transactions, amusements, promissory notes, insurance policies, bills of lading, telegraph and telephone messages, all kinds of train tickets, and on and on, rather than issuing Treasury bonds. Income tax on business and individuals was doubled, federal taxes on inheritances could be assessed at up to 10 percent, tax on net profit from the manufacture of munitions, explosives and firearms was at 12.5%, and amazingly there was no objection except from the Republicans, who called it "war taxes in time of peace." But peace was not to last, and expenses would go up. Preparedness was still a problem, as the expedition into Mexico had shown, though those troops did actually gain some experience.

Although Germany had attempted a peace conference on 1 December1916, which was then followed by Wilson's "peace overtures,' albeit through non-official channels, he was courting only the Allies. But what was the US becoming embroiled in? In April 1917, British combat pilots were suffering such high losses that the life expectancy was less than a month. Aircraft were being lost at extreme cost, and German offenses against London had residents becoming accustomed to the nightly air raid warnings, and the cold demoralizing fear that wore against already frazzled nerves. Germany's aircraft were superior, and they were first to engineer the synchronization of the propellers and machine guns so that they didn't shoot off the blades of their propellers. At the entrance of the US into the war, the nature of her involvement was still uncertain. The American public still generally viewed it as a crusade of a high moralistic nature. Germany, whose population was suffering from lack of food and severe economic difficulty under the civil control of von Hindenburg's policies was showing signs of unrest. Gen von Ludendorff, then known as the "robot Napoleon," who was officially the Quartermaster General, and second in command to von Hindenburg, began to take greater command of Germany's forces. Since von Ludendorff was so much more cognizant of political interactions among the enemies, particularly Britain and France, he began to study it carefully. The one thing that bothered him was the bulge in the Hindenburg Line (Siegfried Line), but fortuitously for planning purposes, that occurred at the weak point between British and French forces. There had long been squabbling between the highest commanders of those forces, and the French troops were on the verge of mutiny. They were unable to function efficiently due to lack of food, typhus, trench foot, dysentery, inadequate clothing, and most importantly, lack of ammunition.

In America, modification of the old term "peace without victory" was gentrified by Wilson to "a noble charter of international order." He had a talent for obfuscation with verbiage things that might arouse animosity on the world stage, while hiding the underlying intent. This was influenced by the flat refusal from the Entente to Germany's bid for a peace conference on 1 December 1916, and their demand that Germany offer complete reparations, restitution, and guarantee against any further aggression. By mid-December, Wilson was trying to get his own peace efforts accepted. He also let the rest of the world know that the US was not holding back from lack of concern, but because she must first be convinced that her efforts would be for the "rights of mankind." These were certainly idealistic ideas, but obscured the underlying intent. Wilson still seemed to believe that we might have the good fortune to bring the war to termination, preferably without shedding American blood, or economic assets, thereby assuring him of an historical prominence unequaled by any President since Lincoln. The isolationists were waning in their political fervor, and it became obvious to the general public that the country must, without a doubt, become prepared to actually become involved in the war in other than a neutral capacity. The division among them due to diverse ancestral origins was essentially laid aside, and the troops would proudly say they were AMERICANS.

My grandparents on both sides would still argued that despite the unification of the American population, it might have been handled better in many ways, without the monumental loss of human lives. Germany, at this juncture in April of 1917 had none of her country held by the enemy, and her lines extended into Belgium, France, over all of Serbia, most of Poland, as well as Rumania. Though she had suffered heavy losses in ferocious battles, still the German losses were less than those of the Allies, despite the addition of Italy to the Entente and British control of the sea. Given the lack of peace overtures, and because the blockade was severely negatively affecting the German civilian population, unrestricted U-boat operations resumed in an effort to blockade Britain. If Britain was disabled, France and her allies could not stand alone. This resulted in Berlin notifying the US that since an equitable agreement could not be reached, that the U-boat campaign was to resume immediately, and it did on 31 January 1917. Wilson's administration had sought to arm the merchant ships, and the Senate knocked that move down, but trouble was definitely brewing. The impasse with the US triggered the "Zimmerman telegram," previously mentioned. It was sent to Mexico by Germany, stating that if America were to enter the war against Germany, then Mexico should enter an alliance with Germany. She was to create a strong enough disturbance along the US/Mexican border to distract the US and divert some of the troops bound for Europe to protect the US southern border. Then, as a reward, Mexico was to receive Texas, New Mexico and

What Price Honor, Memoir of Eugene Adams

Arizona. Mexico was also to mediate between Germany and Japan. This telegram was intercepted by the British, since all cables had to go through a complex process to arrive at their destinations. The encrypted message went through a communications center at Land's End in Britain, where the signal was boosted for transoceanic transmission. However, the British had an intelligence center there, which, though they were not supposed to do it, decoded and forwarded the message to the US. There was quite a bit of discussion, plotting, and consternation over the Wilson government's determination to publicize possession of it, because it would reveal that the British were decoding German messages and Germany would cease to send them by that route. However, Wilson utilized that opportunity to his own advantage. Once announced to the American public, Germany's gamble unwittingly galvanized the unity of US citizens, and in particular, Texans, because there was and is a heavy population in Texas of people of German ancestry, who ceased to be "hyphenated". Also, Wilson had previously authorized an attack on Vera Cruz, so relationships were not good between Mexico and the United States. The new President of Mexico, Carranza, who had replaced Madero after an internal uprising, certainly didn't want to throw fuel on the fire between the two nations, primarily because the US was militarily much stronger, and also had alliances with nations that could easily strike Mexico's southern border or along her extensive coast lines. Mexico declined Germany's request.

Russian turmoil continued, as the provisional government, established in March in the republican format, teetered, and though the Eastern Front ceased to distract Germany from the primary objective, Austria-Hungary was becoming even weaker. The huge sums of money loaned to the Russians by France were now forfeit, and France had her own other economic difficulties as well. The careful German organization of her food supplies and ruthless plundering of occupied regions of Poland, Belgium, Rumania, and the Ukraine kept Germany from outright famine, but underfeeding was beginning to take its toll on civilians, decreasing the civilian will for absolute victory. Austria-Hungary was of little help, because she was threatened by unrest and outright hostility from

Slavs within her borders. Czechs and Slovaks who had been captured by the Russians managed during the Russian collapse to get to the armies of the Entente by going through Siberia, and they fought with the remaining Entente forces. The new emperor of Austria-Hungary, Charles, sent messages to the Entente Headquarters that Austria-Hungary wanted peace, as long as it didn't mean dismemberment. Italian defeats actually led the way to Austria-Hungarian defeat in the winter of 1917. By then, in France, Clemenceau had become Premier, with almost dictatorial power. He would tolerate no defeatists. Predictably, there were changes in military and political leadership. In Britain, during the Easter week of 1916, there had been an Irish rebellion, so when Britain introduced conscription, they dared not draft the Irish for fear that another rebellion would break out. In summary, the broad-based instability among both combatants and noncombatants of nations embroiled in the global conflagration indicated that many of them would shortly fall victim to the fate of Russia. Chaos would certainly rule.

It was taking time for the US to raise its Expeditionary Force under Blackjack Pershing. The willingness of German civilians to continue the massive war effort was definitely waning. Even though Spring was lifting the green shoots from the earth, and it was warmer to stand in the long lines for them to get their meager rations of flour, sugar and a few staples, the mood grew more dreary by the day. The people were asking why the war couldn't end while Germany was seemingly ahead – but von Ludendorff was acutely aware that since the US was training up an Expeditionary Force, behind which was a virtually inexhaustible wealth of more men and war materiel, being ahead was a mere illusion. Advantages in force numbers, despite military excellence, and supplies of munitions and better weapons could soon be lost. The time to break the deadlock on the Western Front was running out, and Germany was teetering on the edge of collapse at home. As a result of the collapse of Russia and the signing of the Treaty of Brest-Litovsk in March of 1918, full force could be turned to the strategically and critically important offensive von Ludendorff had already planned in November 1917 with the German military hierarchy. It had to be launched, immediately if not sooner.

What Price Honor, Memoir of Eugene Adams

Kaiser Wilhelm II had slowly been moving to the background and von Hindenburg had to lessen his command presence in combat offensives. The problems von Ludendorff was facing were primarily logistical, due to shortages of literally everything, due to the years of non-relenting naval blockade of Germany. As probably the most militarily excellent of the commanders on either side of the impending last major campaign in a war that had lasted over four years, von Ludendorff took under careful consideration all strategic and tactical aspects of his last great offensive. He first considered that the British, if defeated would probably end the war, because the French would simply give up. However, the terrain and overall geographic conditions mitigated against striking against the British lines at the point of their greatest strength toward the west. Ludendorff was aware of the less than cooperative interactions between British and French forces, and the mutinous attitude of the French troops, so he sought to strike at a point which would sever the two. That would exacerbate the lack of cooperation between them. The biggest obstacle the Germans would face by avoiding the mud of the flatlands like Flanders was the burnt earth desolation they, themselves, had left across the plains when retreating from the Battle of the Somme a year before. However, due to the conflict between the British and French, there would be a possible corridor between them of 20-25 miles, which would be poorly guarded due to the French withdrawal of their troops at that point. That stretched the British line, and was to be guarded by the least capable of their armies. The other advantage was that the German troops could be safely withdrawn through land they held, but the Allies had almost no room to withdraw. For this last powerful offensive, von Ludendorff moved three full armies forward to attack along a line of nearly fifty miles. In his carefully conceived plan, once the Germans, close to a million strong, broke through, they would wheel on the right flank to push the remaining Brits to the sea. The connection between the French and British would be broken. On the left flank, the German forces would advance as far as the Somme River and hold as a foil against counterattacks that might strike the German rear. Should that be in any way unsuccessful, the backup plan was equally well designed and would pin down the British so that the main offensive literally ripped them from any access to the sea, severing any opportunity for logistic support or reinforcements by that route. It was a brilliant plan, and von Ludendorff had announced that he was willing to lose a million men to accomplish that goal before the American Expeditionary force could get there, and that Germany would "be in Paris before April." Had the plan succeeded, Grandpa John Crouch said that we all might have been speaking German after that.

During the German pre-battle build up, there was a pervasive tension in the trenches on both sides. As usual, at night, both sides had patrols slinking around between the trenches to gather intelligence. Nights became fairly quiet and the warmer weather was very welcome. The artillery was essentially silent for a while, with gun crews lolling about and catching up on much needed rest. Though Ludendorff couldn't hide his chosen point of attack, he successfully disguised the magnitude of it, and in March, he had begun training up what would later be called "storm troopers." Large ammo dumps were concealed under mountains of hay. Gun emplacements were carefully camouflaged, as were the locations of the machine gun crews. The activity was apparent to the British, but veiled both by the heavy morning mists and clever facades. The extent of the plan was completely unanticipated. Instead of the previous lengthy bombardment prior to attack, it would be only an intense initial barrage, early on the morning of the advancement of the storm troopers, dressed in gray and slinking across along the ground under the cover of fog, either on their stomachs, or bobbing up and down between shell craters. It offered the best defense against presenting easy targets and maximized the element of surprise. The storm troops were to open gaps in the enemy lines and they would be followed by a flood of infantry to wedge them open, then more troops to widen the holes in the line. For the first time, these troops would be Reserve soldiers, and though that had never been done before, it was necessary given the manpower constraints. But the weather wasn't cooperating. A cold rainfall, and a wind came up. The latter might affect efficient use of gas or flame throwers, but because of the fog, there hadn't been many British patrols on the night of 20 March. However, they had discovered some places where there were holes cut in the German barbed wire, which they thought might be so that infantry could slip through. This was reported, but probably not really considered until more intelligence was gained from German prisoners who had been captured by the British, about a great offensive which was to begin on the 21st, and the prisoners wanted to be moved to the rear to avoid being killed by their own artillery and countrymen. British troops drew lots to see who would have to go forward, and some others were sent to hide out in No Man's Land, armed with flare pistols to shoot up flares if an enemy advance was detected.

Early that morning, the last great battle, which would determine the fate of Europe, began. At between 0430 and 0440, an earthshattering series of flashes and explosions lit up the sky and deafened anyone, even behind the lines on either side. Winston Churchill, who had been visiting the front, and was quartered about five miles behind the British lines described the cannonade as the "most tremendous" he had ever heard or was likely to ever hear again. The sky was aflame, the ground was trembling, and smoke filled the air. More than a million men, collectively, participated in that greatest onslaught in the history of warfare. The Germans even broke through at some places to the "lines behind the lines," where Britain was practicing something called "in depth defense." The concept was that the battle lines were to hold as long as they could, but when they were no longer able to do so, units had been placed behind the battle line to stop the enemy advance. This redundancy was not always completely successful, and at some point, cooks, clerks, and other non-combatants were called upon to stop the German advances. The flare pistols had been fired, but flares could not be seen in the heavy mist, and those British soldiers died quickly. Overall, the first day was a success for German forces, and for the Grim Reaper, who was collecting a bumper crop. The 22nd would not begin or end as well. When the cacophony of artillery and gunfire erupted that day, some German troops, to their horror and mortification, realized that they were being bombarded by shells from their own side. What had happened was that during the night, the artillery pieces had not been pulled up for the next onslaught. Bullets were flying and death was lurking everywhere in that heavy morning mist. Also, as light began to filter through and the sun dispersed the fog, British airplanes provided close air support to their ground troops by heavily strafing the closely packed German soldiers. But though it had begun badly on the 22nd, through the 24th of March, the Germans were advancing still, over a landscape surreal in its ghastly horror of unbelievable destruction. But ultimately, other events finally led to the inability of the Germans to secure a final victory, and the American Expeditionary Force had landed. On 9 April, Ludendorff called off the offensive, after having gained over a thousand square miles of Allied territory, captured 90,000 prisoners, over 1,000 guns, and unknown quantities of supplies and provisions. Though it sounds like a great victory, it wasn't worth the cost, because Ludendorff had a greater distance to defend, less ammunition, and massive casualties. The connection between the British and French had not been severed. The French had not given up. Those major objectives had not been achieved. By November, Germany's homeland was caving, the Turks had given up, Austria-Hungary had lain down their arms, and the Kaiser had fled to the Netherlands. The Yanks, once they learned not to march shoulder to shoulder into enemy fire in the old way, achieved some victories, and the outlook for Germany to continue the struggle was bleak.

Germany sued for peace, and an Armistice was declared at 1100 hours on the 11th day of November. Little did they know that they would not even be invited for the construction of the final treaty, nor what would be the result thereof. Someone once said "All is well that ends well," and this did not end well.

Chapter Ten – Beginning of the End

For Germany, it was the beginning of the end, for America, it was the beginning, and for the Allies, the winds of Fate had blown favorably in their direction. But all of Europe was bleeding, and there was naught to bind her wounds. An ill-conceived treaty would insure that another horrific war would ensue. World War I lasted four and a half years, 29 July 1914-11 November 1918

At the end of his offensive, which conceivably could have won the war for Germany, von Ludendorff now had a longer front to defend and flagging support from home. Germany was on the verge of revolution, the monarchy essentially didn't exist, communist and socialist agitators were at work, but the people set up a provisional government along the constitutional republican lines. The people were demanding peace and an end to the misery and privation of the war effort. Hungary was falling away from Austria, and the Central Powers were dissolving. Bulgaria and Turkey surrendered in October, Austria-Hungary collapsed in November, Czechoslovakia formed a provisional government, Hungary separated from Austria, and the old empire on the Danube ceased to exist. The naval actions of von Tirpitz ensured the Americans would become involved and alienated liberals and socialists in Germany, which influenced reform of the German constitution. Changes in the leadership of the Allies was to have a profound effect, as well. At a joint Allied meeting, Gen Haig, commander of British forces, suggested that Gen Foch, recently put in charge of the French forces under the Premier of France, Clemenceau, be designated the supreme commander of all Allied Forces for the duration. It was a masterful move that united the Allies into one military body, although there was to be no dismemberment of British units to reinforce within forces of other nations, to include France. Whole units would have to be reassigned intact to meet any need. That, too, was a stroke of genius. Foch agreed, and the disunity between Britain and French military was essentially eliminated. Gen Ferdinand Foch would brook no disloyalty, and would not hesitate to execute those who mutinied. He was a short, bandy-legged man, but he emanated determination, discipline, and dedication to military success.

The Yanks were definitely making their presence known. Pershing, after the declaration of war in Congress and his appointment over all American forces in Europe, was dispatched by President Wilson with a small contingent of soldiers to France. On June 8, 1917, Pershing arrived in Liverpool with a staff of 53 officers and 146 enlisted soldiers, as a sign of good will. They were welcomed even by King George V, who said it had answered a dream of his life "to see the two great English speaking nations more closely united." When Gen Pershing got to France on 13 June, he was received with great joy, and a unique honor was bestowed on him. Marshal Joffre led him to Napoleon's crypt, where he was permitted to hold Napoleon's sword, a gesture which had never been offered before. While Pershing coordinated with the French War Office for communications, base locations, depot locations, and all ancillary arrangements for operational efficiency, he organized his staff as a template for units subsequently to report to the Theater. He was responsible for the system used today for specific staff responsibilities which are G1, administration, G2, intelligence, G3, operations, G4, logistics and transportation. If lower than General Staff, the prefix was changed to "S." These are still used today. He then informed Washington in July that the smallest force to properly execute the mission in Europe would be 1,000,000 men. They should be trained, equipped and transported to France by May 1918, and furthermore, he recommended raising an army of 3,000,000 to be prepared immediately, 1/3 of which would be transported to fill the immediate requirement, and the remainder to provide adequate replacements or reinforcement, as required according to need. Also, they would be available for any national emergency.

I spent a lot of time at the library at Ft. Benning, GA, Home of the Infantry, studying General Pershing, and was fascinated by his tremendous organizational ability and military excellence. There can be no doubt that he was the right man for the job. Lead elements of the AEF arrived and engaged the Germans. The victory at Chateau-Thierry, Battle of Belleau Woods, and capture of Vaux had tested those troops and halted the German advance in their Great Offensive, and it had also resulted in casualties, but the morale factor the Americans generated in the Allied Forces through these and other successes was significant. At first, Gen Foch sought to take American troops and integrate them into French units, but that was absolutely refused by Gen Pershing. They would support the French, but only as units, so. After they were assigned a sector, from Reims to the Swiss border, Pershing realized that the distance between the ports of disembarkment was logistically unacceptable for coherent offensive operations. He therefore busied himself over the last half of 1917 getting rails and locomotives, as well as building materials shipped over from the United States to address that shortfall. Deficiencies in port facilities used by the Americans at Brest, St. Nazaire, and Bordeaux were upgraded and enlarged, cranes were brought in, as well as other equipment for handling cargo. Since the French railway system in Southern France was inadequate and exhausted, more than 1,000 miles of lines, standard guage with double tracking, cut offs, and tracks in the yards at ports and depots were laid. Over 1700 locomotives were brought over, 27,000 freight cars, and 430,000 tons of rails and other equipment were brought over and installed. Barracks, hospitals, stables and 20,000,000 square feet of storage were constructed and manned. One of the hospitals (Mons) covered 33 acres. The British and French began to question the necessity of such massive facilities, since by the end of 1917 less than two hundred thousand US troops had arrived, and only 300,000 by the beginning of the opening of the German offensive in March.

Pershing ignored that, and continued to both prepare adequate transportation and facilities while simultaneously assuring that the arriving troops were further trained in the kind of warfare in which they were to be engaged. After arriving in France, both officers and enlisted men received a system of rigidly intensive training to match the advanced requirements of the European war. Gen Pershing had no doubt of the inherent ability of American soldiers, but was determined that they be properly trained so that combat operations were successful and casualties minimized. At one point, the French were questioning the length of time it would take to get reinforcements from the US to the front. They were soon relieved that troop movements were rapid, and in larger numbers than they had hoped for.

An American Expeditionary Force (AEF) landed at St. Nazaire, France in November of 1917, as the 42nd (Rainbow) Infantry Division, with units contributed from 26 states, 27,000 strong, dedicated to victory. The number of troops in just that one contingent seemed to somewhat relieve anxiety in the minds of the Allies. The 42nd, commanded by Gen Mann, with Douglas McArthur as Chief of Staff, had sailed from Hoboken to France on a Troop Transport craft, the Covington, escorted by Navy CPT Arthur McArthur's ship, the Chattanooga. Units were made up of active Army, Army draft, and Reserves, taken from 26 states, which had coalesced into a cooperative, cohesive, determined division.. They were solid both in officer and enlisted ranks, cohesive, enthusiastic, and despite having to dodge mines and U-boats, made the voyage in 14 days. While on board, they had been drilled daily for long hours, and definitely were glad to get rid of the sea legs and a short rest from the intensity of continuing training. The Covington had made it safely across the Atlantic, but she was sunk by a U-boat on her way back out. The 42nd was to acquit itself well in Europe, and would appear again in WW II. The presence of American forces in massive numbers, complete with equipment, facilities, transportation and logistical support orchestrated by the Supply Service created for that purpose by Gen Pershing was, as German Gen von Ludendorff had anticipated, the death knell for Germany's possibility for victory.

Until September of 1918, the German military dictatorship had demanded war until victory, but by then it was impossible. The delay, however, had made favorable compromise to end the conflict, equally impossible. Prince Max of Baden, as chancellor of a peace ministry, negotiated for an Armistice. Wilson said he would only deal with a representative of the German nation as a whole, but was assured by Baden that the ministry represented the majority of the Reichstag. However, during the peace negotiations, a revolution swept the monarchy away completely. In Early November there were mutinies in the fleet, strikes in the factories, socialist and communist outbreaks in cities, desertions in the army, and the abdication of the lesser princes, so Prince Max surrendered his authority to the newborn German Republic. All the military details of the Armistice were devised by marshal Foch, and the outline of peace was predicated on the 14 Points President Wilson had presented in a speech made in January of 1918. These are summarized as:

    (1) Open covenants of peace, openly arrived at. (no secret diplomacy)
    (2) Freedom of the seas
    (3) Equal trade conditions to all nations
    (4) Reduction of armaments
    (5) Impartial adjustment of colonial claims
    (6) Evacuation of Russia
    (7) Restoration of Belgian independence
    (8) Evacuation of France and return of Alsace-Lorraine to that country
    (9) Readjustment of Italian borders along national lines
    (10) Autonomous development for the different peoples of Austria-Hungary
    (11) Evacuation of Rumania, Serbia, and Montenegro, with access to the sea for Serbia
    (12) Freedom for people of the Ottoman Empire and opening of the Straits to commerce at all times.
    (13) Independent Poland with access to the sea
    (14) A general association of nations.

But the European allies insisted on two amendments during the negotiations.

    (1) Reserve freedom of the seas for further discussion
    (2) Restoration of invaded territory to allow reparation for all damage done to civilian life or property by Germany and her allies, by land, sea, or air.

Germany agreed to make peace, based on the provisions by Foch and the 14 points as amended. There were also considerations to be made of treaties made by the Entente during the war, and some nations that had existed before the war no longer existed. New nations formed, though they were not always along national lines based on ethnicity of the people, and they were usually in the republican format. The blockade of food for Germany was supposed to be lifted, but it was not. The German people were starving by the droves, and so they had been lied to and the civilian population victimized further. The Versailles Treaty was a document that further wrecked Europe on the eve of her bloodiest war. It would overlook the Armenian and Greek Genocides in the Ottoman Empire. It would disavow the rights of multiple ethnic groups to determine their fate, for it would ignore the desires of the people living in various areas, and engender in those so harmed a burning hatred, as starvation in some countries began to take more lives than had been lost in battle. It was also based on a contract signed under duress in Allied absolute hatred of those who had sued for peace and who were denied a voice in creation of the final document. I used to hear the expression: "Etiam diablus audiatur" from one of my grandfathers. How could this happen among "civilized" nations?

Germany had agreed to come to the negotiation table, not the guillotine. Though she and her allies had lost fewer combat casualties than the Allies, the privation and starvation of the civilian public probably killed more of the German public than battlefield losses. The British, then later American, blockade had been extremely effective during the war, and under the terms of the Armistice, it was supposed to be lifted, but that didn't occur until July of the next year. Then the wholesale butchering of national lines began in earnest, in vengeful determination to satisfy the land lust of the "victors." Bluntly, no one really won, because the stage was set for the war I would eventually be fighting. Czechoslovakia was a new nation established with the dismemberment of Austria-Hungary where 4 ½ million Germans and Hungarians, 3 million Slovaks, and a smattering of other ethnic groups were to be ruled by 7 million Czechs. At this, the Chief of the American Delegation filed, Archibald Coolidge, a memorandum objecting to this action, but it was ignored. The French wanted all of the Rhineland, in addition, of course, to Alsace-Lorraine, as a buffer zone for them in case of subsequent action by the Germans. They were unable to get that entirely, to Foch's consternation, but were, with US backing, able to get occupation rights for 15 years to ensure a safety region considered equivalent to that of the British and Americans with their sea protection and naval capability. Greed for new territory by all those who claimed victory was backed by the United States. Wilson's stated claim to Congress that the settlement was fair was simply a lie. There was no honoring of plebiscites from any of the butchered parts of Germany, Austria, Hungary, Bulgaria, and Russia to see by whom they wanted to be governed. If there were winners in the Versailles conference, it would have to be the Czechs, Serbs, Poles, and Rumanians. The "victors" hovered over the carcasses of the conquered like butchers over a carcass of prime beef, and sharpened their knives for measures of humiliation to flavor the cuts. Hatred and emotional vitriol was served up to the German representative sent to sign the treaty. In the "agreement," to use the term loosely, Germany was to accept responsibility for the entire war, and destruction of civilian life, property, military losses, and anything else that could be thrown in, including reparations to include payment of pensions to British soldiers who had fought in the war. That was the biggest lie. In any argument, there are two sides to the story, and there were many other factors in the pre-war balance of power that led to the outbreak of conflict, not the least of which was the French anger over the humiliation of having lost Alsace-Lorraine to the Germans in the Franco-Prussian war, which was a move to assuage the German humiliation for having lost it during the Napoleonic Wars. Not only had the political and economic life of all nations participating in the Great War been altered materially to meet the needs of armed forces on the battle fields, hundreds of billions of the world's wealth had been destroyed, and millions of acres of fertile land had been desolated. Actually the United States emerged as the world's financier after the conflict was over, but the "victors" were drooling over the price that could be exacted from the Central Powers. The peace that Wilson had often described as the peace of justice was clearly a peace of revenge. Lloyd George of Great Britain actually won his sweeping election victory by demanding that Germany pay for the entire cost of the war. Reparations that Germany was to pay were set at 132 billion gold marks, equivalent to $31,400,000,000 at the time, as well as the Belgian war debt, and the cost of Allied Occupation Forces along the Rhine, and return of treasures such as the original Koran of the Caliph Othman and the skull of the Sultan Mkwawa. Austria-Hungary, Bulgaria, and Turkey were assessed far smaller indemnities, because it was clear that they didn't have the funds to pay large sums. Since much of the industrial and natural resources of Germany were sliced off with the establishment of new nations and seizure of territory by the Allies, neither did she. At first, she was able to make payments with goods and what remained of her natural resources like coal. Of the reparations and other indemnities, the bulk of it was paid to France.

During this lengthy procedure, German representatives were at first excluded for several months, and though later admitted, were not permitted to speak at all. They could only submit comments in writing, which might or might not be read or considered. The reason for not allowing them to attend the initial negotiations was the fear that any disagreements among the victors might be used by Germany to her advantage, therefore the first of Wilson's 14 points was ignored. Certainly not all negotiations were conducted openly, and certainly not the ones to which the Germans would have the most stringent objections. Therefore, secret diplomacy was most assuredly utilized, particularly in the case of things like the "Polish Corridor," which included Posen and West Prussia, all the way to the Baltic Sea. That separated East Prussia from the rest of Germany, and Poland was also given a large portion of Silesia. This is only one example, and while there were some plebiscites conducted, if the result was unsatisfactory to those wishing division of territory to suit themselves, the results were ignored, therefore it was the same as if they had not been conducted at all. No more were conducted once Germany was permitted to have delegates present, though not participatory in the negotiations. Ultimately, the Treaty was not one of mutual agreement but a declaration of terms under force. Austria and Hungary fared even worse. New nations like Czechoslovakia and Yugoslavia gathered in spoils, as did Denmark, Italy, and Serbia. The Turks also lost significant territory, but were able to retain Armenia, despite their virtual genocide against the inhabitants, and the Middle East was parsed out primarily to Britain and France. There were also other changes in the way countries dealt with distribution of some of the colonies and property through a legal device called a "mandate," which was monitored by the League of Nations through mandatory reports to that agency by the country holding the mandate.

Disarmament was severe, though it was supposed to occur for all nations as stated, "to render possible the initiation of a general limitation of the armaments of all nations." This was embodied in the 4th of the 14 Points, but was ignored by the victors. Only Germany was denuded of large stocks of military equipment, her army limited to 100,000 regular soldiers, none of whom could be maintained west of the Rhine, nor fortifications established along its banks. The river itself, was internationalized for traffic, as were all rivers in Germany. Naval installations, like Helgoland, were dismantled. Her navy was to be restricted in size and zones of operation, and most of the ships were surrendered. Some, as pointed out previously, were sunk before they could be taken, and the British sailors fired at the unarmed German sailors as they left their sinking ships in lifeboats. Germany was never to have any submarines in the future. This was punitive, but the inhumane treatment of the German civilian population was and is inexcusable. On 7 May 1919, when Clemenceau, with Wilson accompanying him, presented the completed document, the German Foreign Minister, von Brockdorff-Rantzau not only addressed in his written note, as required, the powerful hatred their delegation had received, but the unjust accusation that only Germany had caused the Great War. He stated that for him to admit guilt for the war would simply be a lie. He also mentioned the hundreds of thousands of non-combatants who had been killed "in cold blood" since Germany's surrender by privation and starvation, and advised them to think about that when they were assessing guilt and punishment. This angered Wilson, Clemenceau and Lloyd George. Later, when Phillip Schneidermann was led into an office like a criminal to sign the document, he refused to sign and resigned his office as Chancellor. However, a disarmed Germany was facing threats on every side besides the starving, and Foch was preparing to lead an attack on Berlin with a full army if Germany didn't capitulate. On the 28th of July in 1919, two

German delegates were escorted like prisoners through a large crowd and the Treaty of Versailles was signed.

Why it was not understood that an undying hatred can be engendered when someone is forced at literal gunpoint to admit to a crime he/she did not commit is absolutely astounding. This and the continued mistreatment of members of the Central Powers in the post war years were predictably seen by some, like even Lloyd George, as fuel for another war, but Wilson was angered by anyone that denigrated what he was so proud of. Besides, he had been able to get the League of Nations charter and organization initiated during the lengthy negotiations for the Treaty of Versailles, and planned to get Congress to approve the entry of the United States to become a member of it. Sixty other nations had already joined. His grandiose plans and expectations were dashed when Congress was neither enamored with the provisions of the Treaty nor willing to enter into the League of Nations. When the American press began to try to propagandize about starvation in Belgium, it was such an obvious misdirection of attention that it was hard not to hear Hoover objecting to the far more pitiful situation in Germany. He said Americans "have been brought up not to kick a man in the stomach after we have licked him." Wilson called Hoover a "son of a bitch." Hoover tried to get food for the German civilians, but Congress refused. They did approve a huge appropriation for sending food to Europe, but Germany wasn't to get a single crumb of it. It seemed unfathomable to me that the innocent women, children, elderly, and ill people of Germany should be cold bloodedly starved to death by the vengeful "winners." According to my own elders, nobody won, and as it turned out, they couldn't have been more right. The biggest winners would eventually face the biggest losers of this travesty in 25 years.

I was only an infant when the Treaty of Versailles was signed. Life in the United States was invigorating to my mother, who had completed her training as a surgical nurse, and to my father who was returning from service in the US Navy. However, I was to later learn that the effects on soldiers, sailors, marines and airmen who were called upon to serve during WW I were to be long lasting in many ways for many people. Though the US suffered only about 116,000 killed and thousands of men crippled, maimed, and suffering from "shell shock," the effects had been felt at home as well. Those are the wounds that seem never to be noticed or counted. Everyone was glad that the rationing was over, and that many of the over 2 million men who fought in the war had returned…or had joined that innumerable caravan of warriors that wind their way through the endless corridors of death to their final resting places…The horrible flu epidemic had come in 1918, but I didn't remember anything about the flu pandemic that killed between 50 to 100 million people, but according to everyone, I didn't get it, even though some of my relatives did. Nobody had any verifiable facts as to where it had come from, but they all would mention Fr. Riley, KS in relation to it, and would discuss why it was called the "Spanish" flu.

As I grew, I still spent time with both sets of grandparents, and had access both to their wisdom and their libraries. Every summer, I worked on Grandpa Alva's farm in Illinois, and he continued to impart wisdom about many things. Both sets of grandparents emphasized the importance of an education, so I studied hard enough to finally earn a scholarship, but that is getting ahead of the story, and there was much more in post-war Europe to try to understand. Grandpa and Grandma Crouch both agreed that Germany would eventually emerge from the terrible humiliation, privation and unnecessary civilian death and they were not surprised when 15 years after the Treaty of Versailles was signed, Germany began to re-arm. After all, none of the other countries had "given a fig," as Grandma Crouch said, for the restriction of armaments to prevent another conflagration, therefore she agreed that Germany should not be bound by it, either. I was a teenager then, and didn't really worry about the continued upheavals in Ireland, or their comments that someday they would see me march off to war. I just went to the farm in Illinois, where Grandpa Alva was paying me $1.00 per day to bale hay, plow, and do chores. A whole dollar per day was a lot of money back then, and he was always encouraging me to save it against an education. He was definitely beginning to show his age by then, and though my parents had divorced because of conflicts that had arisen during my father's absence, Grandpa Alva didn't want to lose touch with me. I will always be grateful for that. Grandma Ida was gone, and I think he needed the company, so he was more loquacious than ever before, as though he needed to impart as much knowledge to me as he possibly could in what time we had left together.

Part II The Interim

Chapter Eleven – Planting of the Weeds

Just as twisting vines will bind together and eventually choke life-giving plants, so the vines of revenge, injustice, and hatred wound themselves ever tighter around those who had imposed an unjust peace settlement and cruel, punitive penalties. Only the bitter weeds of revenge would sprout and grow.

    In the years following the imposition of the conditions of the Treaty of Versailles, from 1919 to 1941, the ravages of war began to heal, but the underlying conflicts boiled in a rich cauldron of dissatisfaction, spiced by hatred from the disenfranchised. Military imperialism had been defeated but the surgery had not been successful, so there was not rejoicing but an exhausted world moving forward slowly, weakly, and uncertainly. The universal desire for peace and return to the pre-war liberty and prosperity was prevalent, but the will power to achieve it and secure it was somehow missing. During the intense sacrifices made in the expediency of war, things had moved quickly, but in other respects, there had been a great deterioration. The generous spirits which had freely sacrificed themselves under the rapidly changing demands of war had not seen the rise of sly, base movement in the worlds of business and money, which had seized a stranglehold upon the material resources and political power of their countries. A large number of newly rich, newly powerful men emerged from the shadows of exhausted nations to eradicate the feeling of patriotism and brotherhood which had existed in nations at war. The expediency during wartime had been well learned by these shady operators, and new agencies were set up by and for them, like the Ministry of Reconstruction in Great Britain, which was supposed to plan a new and better social order, better labor conditions, better housing, extended education, and revision of the economic system. Other countries established similar governmental organizations with the same stated aims. The word "reconstruction" fell upon unsuspecting ears as a marvelous effort for the good of the common citizens, but by the middle of 1919, the masses were profoundly disappointed, because there would not be a reconstruction but only a restoration of the old order in a harsher, more bleak form due to the poverty in the chaotic, poverty stricken world. It was also not just a poverty in money, but in morality as well.

The epilogue of disaster would continue unabated through the successive Presidencies of Harding, Coolidge, Hoover, and then Franklin Delano Roosevelt (FDR). Post war private enterprise never recognized nor cared about the urgent needs of the times, so upon its release from governmental control, it went rampant globally into speculation, luxury, production and maximum profit. There was a studied obliviousness to the unwillingness of European and American masses to continue the privation and inconveniences experienced during 1914 through 1919. The people had been uprooted and brutalized by training to be ferocious in war, which engendered unwillingness to acquiesce to denial and disenfranchisement, and it had instilled enhanced capability for desperate action. In short, social unrest had become much more dangerous. It wasn't that they had any political, social, or economic plans for a new system, but rather that their disgust with the system of luxury for the few, waste, poverty, and their own general misery made them uncaring about what might follow, as long as they destroyed the existing system. The inadequacy of the profiteering in the past war years to solve problems of housing, crowding, dislocation of goods, poor road and rail transport thereof, and discrepancies in wages made civil unrest a natural result. For the returning worker, after business was released from governments to the private sector, his pay did not increase to match price increases, or even enable him to pay for food, housing, clothing or any essentials. Appeals to employers were simply ignored, therefore providing a ubiquitous environment for social unrest. It was particularly prevalent in Germany and Italy, where there was a distinct slide toward communism.

This continued during 1921, with violence and rioting throughout Italy by those who wanted private property. They organized as the black shirted Fascioti, who were not only nationalistic, but against socialism. Benito Mussolini, who had once been a radical journalist, emerged as an energetic, unscrupulous leader. They were able to silence the rather sentimental published outrages expressed by communists, and they simply beat liberals with clubs, or fed dissidents massive doses of castor oil to punish them for criticizing the Fascioti. They also destroyed liberal private property, beat, tortured, or murdered them. Communist rule was replaced by brigand rule. Germany was being occupied by British forces, and being embargoed so that her starving, shivering population was vulnerable to communist and socialist ideology. Among those Germans, humiliated and downtrodden, an injured Corporal was recovering from an attack of mustard gas while he was in the trenches. The country had been denuded of much of her agricultural and industrial capability, factories, natural resources, territory, some of which she had ruled for centuries, population, loss of sovereignty over her rivers, and was faced with an almost unimaginable reparation assessment. Because of her difficulty in paying the reparations as quickly as France desired it, French armies had marched into the Ruhr region, which threatened the peace of Europe. Britain was suffering economically due to the collapse of markets on the European Continent, and from the impact of the doles she was having to pay to her huge number of the unemployed. Poland and Spain were in chaos. American markets were suffering because Europe could not afford to purchase goods, nor were they able to even pay for goods already ordered and received. Though there was a gradual withdrawal of government from business functions assumed during the war, there were still many unresolved issues, and the abnormally high prices established during the war continued until the middle to the end of 1920. The greedy profiteers dominated at every level, and the cost of goods compared with 1913 prices were hiked from 20 to over 200%. Labor organizations were striking to try to get their share of the inflated profits, and while wages were higher, the value of, for example, the US dollar had plummeted by 25-30% of its value in 1913. The cost of living was higher than ever before, so there were actual 'buyer's strikes' in the big cities, which actually caused some of the major retailers, including Ford Motor Company, to lower prices, but on all actuality, there was a depression in the United States in 1920.

Congress was struggling with issues such as ratification of the Treaty of Versailles, providing definite policy for a soldier's pension, soldier's bonus (for those who had served), demobilization of literally millions of soldiers into an already glutted work force, railroads, highways, merchant marines, taxes, the tariff, and many other questions. Because of the economic downturn in Europe, there was essentially a lack of foreign markets for the surplus of US goods, so every industry, particularly agriculture, felt the pinch in 1920 through 1921. President Wilson prevailed upon Congress to pass a Budget and Accounting Act in June of 1921, which was also recommended by the new president, Warren Harding, to centralize budget control for the government. A Budget Bureau was created in the Department of the Treasury. There was a move, with this new bureaucracy, to decrease expenditures as well as taxes. However, the end result was that revenue from customs went down from nearly 50% of the total governmental revenue to approximately 40% and the internal revenue resource which included corporate taxes, went from near 50% to 60%. The source of federal income had begun to shift. Wilson held some conferences to try to arbitrate the disagreements among labor, capital, and the public, but no agreement was reached, though Mr. Gompers gained name recognition during this time. He made his famous bid for the right of wage earners to organize and bargain collectively, without discrimination against them from employers, over wages, hours, conditions of labor, and conditions of employment. Employers flatly didn't agree. After that, there were major strikes, like for example, that of the steel workers, involving 370,000 workers for several months, and there was a failure of the strike, despite deplorable conditions and unfair labor conditions. A Senate investigating committee claimed that one of the strike leaders was working with a radical, semi-communist organization, the Industrial Workers of the World (IWW). The investigating committee claimed that due to the IWW presence, the strike was composed of anarchists, revolutionists, and Russian Soviets. This was later shown to be untrue, but there had been an influx of radical socialists, encouraged by Russia, where a totalitarian Soviet government had become well entrenched. Though the American labor force withdrew from this and other conflicts involving violence or Soviet influence, the public sentiment began to turn against labor. Grandpa Alva commented that "Tell me what you're looking for, and I'll tell you what you'll find." While he was leery of the labor unions, he certainly understood why they had been formed, but tried to warn my father, Fred Dewey Adams, not to become involved with the railroad unions. Meanwhile, he was struggling with his own economic concerns, because agriculture was hit harder than virtually anything else. However, though farmers were hit particularly hard, conditions gradually adjusted themselves to, as President Harding had called it "a satisfactory state of normalcy" by 1924.

The US rural population was decreasing in the post war years, and farmers had experienced only a small part of the wartime prosperity, and certainly no prosperity in the period 1924 to 1928. But improvements in efficiency and industrialization of agriculture continued unabated. Old Bob, Grandpa Alva's faithful old plough horse was growing old, and I can remember asking him in 1925 when he was going to train a new one. That brought about a lengthy discussion about the internal combustion engine, and how Grandpa Alva had been saving for years to buy a tractor, as well as some more land. He let me know in no uncertain terms that he never bought anything he didn't have the money to pay for outright, because debt is a goblin that can eat a man up. Old Bob was to be his last plough horse, and he was using him to help clear some more land he already owned to put it under cultivation. The number of farms was rapidly decreasing during those times and the size of those remaining increased. Farming became big business and though there was less demand for products to support horses, like hay, corn, or feed, since when tractors became more common other products took their place. During the war, the demand for food had caused agriculture to expand beyond what could profitably be maintained in peace time. Also there had been speculation on a grand scale, planting of extra acreage to reap war time profits, but even during the boom years, farmers were only making about 6% on their investment. Then, in 1920, the sale price of produce of produce often fell below the outlay. For example, corn fell in 1921 from $1.56/bushel to 57 cents, wheat from $2.14 to $1.19, and cotton from 30 cents/lb. to 12 cents/lb., and meat suffered similarly. Land values dropped like a rock, up to 70%, but taxes didn't follow suit. Farmers couldn't pay the high taxes, freight rates, interest rates, or even afford seed. Bankruptcies were almost ten times as high, and agricultural products being produced were far more than could be sold. The farmers began to form organizations in an effort to protect themselves and to lobby for farm relief, which was generally met with hostility. Despite new legislation and their efforts, by 1924, farmers received an average of only 4% return on their investment. Only those who owned their property outright were able to hang on. The more I learned about this, the more I appreciated Grandpa Alva's frugality and business acumen, and later on, because of that understanding, I truly appreciated the generous $1.00/day he paid me for working summers on his farm. He also told me that $1.00/day was what the drafted soldiers were paid during the war. The agricultural conditions ultimately led to what was called the "Farm Problem" in the late 1950s, which my daughter was to debate in both high school and college. This will be discussed later, but due to my familiarity with the origin of it, I was able to give her insight that the later historians had obscured with their alterations of facts to suit their own interpretations, just as they failed to mention that the US Congress did not ever ratify the Versailles Treaty.

In the preparation for war, transportation, to include highways and railways, fuel production, port construction, port utilization, ship building, steel and manufacturing were brought under tight federal control. Wages for those engaged in occupations thought to be essential to the war effort were high, compared with the $1.00 per day for soldiers, sailors, marines, and airmen, which naturally engendered dissatisfaction among those who were expected to lay down their lives if need be in lands far from home. In addition, those in these "essential" jobs were exempt from the draft. Cantonments for the military were essentially small cities with hospitals, water supplies, sewage, lighting, heating, and all the adjunct facilities necessary for self-sufficient communities. There were 36 of these constructed, at great cost to the taxpayers. Those camps with permanent buildings cost about $8,000,000 apiece, and those for the National Guard, which were much less substantial, about $2,000,000 each. Facilities for the regular Army were completed in approximately three months and it was, as stated, both expensive and subject to graft from greedy construction companies and their suppliers. Supplies for the soldiers drafted and in training required very large bulk quantities of food, clothing, munitions, fodder, horses, weapons, ammunition, motorized transport, and all ancillary supplies for execution of warfare for over 4,000,000 troops were stupendously costly. Because of the expense, and Emergency Loan Act was passed for a bond issue of five billion dollars and issuance of two billion in sort term notes to meet the governmental need. Wilson wanted the greatest part of the cost of the war to be borne by the "present generation," by what he called well-conceived taxation. The measures raised over three and a half billion dollars, but that didn't cover the rising costs. Various manipulations of taxation, however, had raised over eleven billion dollars, which was a larger percentage of the war budget than in any other country. They had also borrowed nine and a half billion dollars initially. The total expenditures for three years was in excess of $35,500,000,000. The monumental expenditures were believed to have been more than it cost to run the entire government from 1791 to 1914. The number of governmental employees, due to the ballooning of federal bureaucracies swelled in direct correlation. Government became bigger, but not necessarily better. Subsequent Presidencies would be faced with both the $16 billion in debt and the continuing proliferation of the size, expense and complexity of government.

At the death of Warren G. Harding (29th President, 1921-1923), almost simultaneously with the discovery of some corruption in the oil industry, a virtual unknown, Calvin Coolidge, the Vice President, assumed the responsibility of the United States Presidency. Prior to his death in 1923, Harding had been a jovial, well liked man, who enjoyed life, and scandals only emerged post mortem. Calvin Coolidge was quite different from his predecessor. He was a quiet, thoughtful man, and when he did speak, that trait was well demonstrated. His immediate attention was turned to the economy, and to the unwieldy expansion of both federal government and employment that had resulted from it. He was a typical Yankee, who played no poker, drank no liquor, and was simple in habits and manner, therefore he lacked many of the graces and personality traits to make him a popular political leader. He did, however, have a very good analytical mind, absorbed facts quickly, and knew where to find authoritative information when he needed it. He was a college graduate, conscientious, courageous and of unquestionable integrity.

A government which lays taxes on the people not required by urgent public necessity and sound public policy is not a protector of liberty, but an instrument of tyranny. It condemns the citizen to servitude.

Calvin Coolidge

Image from the Library of Congress cph 3g10777

He vetoed the Bonus Bill and the McNay/Haugen farm relief bills and some others Congress favored, not because he didn't see the need for help for both farmers and veterans, but because of the actual underlying chances for fraud and abuse buried in them, but that certainly didn't make him popular. The press took it as an excellent opportunity to attack him. However, he was a devoted conservative with an innate interest in the economy, a sincere love of the country, and his honesty and forthrightness soon made him popular. He resisted ex-President Wilson's stirring of the cauldron of discontent, and foolish "reforms" from Bolshevik fringe elements and concentrated on tax reductions, which ultimately made him a trusted leader of the nation. Also when he ascended in power, he abided by a policy frequently used by successful leaders in the military since the time of George Washington in that he made no drastic changes to Harding's policies until he had assessed the situation. He kept the cabinet, continued existing policies, and took over the reins of government so quietly and effectively that there were no disruptions. Those cabinet members associated with scandals were quietly replaced and movement to obtain justice for culprits who sought to defraud the government and the people moved quickly forward without publicity or anxiety over the situation that dishonesty had caused. By 1924, prosperity was quickly returning, though agricultural recovery was moving more slowly. In the 1924 Presidential campaign, Coolidge was not only known for his practicality and efficiency, he was also free from contamination by previous scandals associated with his predecessor. He had just returned from Europe after being instrumental in formulating a practical, workable plan (Dawes Plan) for Germany's reparation payments. He was determined that in a second term, he would reduce the national debt through economy and careful consideration. Frugality was a fundamental hallmark of his personality, and that resonated with the public as well as with business, because he said in 1923, "the business of America is business." He was supported by the business community as well as the general public, and he won the election with twice as many votes as his opponent, Alfred Smith, who had based his platform on praising Wilson. At the time, the Democrats were promoting the continued control of merchant marines, regulation of anthracite coal, government relief and control of agriculture, and denouncing the corruption and foreign policy of Republicans in general. Since Coolidge had addressed the former by steadfast opposition to big government and governmental controls of segments of the economy which should belong to states and the people, and the latter by having completely been exonerated of any corruption, plus increasing worldwide respect for American foreign policy. He stood firm against incursion of communist and socialist elements which continued to slither about the nation. At the end of his term, however, he declined running again and backed Herbert Hoover for the next election, having briefed him about the existing economic problems which were yet unsolved.

An interesting component of the previous Coolidge campaign was the appearance of the "Progressive Party," containing the dissatisfied, disaffected elements of both major parties. They ran LaFollette, an independent Republican from Wisconsin, and Wheeler, a Montana Democrat. They ran on a ticket endorsed by the Socialist and Farmer Labor Parties, which had sprung up in the early years of Harding's administration. They advocated bigger government, with control of railroads, water power, finance, and industry in general, to include agriculture. They lost, and even if all the votes going to the Progressives were added to the Democrat, Davis, it would not have changed the outcome. In 1924, the GOP had managed to hold on to Congress, but the political situation in the US was undergoing a significant transformation. By the end of 1926, many of the strong former shapers of national policy for the previous quarter century, like Theodore Roosevelt, Lodge, LaFollette, Debs, Gompers, and others, had either died or been replaced by a younger group of leaders. Party lines were often frayed or even obliterated, and issues were often confused. The basic difference in the two major political parties was more drastically reduced than it had been in over 75 years. The US had even joined the World Court, restricted immigration, introduced flood control, enforced prohibition, farm relief, and the Latin American question became more important as the 1928 campaign approached.

Though there was a strong movement to draft Coolidge, he declined, as mentioned before, while just ignoring the opposition denouncement of a possible "third term" for him. He backed Hoover. The Progressives were determined to run a candidate. The platform of the GOP was strongly influenced by Coolidge's success in greatly reducing national debt, tax reduction, protection of American foreign interests, and other measures proposed to give farm relief, support of labor, and dedicated enforcement of the 18th Amendment. Grandpa Alva said that the 18th Amendment had been a mistaken idea that morality can be legislated, and Grandpa Crouch thoroughly agreed. He said it simply opened a doorway to criminal activity and gang rule of something that was a personal decision, and tax revenue to the government. Their wisdom was later to be proven true. Though Hoover has often been maligned by subsequent "experts" and blame mongers, he was to face many problems, but actually did a great deal of good under very difficult circumstances. Hoover adhered strongly to Republican policies, though he did express his own opinions on the interrelationship between the government and business. During the campaign, Smith's states- rights attitude for Prohibition was acceptable to the public, but his position on Roman Catholicism and Protestantism lost him most of the Southern states. In summary, Hoover had won because many from both parties either voted for Hoover or not at all. The electoral vote for Hoover had been 444 to 87, and the popular majority was over six million. This could clearly have been a mandate, and the Congress had maintained control by a large majority. However, the success was to be obscured by events which had long been festering. Though his cabinet was composed of men of great integrity and past real experience and accomplishment Hoover failed to dominate his party in the Congressional branch. The sincerity of his intentions was above reproach, but they were often in conflict with desires and intentions of sitting members in Congress, some of whom were well entrenched. The first thing on his agenda was a farm relief program, hindered by the fact that great surpluses of certain products had begun to accumulate, particularly in the Midwestern wheat and livestock industries. The McNary/Haughton bill would place governmental controls over pricing of a given product, and excesses would be sold on the world market at prices set by a new Federal Board. That was complicated, but the end result would be that the price would be fixed, <u>minus</u> an equalization fee, so lower return on their money would force farmers to control their "over production." Coolidge had previously vetoed it, along with several other similar legislations, because price fixing would give a special advantage to certain crops, and because price fixing, itself, was both unsound and un-American. It would contribute to higher domestic prices with attendant speculation. Hoover favored another method that would, unfortunately, include another federal board, called the Jardine-Coolidge program. This was definitely a complicated issue which Hoover tried to solve, and a modified version of the Jardine-Coolidge Program was adopted in June of 1929, with the creation of the Federal Farm Board to supervise its administration and a very large appropriation ($500,000,000) to do so. Alexander Lodge, President of International Harvester was appointed to run the board.

Herbert Hoover had only been in office for about eight months when the "defecation hit the revolving agitator" in the US economy and there was the Bonus March. The clouds of depression had never fully dissipated, and began to intensify. What became called the Teapot Dome Scandal, formerly known as the Oil Scandal, from the Harding Administration was in the final stages of litigation, so there were multitudinous issues at hand. In the face of farm "over production," many citizens, particularly unemployed veterans, were often going hungry. One source from 1939 says that the march began on the third year of the Great Depression, and millions of unemployed people in the US were suffering from hunger, deprivation, and despair. References from that time period vary on dates and participation in the march, but Army records are quite detailed on the issue. Gen Douglas McArthur was the Army Chief of Staff at the time, and though I have never been enamored of him, he was always meticulous in his record keeping. In late May, in 1932, a contingent of unemployed, desperate veterans went to Washington, D.C. in hopes of influencing Congress to grant an immediate cash bonus to alleviate their situation. For two months, they made daily visits to the Capitol Building and the White House, hoping to get the help they desperately needed. In 1924, the Bonus Compensation Bill had been passed, which approved compensation for veterans in lieu of the higher wages earned by those who did not serve in the military during WWI, however no payments had been forthcoming. The American Legion launched a movement for the amounts to be paid in cash and not in 1945. Originally, the movement was led by Walter W. Waters, an Oregonian veteran, who met with Gen McArthur, then the Army Chief of Staff, and they agreed that if the Army was called in, Waters and the veterans would withdraw without violence. Because many of them were in a shanty town of partially demolished buildings along Pennsylvania Avenue, McArthur sent tents, field kitchens, hygiene instruction on latrine construction, and water to Anaconda Flats to alleviate suffering, prevent disease, and get them moved from Pennsylvania Avenue. This angered some of the Congressmen, who threw a great enough temper tantrum that the kitchens were finally withdrawn. In June, tension mounted and the numbers rose to 17,000, but only one in ten, at the most, was a military veteran. The vast majority were Communists or protesters recruited by them. The then Governor of New York, Franklin Delano Roosevelt, sent a message to New York veterans in the movement that if they would return home, the state would pay their railroad fares back to New York. President Hoover got a bill through Congress for transportation loans to pay for return of veterans to their homes and most of the veterans left. The privation, heat, lack of success, and invasion of the movement by undesirable elements had thoroughly disenchanted the veterans, who had a valid complaint. The hard core of the Communist bloc not only stayed, but grew. The FBI reported that out of 4,773 marchers fingerprinted, over 1,000 of them had criminal records to include drunkenness, rape, and murder. By that time, Waters had been deposed as leader of the movement, and violence was increasing to the point that the DC Police Force could no longer control it. Twice, to no avail, they had asked for the Army to come in, because they were being assaulted and pelted by rocks, bottles, broken glass, and debris. So, when on 28 July, when a mob of 5,000 began to march up Pennsylvania Avenue, the police were outnumbered, attacked, and mauled. Gunfire broke out and two men were killed, others injured – and it was not unilateral. The condition had clearly gone beyond the capability of the local police force. The Board of Commissioners of the District of Columbia formally requested federal troops to assist, because otherwise it would be impossible for the police to control the violence except with "free use of firearms." Commissioner Richelderfer stated that a small number of federal troops would "obviate the seriousness" of the situation, and reduce the potential violence and bloodshed. President Hoover consulted with the Secretary of War, Patrick Hurley, and placed him in charge. A copy of Hurley's order to Gen McArthur is given below:

Dorothy A Adams

TO: General McArthur

Chief of Staff, US Army
The President has just informed me that the civil government of the District of Columbia has reported to him that it is unable to maintain law and order in the District. You will have United States troops proceed immediately to the scene of disorder. Cooperate fully with the District of Columbia police force which is now in charge. Surround the affected area and clear it without delay.
Turn over all prisoners to the civil authorities.
In your orders insist that any women or children who may be in the affected area be accorded every consideration and kindness. Use all humanity consistent with the due execution of the order.
                Patrick J. Hurley
                Secretary of War

600 soldiers, under the command of Gen Perry L. Miles were drawn from units near Washington, and he issued the following order:

"We are acting on the order of the President of the United States. The cavalry will make a demonstration down Pennsylvania Avenue. The infantry will deploy in line of skirmishers in the rear of the cavalry. You will surround the area and evict the men in possession there. Use care and consideration toward all women and children who may be in the area."

In accordance with the request by President Hoover, Gen McArthur, accompanied by Major George S. Patton and Major Dwight D. Eisenhower, accompanied Gen Miles' contingent. No shots were fired by the military, and Gen McArthur and his detail wore the same uniforms as the soldiers. The sticks and stones of the rioters were met with tear gas and steady pressure from the infantry and cavalry. No one was killed, and there were no serious injuries on either side. By 2130 hours (9:30 PM to non-military personnel) the area was cleared back to Anaconda flats. At that point, Gen McArthur received notification from the Secretary of War, Hurley, to cease the operation at his own discretion, so he halted the command at the bridge. The rioters then set fire to their own encampment. By 2330 hours that night, McArthur had concluded a mandatory meeting with Secretary Hurley and was instructed to give a statement to newspaper men who were waiting outside. The statement he gave was direct and to the point that had Hoover not acted quickly and judiciously, the government might have been in peril, and he would have been derelict in his duty to the American people. The day after the riot, police rounded up 36 of the leaders, including the American Communist Party candidate for the Presidency of the US, and several major Communist leaders. That broke up their DC riot organization, and the rest of them vanished. Three days after the uprising, the New York Times reported:

"The Communist Party, at its headquarters here, accepted responsibility for the demonstration that resulted in the bonus-army riots in Washington. "We agitated for the bonus and led the demonstration of the veterans in Washington" a spokesman for the party said at the headquarters at 50 East 13th Street. "We stand ready to go to Washington again and fight for the working men. We started the march from here for Washington, and we will lead the way again."

But the newspapers violently attacked Gen McArthur as well, and their action with rather elaborate distortions were blatantly debated before Congress as well as in the press. According to Army records, there was no cavalry charge, brandishing of swords, dress uniforms, or firing on citizens, but it became an often repeated legend. It gave credence to the saying that "a lie told three times or more is then accepted as fact," and exposure of the untruths was not fully revealed until 1948 and 1949, when Communists, themselves, in the book by Benjamin Gitlow, "The Whole of Their Lives," and testimony under oath by John T. Pace before a Congressional committee admitted complicity. They both revealed the Communist conspiracy and direction of it by Moscow.

Though President Hoover, noted for a life dedicated to human service, accomplished many positive things during his administration, he received the blame from the media for the fantasized violent put down of the Bonus March insurrection and the whole Great Depression. How he was to have prevented the horrible crash of the stock market on Thursday, October 24, 1929 is a mystery. He was to be followed by Franklin Delano Roosevelt (FDR) as the 32nd President of the United States, and a great part of FDR's New Deal had been outlined and implemented by Hoover in response to the depression, which was worldwide. After the Great War, there were hard times throughout Europe, with a great depression in 1929 from internal debts and reconstruction costs. The industrial nations, Britain, Germany and the US, were hit particularly hard because there was a decrease in demand for goods, leading to an increased unemployment of millions of "town-bred" workingmen. President Hoover proposed a "holiday for all war debt," which was accepted for only a year. By the later Lusanne Agreement in 1932, Germany promised a lump sum payment in lieu of any further obligations, but since it was contingent upon other negotiations involving the US, which didn't come through, it simply ended reparation payments. By that time, Germany had paid 1/3 of the stupendous amount demanded of her, or approximately over ten billion dollars of the thirty-five billion, and she would not pay more. She had rearmed, as had most of the other European countries, to include Russia. The upcoming generation was aware of the political intrigues, assassinations, and unrest in Asia, Europe and the USA. As always, those of the generation who "will be" were knocking at the door of the future with a mailed fist. Hungry people are not likely to be reasonable, so there were international controversies, wars, and rumors of wars. The Elders prayed for the return of prosperity as the foil against war, but the young, who had not grown up facing trenches or gunfire, but in the privation, hunger, hardships and humiliation of the aftermath of the Great War, wanted even war to dispel the dull, grey, miserable existence in which they were living. Militaristic spirit was to be found everywhere. WWII was inevitable.

Chapter Twelve – Storm Clouds Gather

Peace was but an illusion, hidden beneath the poppies that still grow among those crosses in Flanders Fields, and restless discontent would rise up again in vehemence no mortal could yet imagine. It was not a Peace, but a Cease Fire for 25 years with tangled vines of political strife, across the ambitions of mankind. All that glitters is not gold, but paper can never replace it.

Salvaging a wrecked world was the objective of the Peace Conference which resulted in the carving up of the Balkans, and the loss of the people of many of the "old" nations the right to remain in countries which were reflective of their ancestry, language, and culture. No nations had been defeated in WWI, and many were discontented with the peace, in name only. Fascists, led by the veteran who had been wounded in the war, Benito Mussolini, in Italy, believed that the world was divided into classes of nations – those with wealth, prosperity, power (Britain, France, and the USA), and the proletarian nations peopled by millions who were forced to eke out a poverty stricken existence in overcrowded, small, impoverished nations. Italy felt she had been cheated in the division of spoils by the Treaty of Versailles. Nor was Japan satisfied, but her dissatisfaction made them, as with Italy, fully sympathetic with Germany. Failure of Britain to renew the prewar existing treaty with Japan, which gave that small nation protection from China by British naval power contributed to their discomfiture. Japan and China had participated in the Great War, but hadn't been involved in much combat, and they had a long lasting traditionally antagonistic relationship.

Japan had been awarded the German possession on the coast of China and several colonies down to the equator. She was determined not only to hold the German fortress of Kiaochow, the Pacific Islands she had been awarded, and the commercial concessions on the Shantung Peninsula, but Japan had forced China into commercial and territorial access in Manchuria. By 1931, the Japanese took forcible possession of Manchuria, so the Chinese boycotted all Japanese trade. That was a severe blow to Japan, whose survival on an archipelago the size of California, and population greater than all of Germany was completely dependent upon commerce, so she occupied Mongolia and landed troops at the port of Shanghai. The aggression might have been avoided had China not been engaged in a civil war, and Japanese commerce had been protected by the pact with the British Empire, but clearly, Japan had violated the Covenant of the League of Nations, the Paris Peace Pact, and the Washington agreement for China's national integrity. China protested to the League of Nations, and Japan not only thumbed her nose, but defiantly withdrew from the League of Nations. She didn't annex Manchuria, but made it a protectorate as the Empire of Manchukuo under the nominal rule of the deposed Manchu emperor of China. Japan's militaristic spirit was rising rapidly, and she publically announced that she would no longer tolerate naval inferiority but announced her intention to build warships to seek parity with Britain and the US, in order to insure her national security. That success, bringing no reprisal from the major powers, resulted in further rise of militarism, and both anti-pacifism or internationalism. Military expenditures rose, any statesman who opposed them was summarily killed, Premier Inukai was assassinated, and an unsuccessful attempt was made on the life of his successor, Premier Okada. Though it was slower in China, national spirit supported by student activists rose up in anti-foreign agitation and against Christian missionaries. Though no formal declaration of war was made in 1937, Japan extensively invaded northern China, despite protests from Europe and the USA.

  Italy began colonial expansion in Africa against Abyssinia (Ethiopia), the one remaining unconquered monarchy, inhabited by an ununified conglomerate of whites, blacks, Moslems, Christians, pagans, civilized people and barbarians. The most probable inducement was Premier Mussolini's desire to avenge the defeat of Italian troops in Ethiopia in 1896 by Ethiopian Emperor Menelik II. He used the excuse of border raids and boundary disputes against bordering Italian colonies to make war on Ethiopia, then under the rule of Emperor Haile Selassie, who defended his nation without the benefit of modern methods of warfare. The Italian aggression was very close to British colonies, so the League of Nations prevailed upon Britain to address the incursion. Though Great Britain did not dispatch troops, they did punish Italy with severe commercial boycotts, but Ethiopia had to fight her own battles, unassisted otherwise. Fear arose in the League of Nations that pushing Italy too far might cause an Italian-German alliance. The League was embarrassed, and Britain feared a naval war with Italy, so the Suez Canal was left open to Italian warships, and sanctions were not placed on oil or general trade, but they were relieved to hear that Ethiopia was in revolt, and Haile Selassie was in hiding. The last truly independent African nation was effectively made an Italian colony. Though the League acquiesced to the result, it had suffered its greatest defeat.

More dangerous than either of these magniloquent moves by Japan or Italy was the mounting aggressive spirit in Germany, growing hand in hand with deepening depression, and being fanned into a roaring inferno with the accession in 1933 by Adolf Hitler and the Nationalist Social Party to supreme power. Adolf Hitler was also a WWI veteran who had been injured in the trenches, and he established the machinery of dictatorship extremely rapidly by decrying the fourteen year democratic government preceding him. He capitalized on the humiliation and punitive actions imposed on Germany by the Treaty of Versailles, and the failure of the new constitution drawn up at the national convention at Weimar, which was drawn up along liberal lines.

That particular government, suffering from its inception an inability to balance the budget and production of worthless paper currency, since the gold had gone to pay reparations, was failing. Many political parties sprang up, but the spirit of cooperation among them was virtually non-existent. The French occupation of the Ruhr's manufacturing district to force payment of reparations was a solid, festering source of bitterness, as were the unjust conditions of the Treaty of Versailles. Some parties in the Reichstag were openly disloyal to the German constitution, while on the left, the Communists wanted a government like the one in Russia, a dictatorship of the proletariat. On the extreme right, the Nationalists wanted a restoration of the monarchy. Most of the major entities, like the army, civil servants, students, and even the general public, were royalists. Business was willing to support anything that worked and supported stability.

Most people were actually preoccupied with getting enough food, so bread and butter took precedence over political machinations. The worldwide depression in 1929 did more to elevate the radical ex-soldier to power than anything else. Though he had been born in Austria in 1889, as an ardent patriot for all Germans, he enlisted in the German instead of the Austrian army during WWI. As an equally ardent believer in the greater Fatherland, after the war, he joined the National Socialist German Worker's Party, known as Nazi for short, with a platform calling for union of Austria with Germany, repudiation of the Treaty of Versailles, exclusion of Jews from citizenship, elimination of war profits, nationalization of trusts and chain stores, restoration of military conscription, suppression of all non-German media, and a strong central government to put public interest before private interests. He had been jailed in 1923 for inciting an insurrection in Munich, but that didn't stop his rise to prominence and leadership in 1933. In 1932, he ran against the reelection of von Hindenburg, then in his 80s, and though Hitler won a respectable number of votes, primarily because of the showy flag-waving Brown Shirts, songs, and energy of his campaign, he lost the election. His party, however, had won many seats in the Reichstag. When von Hindenburg offered him the office of Chancellor in January of 1933, he took it, but demanded a new election, and people, attracted to the word "National" in his party name, and weary of the status quo, were susceptible to his campaign. Discrediting the Communists with an accusation of having burned down the Reichstag building, Chancellor Hitler and his allies held a majority in the new Reichstag, so he pushed a law through suspending the constitution and making the government dictatorial for four years. The Communists were definitely ousted, and remaining political parties quickly dissolved, leaving only the Nazis.

In this transition, von Hindenburg was left with prestige and the title of President, but was as completely stripped of power as the King of Italy had been. Hitler, however, still focused on the "national" aspect of his power rather than the socialist philosophy of the party that had fostered his success. He concentrated centrally on purifying Germany from all alien influence. Hitler as nominally Catholic, professing a friendship with Rome and Christianity, was opposed to what he labelled as "Marxist materialism." He didn't emerge completely during the first few years, maintaining the association with the League of Nations, and initially avoiding the re-establishment of previous German borders, though Germany did reoccupy the Rhineland. It was an extreme nationalism, with the introduction of the Aryan myth that he voiced as the concept of the "Third Reich," the first having been the Holy Roman Empire, and the second, the Germany built by von Bismarck. The third he designated as having been from 1918 to 1932 and the transition to the Nazi Empire. This emphasis which focused on the German race was a clear demarcation of distinction from the Russian communists. The swastika was supposed to symbolize "pure Aryan blood," and it appeared on all flags, on buildings, and in places of honor.

Soviet Russia, as mentioned before, arose rapidly when the Bolsheviki seized the government in 1917, but they had no intention of it being an isolated experiment. Their master plan was that it should spread worldwide, and had expected it to rise by revolution in all industrialized nations, like France, Germany, Britain, and the United States. Many such insurrections did arise, but were rapidly suppressed, to the consternation of the Georgian, Joseph Stalin, so a line was sharply drawn between Communist Russia and the capitalistic remainder of the world. Between Russia and Germany, there was a new belt of smaller, weaker, independent nations: Finland, Estonia, Latvia, Lithuania, Poland, Czechoslovakia, Austria, Hungary, Rumania, Bulgaria, Yugoslavia, Albania, Greece, and Turkey. They all had new or renovated constitutions supposedly based on popular sovereignty. This was, however, in most of them, a transition period to nationalistic, militaristic dictatorships and not toward Communism. For a long while, exactly where Russia's borders lay was uncertain, and many of those small nations, like Finland, were experiencing internal civil wars. Some, like Latvia, Estonia, and Lithuania, had poorly defined borders; Poland was recognized nominally, but with ill-defined borders and a mixed population of Poles, Ukrainians, White Russians, Lithuanians, and Jews. Ukrainia was in anarchy, with pockets of Communists, Ukrainian nationalists, Russian royalists, and rampant brigands.

On the Black Sea, the territory was held by Cossacks, who were absolutely hostile to the Soviet government, nationalists in the Caucasus wanted independence, Western Siberia was under a separate dictatorship, and Eastern Siberia was controlled by Japan. Counter revolutionists were unable to succeed because all nationalities and races were given complete equality, and Soviet Russia became federally based. Also, no revolutionary group was able to convince the peasantry that they would be protected from restoration of the old landlords or monarchs, so ultimately, they submitted to a modern serfdom. Though composed of many "states," all fell under the iron hand of the control of the U.S.S.R., despite the proliferation of interlocking councils, commissariats, and ministries. The Communist Party was the *only* party, and the government was a dictatorship, less of the proletariat, and more of the firm hand of Joseph Dzugashvili, known under his revolutionary alias, Joseph Stalin. A complex system of espionage, similar to the deposed, executed Czar's secret police efficiently nipped any rebellion in the bud, with the large, growing Red Army in place to crush any residual resistance.

Lenin had died in 1924, and Stalin's only real rival was Leon Trotsky, who still saw the revolution as a worldwide movement, but Stalin concentrated on purely Russian affairs. Trotsky was ultimately banished from Russia due to his opposition. Confiscation of industrial assets and crops was the result of socializing under national planning, which gave way to Stalin's belief that industrialization was as important as socialization. The Five Year Plan (1928-1933) developed heavy industry, power plants, railroads and manufacture of both motor vehicles and farm machinery. The remaining independent peasants were coaxed into giving their land into collective farms. Progress was rapid, as was harvesting and utilization of natural resources such as coal, minerals, metal, and oil. There were problems with distribution lagging behind production, leading to starvation or waste, which was often blamed on sabotage and brutally punished. Religious organizations and ministries came under attack, and clergymen were denied the vote. Those who attended churches, synagogues, or mosques were considered suspect. No organized religious training for children was permitted, and all churches were tightly controlled due to the governmental belief that "Religion is the opiate of the people." The Communist foreign policy was remarkably similar to that of the capitalist powers, and Russia was again allied with France, opposed to Japan, antagonistic toward Germany, and to some extent, toward Britain and the USA.

Details on the smaller nations will not be elaborated, mainly because I no longer remember them, but suffice it to say the geopolitical interactions in the Balkans remained essentially the same as in pre-war times. The Baltic nations remained divided in language, religion, and culture. The wide variety in speech and even faith, tended to make these small nations cling to independence rather than seeking security from some form of common union. They relied on both the League of Nations, and to some extent on the good will of more distant powers like France, Britain, and the US. They universally dreaded and rejected the constant Russian propaganda as well as Nazi propaganda, which assaulted them constantly. Poland, the largest of the Baltic States, experienced the greatest danger from the rising schism of the Great Powers, since her border with Germany was bitterly resented and contested by German resurgence of strength and power. Internal strife over governmental structure and policy was rife in Poland, and she was under a strange blend of dictatorship and democracy by 1935. Austria and Hungary had been so thoroughly surgically dismembered and both Yugoslavia (Serbia) and Rumania so greatly enlarged that any resemblance to the old Danubian Empire was only incidental. The League of Nations effectively stopped Austria from uniting with Germany, but it remained a quiet, tranquil, but despairing republic. Hungary chose to be a monarchy, but had no king. Governmental forms in these regions frequently morphed, but the Nazis became politically important in 1930, due to a new threat of famine. In 1933, Austrian Chancellor Engelbert Dollfuss, a Christian Socialist came to power, crushing two other parties, the Social Democrats and National Socialists, putting down any resistance as firmly as any dictator, and authoring a new constitution for what he called a "Christian,

German, Federal State on a Corporate Basis." Elections were abolished and resistance was eliminated. Nazis opposed Dollfuss, because he refused union with Germany, so they kidnapped and "accidently" shot and killed him. There was an upheaval in Austria, and many Austrian Nazis were captured, arrested and executed, but no clear path to an Austrian independent government was easily found. A reunification of Austria and Hungary might have saved them both, but that did not happen, so Hungary underwent tumultuous times as well. The revulsion against Communism was so great that a Hapsburg monarchy was almost restored, but ex-Emperor Charles was seriously threatened with war by Yugoslavia and Rumania if the Hapsburgs were restored to power.

Unrest continued throughout the intervening years between WWI and WWII, and no nation was exempt. Great Britain continued for a while under the wartime coalition under Lloyd George, but that was not to last. Their old two party system gave way to a three party system composed of Liberals, Laborites, and Conservatives. By 1930, the Liberals had sunk into third place and was divided into factions, so the balance was between Labor and Conservatives. The Irish problem was not only present, but intensifying, which was a source of active discussion among my elders, as was the resurgence of Germany under the dictatorship of Hitler. The Irish problem was about the only thing the three remaining grandparents didn't blame on Wilsonian politics. They vehemently disagreed with the British, with their denial of "Home Rule" for Ireland, when peace in a longstanding civil war could have been ended in other ways. Prior to the war, a Home Rule bill had been passed, but due to the war, it was to be delayed until the war was over. Then the British refused to honor it without dividing Ireland into Protestant and Catholic dominions. The Ulster (Protestant) dominions of northern Ireland objected to the law so vehemently that Lloyd George introduced a division with two legislatures, one for northern and one for southern Ireland, under British rule. The southerners rejected it outright, and the Sinn Feiners of the Catholic south wanted independence as previously promised. The ever placating George presented another plan where the south could have what he called "The Irish Free State" without representation in Parliament, but with complete control over their local affairs. This split the Sinn Feiners into factions, one of which accepted the proposal, and the other, a minority, did not. The Protestant north accepted the second portion of that proposal, which gave them the conditions as outlined, but civil war and anarchy continues to this day. As an adjunct to this upheaval, other parts of the Empire began to show nationalism, and both Egypt and India began to demand self-determination. Factions arose in India, the most famous of which was led by Mahatma Ghandi; others were advocating active rebellion. Those of the Empire under self-government remained faithful to Britain, and sought only recognition as sovereign nations within a voluntary union with the Empire, and chose to represent themselves as entities in the League of Nations. In 1931, the British Parliament in the Statute of Westminster gave them (Canada, New Zealand, Australia, New Foundland, and South Africa) complete equal dominion over their laws, and freedom from law as enacted by the British Parliament. The more common name after that was "British Commonwealth" instead of British Empire, a move that made the monarchy more important, not in rule, but only a symbolism of sovereignty. Egypt was eventually granted sovereignty under highly qualified conditions, and Britain retained control of the Suez Canal. King George V ruled until his death on 1936, followed by King Edward VIII, who quickly abdicated, so the crown passed King George VI. The great depression continued in Britain, and over two million workers remained unemployed. Lloyd George had retired, and the transition to new leadership was not an easy one. Britain left the gold standard, put in a protective tariff, and balanced the budget, but one of the expenditures drastically cut was unemployment compensation and payment of war debt to the USA. The office of Premier passed back and forth between Stanley Baldwin and Ramsay MacDonald from 1922 through 1937 as the Conservative and Labor parties struggled for control. Baldwin was succeeded then by Neville Chamberlain. There was opposition among all three parties, Liberals, Conservatives and Labor, to the proposal by France to convert the League of Nations into a strictly military alliance. British ministries were becoming more lenient on Germany, but not on Fascism or Communism. The nation was socially stable, but storm clouds were becoming apparent.

Post war France was still dominated by Clemenceau and Foch immediately after the signing of the Treaty of Versailles, but they were aging, and it would not last. The grandparents didn't discuss them to as great a length as they did other nations, except to describe the culpability of France for WWI, and setting the world up for WWII due to her arrogance and greed. They did admit that she had suffered more actual war damage than other regions of Europe, but thought that the control over the Peace Conference and setting of reparations to be paid to her by Germany and continued blockade in peace time were punitive and set up an undying hatred that would one day have to be expressed. My exposure to the French side of the equation would not occur until I married into a family whose paternal heritage traced back to French minor nobility in Alsace. What I learned before that was gleaned from the voluminous literature on the subject in both the libraries of my grandparents, public libraries, and finally in classes on world political geography. I gleaned a consensus that France collaborated with Wilson on the Treaty of Versailles, and Foch was the main moderator of the negotiations, engineering much of the punitive quality of that document against Germany. There was both post war financial and social instability, and the leadership changed so rapidly, sometimes with violent means, that France suffered substantially and was finally taken over in 1936 by a coalition of radical parties called the "People's Front." They borrowed heavily from other nations, particularly the United States, and the debt was never to be repaid.

Other European countries, like Spain and Portugal, were becoming more unstable, with struggles between the politically right and left. Germany and Italy were behind the scenes, supporting the efforts of the discontented radical elements which advocated dictatorship. If Spain and Portugal were to ally with Germany in a future conflict, France would be hemmed in on three sides by German, Italian, and Spanish dictatorships. The 1936 rebellion under Generalissimo Franco, backed by German and Italian sympathy highlighted the growing European instability. German "volunteers" were permitted to enter the Spanish revolution on one side, and Russian volunteers on the other. Britain and the "Great Powers" set up a patrol to prevent outside aid in this "mini-world war." By then, I was eighteen years old, and my grandparents and I watched current events with a mixture of anxiety, hope, disappointment, and anticipation. There was finally a compromise in the form of a Spanish constitution promoting unity, but some provinces were permitted to organize regionally and locally as they chose. Other smaller nations of Northwestern Europe made peaceful, steady recovery from WWI, chose neutrality, and remained in the League of Nations.

In the United States, FDR had been elected, took office in 1933, as the first Democrat elected since Wilson, and as a member of a prominent, very wealthy family, was both an excellent politician who capitalized on popular dissatisfaction with the economy, and possessed superior public speaking capability. He used radio and public speaking to cement his relationship with and engender faith in the public. During his campaign, he travelled an estimated 25,000 miles across the country, and in Chicago when accepting his nomination to run against Hoover, he announced his promise of a "New Deal" to bring back prosperity to the nation. He would be elected again in 1936, 1940, and 1944. He had been very successful as Governor of New York state, the office he held when running for the Presidency, and was a near genius politician. Born in southeastern New York, Dutchess County, Hyde Park, 30 January 1882, into a very prominent family, he had the advantage of education, wealth, travel, access to men of influence, and social position. As an only child, he was very close to his mother. He attended private schools, then Harvard as an undergraduate, and went on to law school at Columbia University. He was socially prominent, but academically uninspired. In 1920, he contracted poliomyelitis, and was then deprived of the full use of his legs, but that didn't thwart him in his ultimate goal of establishing a Progressive movement within the Democrat party. An acolyte of Wilson, he was appointed Assistant Secretary of the Navy in 1920, from which he resigned to run for the Vice Presidency on the Democratic ticket. Though unsuccessful in that effort, he continued his climb to the top, despite his physical infirmity, which was treated with the best health care expertise money could buy.

In 1928, FDR ran for and was elected into the governorship of New York at the urgent request of his friend and benefactor, Alfred Smith, then he won again in 1930, providing him with a special position of influence and political exposure. Abraham Lincoln once said "Nearly all men can stand adversity, but if you want to test a man's character, give him power." At this juncture, FDR was attaining power, and as an empiricist, who thought out things through observation and experimentation before acting, he charted his path to the Presidency of the United States of America. Though there were dark shadows in the area of banking hovering over the last few months that Hoover was required to serve after the electoral repudiation, he invited Roosevelt to the White House to talk over policies to alleviate the situation. Roosevelt refused because he didn't want to accept any possible blame for his new administration if the methods somehow failed. Roosevelt did have one plan of his own, which was to eliminate Prohibition, which he estimated would bring $500,000,000 into the nation's impoverished coffers through taxes and industry. It was also a popular move. Once he assumed office, there were many programs which were put into place, and though he spoke about experimentation from time to time, he did not let anyone deter him from initiating or terminating a project he had set into motion, and many of the projects brought very good economic and employment benefits to a weary public. In the general election, the Democrats had won many governorships and Congressional seats, so opposition was at a low level to Roosevelt's progressive programs. Some were successful, and some were not, but he is fondly remembered for those that succeeded, including some that had been instituted by his predecessor. FDR was to serve as President of the United States from March of 1933 to his death in April of 1945. He was to hold the nation together during the Second World War, assisted by his wife, Eleanor Roosevelt, whom he had married in 1905 against the specific disapproval of his doting mother. Some historians believe that she became the *de facto* leader in the White House when he became so debilitated from his health problems. He was succeeded by his Vice President, Harry S. Truman.

PART III WINDS OF WAR

Chapter Thirteen – WWI Epilogue

Slowly the hills and burrows of discontent among the ever expanding population of the human anthill eroded the foundation of the unsteady peace, and as before the globe was riddled with growing upheavals stirred by the slavering jaws of greed for power, control, and money.

Following the close of WWI, and during the interim between the two great wars, a massive reduction in the US standing army took place, much to the chagrin of military proponents. Draft ended in 1918, but an association remained in place in case it had to be reinstated at a later date. However, downsizing of the Army, which is the most numerous in manpower of all US forces, is not a simple task. It is not as simple as picking a number to which the force is to be downgraded, printing out pink slips and releasing the soldiers into a changed and alien environment. Ultimately, force reduction has occurred after each US armed conflict, all the way back to the American Revolution, and it can occur for either one, or a combination of several reasons such as military leadership, civilian public opinion, threat assessment, budget and economy. It is important to note here that force reduction impacts training, readiness and morale of the residual force to the extent that the next battle fought will be inordinately bloody. This occurred at the 1943 Kesserine Pass Battle in Tunisia, Taskforce Smith, Korea, 1950, and then in Ia Drang, South Vietnam in 1965. The Army has even created a Field Manual (FM) 100-17 to cover the precise steps which are to be followed in downsizing the force. The army strength was cut severely in 1919 and 1920, and the glut of returning soldiers, both whole bodied and crippled or injured suffered through unemployment, depression, and lack of adequate medical care.

Both the military and politicians were anxious to demobilize forces rapidly, and one Congressman (William E. Borah of Idaho) declared that "universal military training and conscription in time of peace are the taproots of militarism." However, the Bolshevik Revolution was raging in Russia, threatening to extend into Western Europe, and massive strikes and terrorist bombings at home threatened a possible extension of violence in the US. An attempt was made to create a new kind of standing professional Army, smaller, less expensive, well trained, composed of volunteers, which would work with the civilian forces to meet the military and social needs of the nation. There were, however, opposing views in the Army, because many of the professional soldiers harbored a long-standing dislike of citizen soldiers, because the militia was under the control of the states, poorly equipped and badly trained. In 1919, a bill presented to Congress requested a 500,000 man Army, but a large, vocal contingent of dissenters arose in Congress. One dissenter pointed out that we still had two million soldiers overseas, and that most of them should be transported back to the United States and put back out on the farms. Arguments were made about the cost, and the waste of "men standing around in idleness, drawing salaries, and wasting money." Congress eventually compromised on a strength of 280,000 in the National Defense Act of 1920, but that was cut in 1921, due to Congressional appropriations, to a Regular Army strength of 125,000 due to public pressure. This was less than the original prewar strength when the US was unprepared to even defend herself. Congress debated and gave its unvarnished opinions of how the military should be organized, to be able to accomplish all that would be demanded of it during peacetime. This was to cause difficulties from 1921 to 1940, which was summed up by MG Clair Street: "We have gone overboard to demobilize the Army under a system which to me is not only unsound but positively dangerous." Training, recruitment and retention were to plague the Army for the next 20 years.

What Price Honor, Memoir of Eugene Adams

The Navy after 1918 fared better than the Army and Marines, in that there were some high level conferences on naval strength with Britain, Japan and the United States. There had been some active negotiations going on over naval disarmament since the Versailles Treaty, and the US had been steadfastly demanding parity with Great Britain, while Japan demanded sufficient vessels to protect herself in the Pacific. There was a Treaty of London setting the initial ratios of warships, but arguments continued. Several ratios had been set forward, but the final ratio of 10-Britain, 10-USA, and 7-Japan was finally set. A continued disagreement over armament thereof, numbers of aircraft carriers, and submarines. Also, there was continued resistance to external inspection to insure compliance. Hoover flatly refused, but FDR eventually said that inspectors from other countries would be tolerated. Such inspections were never carried out, which might have raised rancor, but the appeasement worked in the meantime. By 1936, the US had only 18 battleships, but that was deemed sufficient by the Administration for self-defense. After all, the US had signed the Kellogg-Briand Pact under the League of Nations, which outlawed war. Government ownership of Merchant Marine ships at two million tons of ocean going vessels, then under the Jones Merchant Marine Act war emergency legislation, which had energized ship building was to be transferred to the private sector. After this decision, and other legislation, less than 500 of the 2,600 ships remained under government authority. Many had been sold off at enormous financial sacrifice to the British and other foreign countries, as well as to American shipping companies. Often the amount received was less than one tenth the value of the ships.

Demobilization initially returned nearly four million soldiers and sailors to seek peacetime pursuits, along with 11,400,000 civil servants utilized for the war effort. Although this was certainly a difficult undertaking, the reabsorption was achieved with surprising rapidity and less economic difficulty than had been anticipated. The problem with obtaining employment for the returning veterans was taken up by the American Legion, incorporated by Congress in 1919. As delineated before, a bill for compensation was introduced during the administrations of Harding and Coolidge and both vetoed it because in the original form, it called for billions of dollars in expenditures, which was improvident due to the state of the economy at that time. The bill, called the Bonus Bill, was passed by Congress in 1924, authorized payments, but none were made either in cash or immediately in any form. The American Legion continued to champion payment in cash, which was vetoed by FDR, but Congress enacted a bill in 1936, overriding FDR's veto to issue bonds convertible to cash against each veteran's certificate of adjusted compensation.

Overall in the world, the super powers of Europe were essentially destroyed as such, and two new ones were created, one in Russia and one in the United States. The United States was experiencing, as outlined above, economic difficulties both from the loss of the highly profitable markets of the war era, failure of repayment of large loans made to other nations during the war, and distress in the agricultural industry. Two of the bills sponsored by FDR early in his Presidency, to address existing problems were the Agricultural Adjustment Act (AAA), whereby he thought that increasing prices for farmers would cause them to reduce production, and the National Industrial Recovery Act (NIRA), which set industrial "codes." The latter required raising of wages, decreases in hours worked, improving working conditions, eliminating child labor, and requiring negotiation with unions. The Supreme Court declared them both unconstitutional in 1935 and 1936 respectively. Public works began in 1933, and it was found that economic objectives were more likely to be reached by continuing these programs set in motion by his predecessor. A major program was the Tennessee Valley Authority which was to control an unruly river in an impoverished region of the nation, and it was very successful, providing cheap electricity throughout the region, reforestation, restoration of eroded land, and changing it from poverty to a productive, economically stable area. The Wagner Act in 1935 made businessmen recognize and negotiate with unions, which by then had gained political strength.

By December of 1936, I was 18 years old and had graduated from High School. My grandparents were very worried, and I could see it in their eyes and hear it in their voices. I applied for and received a scholarship, which pleased me immensely, because that meant that I didn't have to spend all the money I had been saving for college on tuition, and that I might have some to spend on other pursuits. I thought that I might wait to the beginning of the Fall Semester to enter college, primarily because that was when the scholarship would start. Those months were spent working on the farm and listening to the grandparents discuss every world event in vivid detail. Newspapers from everywhere were read, not just from local sources, but even from Great Britain and Europe. I was amazed to find out that the grandparents were able to read all of them, though sometimes arguing over what a foreign expression meant. They introduced me to the concept of idiomatic and colloquial expressions, some of which were very amusing, but certainly would color the perception by the reader of what was meant. My usually taciturn Grandpa Crouch actually expounded on the critical need for training, experience and leadership in wartime, and denounced the political leadership for their short-sighted, ignorance, and complete lack of foresight. He supported the draft. Grandpa Adams supported a draft also, and pointed out that the final unification of France's population and raising of a highly successful army by Napoleon Bonaparte occurred only because of conscription, which brought people of all levels and from all locals together and forged them into units. The latter was accomplished by a rigorous training program and absolute insistence on utilization of a common language, French. He and Grandpa Crouch agreed completely that Congress, with complicity of the White House, had continued the dismemberment of the US military to very dangerous levels. The grandparents agreed that disarmament happens every time after a conflict, and it began even after the American Revolution. First there is a frantic build up, when danger threatens, then slashing of military assets because "peace has broken out." Unfortunately, I was to witness this first hand later on, but found it an interesting concept to store away. Grandmother Crouch made absolutely sure I was listening, and becoming familiar with names like Chiang Kai-shek and Mao tse Tung. She declared that the conflict between China and Japan was the beginning of WWII. Nobody spoke Russian or Chinese, but they relied upon those stacks of newspapers, and the radio to track what was going on in those countries. The grandfathers even discussed the US government giving away of massive amounts of weaponry, including the new M3 105mm Howitzers to the Chinese, leaving only a very few to be used by American troops, even in training. Training was being provided by the US to Chinese troops on these new weapons, among other pieces of equipment, but nothing equivalent was provided for American troops. It has always puzzled me why these seemingly ordinary working people were so remarkably insightful. They all voted in every election, local, state, and national because they taught me that if you don't care enough to vote, then you can't complain about the governance you get. It is fair to say that I learned more world political geography and political insight from them from any college course I ever took, and I have reflected on how very fortunate I was. The other thing I sometimes wonder about is where family cohesiveness has gone in the intervening years between my youth, adulthood, and advanced age.

I respected the input of the elders, and though like every teenaged male throughout the centuries, occasionally questioned their opinions. To begin with, I couldn't at that time fully understand the wisdom of their comments on the military, and wondered why I should even care about a conflict raging in Asia. But I listened, learned, and read relevant literature to verify facts and either accept or reject concepts. At first, I could not understand why they were not enamored of FDR and mistrusted his policies, but in retrospect the validity of their analyses is clear. I did enter college, thinking that I would become a lawyer, played baseball, joined the figure skating team, studied music for wind instruments, and generally enjoyed life. But I could clearly see that clouds were gathering, darkening, and becoming more ominous. After a great deal of thought, and with advice from the grandfathers, I joined the Army before the draft was reinstated, which later turned out to my advantage. My two years of college didn't give me a diploma, but they did give me advantages, plus, I could sign up for correspondence courses to complete a bachelor's degree at a reduced cost while serving in the Army. I was surprised at the lack of knowledge of the soldier population both about the authorization levels of troop strength, and about the Sino-Japanese conflict. There were plenty of complaints about the lack of funding for equipment, recruitment, and training to meet the demands of being able to fight a war with so few divisions, and those incompletely filled. However, I had definitely learned. The Nationalist, Chiang Kai-shek, had come into power in the giant but decaying Chinese nation in the late 1920s, and had put together policies to provide for improvement of the military, economic, and industrial status of the nation. It was then already under attack by Japan. Ongoing internal conflict from Communist agitators under the leadership of Mao tse Tung paused in 1936, so the Japanese decided to attempt overthrow of Chiang and capture China outright. Across the globe, countries watched with trepidation, as the untrained, unequipped, two million strong Chinese National Government Army kept being subdued by the Japanese. There was no navy, no national reserves, no real air force, no trained pilots, and though Mao's 150,000 guerillas assisted Chiang at first, they, too, lacked the materiel to turn back the Japanese onslaught. Though there were sufficient natural resources, the underdeveloped industry was insufficient to support the Chinese war effort, so the US began its usual "come to the rescue" action, providing equipment, money and military expertise to the struggling Chinese government. Lt. Gen "Vinegar Joe" Stillwell was put in command of a Sino-American force in British-held Burma to clear the Burma Road, an important strategic logistic asset for the Chinese Army. American posters appeared in the United States, calling for assistance for the Chinese, and to win over public opinion.

Elements of the US Army Air Force were sent to train Chinese pilots, multiple training sites were set up to train Chinese soldiers and sailors in the use of the modern weapons provided by the US. Chiang invited Claire Chennault, a retired Army Captain, to be their aeronautics advisor, promoting him to Colonel in their army. Chennault recruited a cadre of trained American fighter pilots, and qualified mechanics, logisticians, and administrators and his organization was called the American Volunteer Group (AVG). He also set up an early warning system so he could get the antiquated, obsolete Chinese planes off the ground before the Japanese could get there. In 1944, when FDR had requested that Stillwell be appointed commander of all Allied Forces in the Theater, Chiang angrily asked for Stillwell be recalled. Maj. Gen Wedemeyer replaced Stillwell and Chiang made him his Chief of Staff.

By comparison with the Chinese, Japan had 300,000 well trained, well equipped regular troops, 150,000 Mongol and Manchurian troops, and two million trained reserves. They were superior on the battlefield, on the sea, and in the air. They took the ports, cutting off the seaborne supply lines, they owned the air, and occupied a large portion of China until the end of 1942. Upon Chennault's arrival, the Chinese really didn't have an air force, and had only a few obsolete aircraft. The US supplied P-40 aircraft, under the supposed "Lend-Lease" arrangement, which gave birth to the "Flying Tigers." Japanese air superiority was significantly eroded. The AVG gave way to the China Air Task Force under Chennault, who was promoted to Brigadier General, and it continued successfully. During the hiatus from Japanese attack, Mao continued to consolidate Communist influence, and he managed an unofficial truce with the Japanese in northwest China, allowing him to use those guerillas who were then unengaged to fight against Chiang in the south. Since the Japanese had enjoyed significant success thus far, they took over the rice crops, but evidently, the Chinese with American assistance were able to repulse them. The conflict continued, but with massive airlift of supplies, materiel, and bomber support from commands under both Stillwell who held the ground, and Chennault who commanded the air, the Japanese were at an impasse. Chiang favored Chennault over Stillwell to such an extent that much of the airlift supplies going over "The Hump" (Himalayas) went to Chennault, allowing him to maintain air superiority over most of China. After his recall from China, Lt. Gen Stillwell, formerly a WWI Intelligence Officer, would serve in WWII as Commander of the US 10th in the Pacific. Claire Chennault would be reintegrated into the US Army Air Force as a Brigadier. The first battles of WWII had indeed been fought in China, and Chiang would eventually be ousted by Mao, whose policy was to "swim in the sea of the people." He became the supreme leader of Communist China, and Chiang fled to a non-descript small island, which the USA still insists on recognizing as the legal authority of China.

Chapter Fourteen – Reductions in Force

Messages come from on high, and somehow the impact does not change.

Message to George Washington

Resolved, that the commanding officer be and he is hereby directed to discharge the troops now in the service of the United States, except twenty-five privates, to guard the stores at Fort Pitt, and fifty-five to guard the stores at West Point and other magazines, with a proportionate number of officers; no officer to remain in service above the rank of captain.

Continental Congress

The Revolutionary War finally ended only when the treaty of peace was signed by the British in Paris on 3 September 1783. Demobilization was to proceed without delay, therefore seventy five privates and officers ranking Captain and below were to provide security for the new nation. The final manpower was 80 "plus an appropriate number of officers." It could not last, of course, but that historically is the first demobilization of troops in American history. The pressure for demobilization is always the same, because the public longs for the societal conditions that existed in the pre-war period, and countries do not wish to bear the burden of expenditures that they swiftly label as unnecessary. Pushed aside are the anxieties of those who had waited in fear of tragic news from the front, and eyes are often averted when a veteran suffering from physical or emotional injuries sustained in battle struggles by. The military tries to adapt to the changing configuration of troops and equipment resulting from Congressional maneuvers to cut expenditures despite actual potential needs. In FM 100-17, a whole chapter of regulations regarding demobilization attempts to minimize chaos, but there is no actual integration with constantly changing legislation on the issues which necessarily arise. An excellent accounting of this is found in DA Pamphlet No. 20-10, *History of Personnel Demobilization in the United States Army* (Washington, DC) July 1952.

A cursory accounting of the interwar years between WWI and the rise of conflict throughout Europe and Asia has been given previously. In short, by 1940, US Army strength was less than the standing Army strength prior to US entry into WWI, which was clearly inadequate. The draft had been halted in 1918, as discussed before. Discussion of preparedness seemed to rise off the banked coals still glowing from the previous catastrophic global conflagration, but what Congress and the civilian population did not understand about what recruitment and training was, and to a large extent is, is encyclopedic. Just raw numbers of ill equipped untrained soldiers does not a fighting force make, and even during the Depression, food, housing and a steady though small paycheck were insufficient to even meet the pitiably small authorization for manpower mandated by Congress. The volunteer force did not even experience real basic training, because training depots were abolished to cut cost, and inductees were sent immediately to their assigned units, where they were to be trained by the officers and NCOs, whether for support or combat functions. For infantry troops, they were still being trained on the old 1903 Springfield rifles, and the artillery on what few French 75mm artillery pieces were available. The Army only managed to obtain fourteen of the new Howitzers for training purposes, and insufficient ammunition to fully utilize them for the artillery units. Motor transport equipment was antiquated, as was communication, air and general materiel. Although their military skills learned as "on the job training," enabled them to be absorbed into the units quickly, they often were employed as cooks, clerks, guards, or in general "housekeeping" occupations. Then the edict came down from the government that they were to receive adequate training, and be concentrated for intensive training events to last for a minimum of two weeks each year, but it unfortunately was not accompanied by assets or funding to accomplish that goal. Miraculously, the military has always been able to retain a small cadre of truly dedicated officers and senior NCOs, or else the demands of the ensuing crises over the years could never have been met.

Demobilization of the Navy has been discussed in a previous chapter, but to summarize, it continued to be a hotly debated issue. In November of 1921, then Secretary of State C. E. Hughes led the charge to decrease the Navy and eliminate building of "capital ships," and had received widespread public support on the issue. His proposal also included restrictions on fortifications, future naval construction, and on fortification of and support of naval bases in the Central Pacific. There was a later move to build cruisers that fell just below the 10,000 ton limit used to define capital ships. There were several other conferences, notably one in Hoover's Presidency, which kept trying to find a "yardstick for arms control," which was still touted as the way to ensure peace. The one Secretary of State Stimson and British Prime Minister MacDonald came up with lasted into the Cold War era. Clearly, manpower reductions without consideration of configuration, training and recruitment factors in an all-volunteer force was worse than ineffective. Arms control cannot be reduced to technological, engineering factors, or mathematical equations if basic political problems are ignored. The limitations on naval assets enraged the naval officers in all three nations (US, Britain, Japan), and shortly after the Second London Conference in 1935, Japan withdrew and began building according to her assessment of national requirements. In December of 1936, quantitative and qualitative limitations on naval armaments ended. Japan's goal was clear. If freed from the above restrictions, she could build her navy to

What Price Honor, Memoir of Eugene Adams

dominate China and Southeast Asia, becoming the foremost power in the entire region.

In summary, the USA, following WWI had definitely wanted to return to traditional values, and there was a resistance to maintenance of a large force. At the onset of WWI, the standing army had consisted of 92,000 regular Army troops and 19,000 of those belonged to administrative and support functions. Estimates of that strength vary depending upon the authorization from Congress for the standing strength, and at the time, the authorization was 142,000, which swelled rapidly during the war to an estimated four million. The immediate post war move was to reduce the larger force, as it returned from war, back to what was considered sufficient for national self-defense. What the public wanted in the 1920s was a small, inexpensive force, composed of volunteers, as far as possible from public sight. With sabers rattling again across the world, some planners were trying to reform the Army so that it would serve both the social and military needs of the nation. A small standing army working closely with larger citizen forces was thought sufficient to produce a well trained and equipped military peacetime force prepared for any contingency that might arise. Compulsory military training for all American males was proposed, to both make them better citizens and more productive, efficient members of society. This was strongly resisted by members of Congress. Ultimately, it became obvious even to the most conservative Americans by 1939 that such a plan of severely limited forces was a recipe for disaster. Reductions in Congressional authorizations for military forces did not cease because Congress didn't understand the danger, and Congress and the American people were oblivious to the fact that "authorization" does not equate to actual boots on the ground. Pershing argued before Congress, but no one listened. The War Department, in 1919, had made justification for a force of 500,000. Instead, Congress steadily reduced the Army from 280,000 to

175,000 to 125,000, and by 1924 to 111,000--only 11,000 more than the Treaty of Versailles allowed a conquered and disarmed Germany. The effects of such a "skeletonized" force will later be considered.

    Early in the administration of FDR, he certainly was busy with many issues, one of which was the instability of the banking system. During WWI, the United States had become the financier of the world, and large loans had been made to other nations, in the expectation that they would be repaid. This has not happened. In actuality, according to my elders, Germany repaid more debt than any other nation, despite her desperate economic conditions. They all tried to strategize on how to send food and medicine to the suffering women, children, and elderly in Germany, because the blockade went on in the face of rank starvation of the public. But privation was striking at the heart of the USA, was well. Prior to the collapse and later closure of banks, they had withdrawn their money from the banks and tucked it away from seizure. I remember, too, arguments for and against conversion of it into gold or silver, to which Grandma Crouch held forth on the belief that those assets would be simply seized, whereas currency could be cleverly hidden and utilized to buy necessities. As usual, she was right. To this day, I don't know where they hid their money, but they did hold on to it, as well as providing their own vegetables and meat from gardens and livestock. I got a few lessons in "canning," and learned that if the cap on the jar is bulged, the food is bad, but if it is not, the food is safe to eat. I also learned that pressure cookers are extremely dangerous, and must be utilized with care. There were a few staples that they horded, like salt, sugar, rice, and flour, in large glass jars, tightly sealed against invasion by hungry little creatures like weevils, or other bugs. Bread was only baked, and never bought, which actually was a marvelous thing, both because of the delightful smells from the oven, the wonderful taste of the bread, and the fact that Grandma

Crouch, when she was angry about something, would go to the kitchen and defuse her anger by pounding on bread dough instead of on the offender(s). They also made their own butter, and Grandpa Alva provided the milk, fresh from his cows. Water was plentiful from the wells, and the families drew ever closer due to the exigency of conditions. Because of their unique knowledge and ability to survive those times essentially unscathed, I benefitted enormously and learned lessons in survival that have never been forgotten.

Others in the US population did not fare so well, particularly in the cities. Business was at a standstill, the default on payments of war debts and decrease of foreign trade were problematic to the Treasury, which in 1933 showed a deficit of an unheard of $3,000,000,000. The status of currencies in Europe was also in flux so the ability of the US to maintain the gold standard came into question. However, the solvency of the banks was an even greater crisis, so both gold and currency was being hoarded. This was one of the issues Hoover had attempted to discuss with FDR before his 4 March inauguration and the takeover by that administration and the newly elected Congress. Because of this impasse at an extremely critical juncture, the 20th Amendment of the Constitution was passed by Congress in February by the required 2/3 vote providing for the inauguration of future Presidents on 20 January and 3 January for the assembly of the new Congress to eliminate the "lame duck" sessions. Prior to his inauguration in March, Roosevelt first concentrated on selecting his cabinet, and sought to represent therein both conservatives and liberals as well as geographical and factional groups. Senator Cordell Hull of Tennessee became the Secretary of State, Francis Perkins, Secretary of Labor, and the first woman to hold such a post; the Secretary of the Treasury was William Woodin, a manufacturer and personal friend of FDR's, and Homer Cummings of Connecticut was selected as Attorney General. In his broadcast inaugural address on March 4th 1933, FDR expressed hope that the normal balance of power among the coequal branches of government would be sufficient to address the serious needs of the nation. However, he qualified it by stating that if there were events which required him to do so, he would ask Congress "for one remaining instrument – broad executive power – to wage a war against an emergency as great as the power that would be given to me if we were, in fact, invaded by a foreign foe." When he returned to the White House from the parades and meetings with multiple congratulatory delegations, he was faced with the collapse of the banking system. Banks had already been closing across the nation in more than half of the states, but the final straw was the collapse of the NYC financial center. With banks closed, there was a shortage of currency to even buy life's necessities. On 5 March, FDR then decided upon a drastic measure, previously suggested by Hoover, to close all US banks, and movement of gold and silver was to be forbidden. On 6 March, he held a conference of governors to discuss a cooperative solution to this problem. This quick response brought him great approval from the public, despite the immediate privation.

By 9 March, he called for the Congress to assemble and discuss his emergency plan of action. The first on the agenda was the Banking and Gold Control Act, the first objective of which was to open all the banks with this legislation, placing them under the control of the Executive Branch to protect the depositors. The legislation called for the authority to reorganize banks "to put them on a sound basis." It passed both houses on the same day. The result embodied in this law was that conservators were put in charge of insolvent banks, liberalized issue of Federal Reserve bank notes were issued, and the Secretary of Treasury was empowered to seize all gold bullion, coins and gold certificates.

The second emergency bill, the Economy Bill, pledged the

government to immediate and drastic reduction of government spending. It passed on 20 March, and authorized salary decreases for government workers by 15% and reduction of some grants to veterans. Costs of government were to be paid by revenues.

On 22 March, the Beer Act set alcohol content of beer at 3 ½ % by weight, and put a high tax on it in states without prohibition laws. The 21st Amendment had repealed the 18th Amendment during the "lame duck" session of Congress, ending overall Prohibition. This had been ratified in December, prior to FDR's inauguration, so in the following year, heavy taxes were placed on all liquor and liquor traffic. The amount of revenue initially collected was not at first what had been projected, but it increased steadily, so that by 1937, it was $600,000,000.

On 31 March FDR's fourth emergency law was enacted, establishing the Civilian Conservation Corps under the nominal Reforestation Relief Act, and under the supervision of the War Department. It would employ an estimated 250,000 unemployed, unmarried men between 18 and 25 years of age at $1.00/day plus food, shelter and clothing. By June of 1933, there were over 1300 camps, and the laborers were employed in road building, reforestation, flood control, and erosion prevention. An educational program was also provided, therefore congress had embarked on both a social and economic reform in which FDR sought to better the lot of the average young man. This would, of course play Hell with military recruitment in the "all volunteer" Army, Navy, and Marine Corps.

Over the years, General Pershing had continued the fight that began in 1919, when he testified before Congress on the necessity for a trained military force, and a compulsory service to the nation. General Pershing made a strong plea for some kind of universal military training. He further emphasized this approach, pointing out the physical fitness and educational advantages. In response, one Congressman cautioned, "We are in danger of having many beautiful schemes for popular education thrust upon us which, if adopted, would make the Army a college rather than a fighting unit." Into succeeding years of the administration, the decimation of the Army and Navy continued, but Pershing never gave up his efforts to fend it off. He was fighting a losing battle, but he never gave up, despite the postwar surge of pacifism. In all assets available to him, be it personal communication, speeches, testimony before Congressional committees, broadcast interviews, or magazine articles, he expounded on the fallacy that "the blind belief in the benevolence of all peoples will prevent wars," and continued to point out that the Army had always been engaged in some kind of military operation for each 18 months of its existence, and a major war every twenty to thirty years. He asked if it was possible that human nature would miraculously change, and also pointed out that conditions in the world weren't any different than what they had been in the last fifteen or twenty centuries. All he was asking for was "reasonable preparedness," and other voices finally began to chime in. Many Congressmen, who were not veterans, believed that the Army was superfluous except for riot duty, but William Wright, former commander of the 89th Division said "The Army is like a yellow dog running down the street with a tin can tied on it, and everybody on the sidewalk throwing rocks." George C. Marshall Jr. noted, "I saw the Army . . . start rapidly on the downgrade to almost extinction." General Pershing's views didn't count at all." Gen MacArthur had been the Army Chief of Staff under Hoover and the first term of FDR, when he observed in 1934 that the entire US Regular Army would fit in Yankee Stadium, so he continued the pressure he had been exerting for over three years for a larger Army. He had been quoted as saying to Congress, "With our present little Regular Army we would be relatively helpless in the event of an invasion by a major power. . . . . [T]he difference between what we have now and what is proposed in this bill marks the difference between relative helplessness and a chance to accomplish our mission of defense. . . . Pass this bill, Mr. Chairman, I beg you, as an old soldier who has probably seen his last battlefield. Pass this bill and give the American Army a chance in the next battle it fights for the life of the country." Congressional appropriations of 1936 and 1937 resulted in some improvements in men and materiel, so Gen MacArthur believed that his arguments had finally been heard, and in 1936, authorization was granted for 165,000 troops. This was as much because the public was beginning to be more cognizant of the Japanese aggression in an undeclared war, and the rearming and change in leadership in Germany, as it was to the continued pressure from the Generals.

The trials and tribulations of the army were only just begun. Defense spending was increased, and the Adjutant General increased the recruiting quotas to 1,500 per month, or 75 new recruits per corps per month, but the recruiters resisted the order. They simply knew that they could not meet the new demands because the depression was no longer supporting recruiting due to the competition from the New Deal and from a moderately improved economy. As mentioned previously, the CCC workers were receiving $1.00/day or $30.00 per month and the pay for Army privates had been reduced to $21.00 per month. In addition, married soldiers, who already lived on the thinnest edge of complete poverty were discouraged from re-enlistment due the dire circumstances in which they and their families had to live. Often, a dependant would be brought to the clinic for extreme weakness, which was always found to be due to the lack of food. Sometimes, officers and NCOs would take up a collection for food, and even milk, for mothers with very young babies. Soldiers had to be careful not to have any unpaid debt, because any negative financial report could disallow them re-enlistment, or even termination of their current enlistment. New recruits were discouraged about getting married; this brought with it more difficulties among the ranks and morale was already at a rock bottom low. So, the uninformed believed that by changing the uniform, the soldiers would be happier, or perhaps the barracks should be renovated, or…bringing to mind that those who have not served do not ever have a clue. For the first time in Army history, even the recruiters weren't re-enlisting. Something definitely had to be done.

By January of 1938, the deterioration in Europe, remilitarization of Germany, and a continued full blown conflict in the Sino-Japanese theater had begun to infiltrate the consciousness of the American public, and of FDR, to the extent that he issued the statement to Congress that "As Commander in Chief . . . it is my constitutional duty to report . . . that our national defense is, in the light of the increasing armaments in other nations, inadequate for purposes of national security and requires increase for that reason." He was suggesting that the draft be reinstated. Still, it would take nearly two years of constant arguing before Congress approved it in September of 1940. I had already joined the Army in 1939, and was submitting my paperwork for Officer Candidate School. The prospects were very good, and I enjoyed the Army. Between 1938 and 1939 there had been changes in the office of the Secretary of the Army, and Stimson had assumed those duties; Gen George C. Marshall had become the Army Chief of Staff, and would remain in that office until almost the end of 1945, whereupon he would become the architect of the post war planning and recovery of an again devastated world. By July of 1941, the Army was training large numbers of draftees at full strength in restored training centers, with new equipment. It was a massive mobilization, and the Army was no longer a naked skeleton, but there was still turmoil within it. Missions had to be met, and command of those elements required to meet them had to be more than recent trainees inexperienced and untried in combat, but by and large, the draftees were eager, overall better educated, from all levels of society, and from every corner of the nation. It unified the Yankees, and had a significant positive impact on the later total victory they would achieve.

But before victory, there were many other events, dangers, and accomplishments to be dealt with. I was sent to receive training as a medic, which was fascinating, and knowledge gained was in an area in which I had never before ventured. The Army is actually very good at teaching skills that might otherwise never be attempted, but are always useful. It was not long after that that I received placement in Officer Candidate School, and I was very pleased that things were definitely coming together for me. And all during that time, my grandparents wrote to me frequently, and once at mail call, I received a tube, which was very unusual. When I opened the top of it and peered inside, much to the chagrin of all my comrades, it wasn't filled with goodies to munch on, but food for the mind. The grandparents had filled the tube with tightly rolled newspapers which had lines underscoring the parts they thought were most important, and great stars next to the headlines of articles to be read. My fellow OCs (Officer Candidates) urged me to tell the grandparents to fill the tube with things for a "goodie gobble," but many of them asked to read the papers, too. In our isolated world, we were unaware of many of the things going on, particularly in Europe. I found it particularly interesting that there appeared to be danger up along the Marine Boundary Line off the coast of Alaska. The Russians had moved in some troops up there on their side of the line, ostensibly to "protect" their northern coast. We OCs debated the likelihood of that, and also discussed the issues that Wjerserkowski, of Polish heritage, had about the conflict that had started, and even ended with the German takeover of Poland. There is much to be dissected there, and he asked if he could keep the articles from the newspapers that gave details of the invasion, and the loss of Warsaw, which was where his ancestors came from. There were also articles about the Sino-Japanese "undeclared" war, and the aid being given to the Chinese by both

Britain and the USA. One of the classmates scoffed about the conflict between "Vinegar Joe" Stilwell, and Chiang Kai-shek, and made some disparaging remarks about the General. I disagreed, and later was to meet, respect, and like Gen Stilwell. Many of my fellow classmates added notes to the letter I wrote back to the grandparents, thanking them for the "touch of the outside world" and asking that they send more, if they could. They could and did, but included some boxes of goodies to be shared. Several of the OCs sent personal letters to the grandparents, wanting to know if they could be adopted as grandsons…to which they received responses in the affirmative.

Chapter Fifteen – The Interim Ends

The steady beat of the marching feet to the time of the Drums of War are softened at first by the distance from your own strong, sturdy door. But as the distance shrinks, the sound is harder to ignore.

    By 1 September 1939, Nazi Germany had moved against Poland, with the firm conviction that East and West Prussia should not be divided, and that the lands ceded to Poland by the Versailles Treaty were definitely part of greater Germany. This included Poznan and Upper Silesia given to Poland after WWI. The Germans had already occupied the Rhineland, and nothing had been done, except for prolific verbalizations by the French, to push them back. Hitler had cleverly negotiated a nonaggression pact with Poland in January of 1934, which was definitely not popular with the German public, but it was with malice of forethought. Hitler didn't want interference from Britain or a French-Polish military alliance against Germany before Germany had a chance to fully rearm. He knew that both Britain and France were following an appeasement foreign policy because they believed that it was the way to maintain peace, and they had made some limited concessions to some German demands during the 1930s. They had turned a blind eye to Germany's rearmament during 1935 through 1937, and ignored the occupation of the Rhineland in 1936, and annexation of Austria in March of 1938. Hitler's first gamble had paid off. At the 1938 Munich Conference, due to pressure at home to revise some of territorial and military provisions of the Versailles Treaty, Britain and France agreed to forcing Czechoslovakia to allow Germany to annex the Sudetenland, which comprised the Czech border region. Though the Czechs were promised protection of the remainder of their state by their allies, Germany dismembered the Czechoslovak state by March of 1939, violating the agreement at the Munich Conference. The

Czechs had simply been betrayed. Neither Britain nor France were either economically or militarily strong enough to fight a war against Nazi Germany, but they did issue a guarantee of the integrity of the Poland. Hitler then negotiated a nonaggression pact with Russia, and the German-Soviet Pact of August 1939 arranged for the partition of Poland between those two nations, therefore, Germany could attack Poland without Soviet intervention. After the 1 September invasion of Poland, the Polish requested assistance from France, and it did not come, although both Britain and France declared war on Germany on 3 September. Unfortunately for Poland, neither of them sent military support as thousands of German tanks rolled across the nation and a thousand aircraft rained death and destruction from the air.

In the background, before Germany invaded Poland on 1 September, there had been a number of Hitler's cleverly designed sleight of hand communications among the involved nations, and admonitions sent to Germany by Chamberlain of Great Britain. In the literal hours before the invasion of Poland, Italy, which on one hand had promised to support Germany, utilizing her sea power to cut supply lines both to Poland and any British or French operations around the Mediterranean Sea, was trying to organize a multinational conference to "solve the Polish problem." Mussolini had been reviewing his own military situation, and was hoping to defuse the potential conflict. This five power conference proposed in late August was to meet on 5 September, with Germany, Britain, France, Italy and Poland to review and negotiate modification of the edicts of the Versailles Treaty, which were "the root of the problem," according to el Duce. Messages were sent and received in Paris and London to this effect late in August 1939, but as early as April of that year, Hitler had approved his military plan for invasion of Poland (Fall Weiss, or Case White), even though von Ribbentrop, Germany's foreign minister, was not fully aware of it. Joachim von Ribbentrop signed the Treaty of Nonaggression between Germany and the Soviet Union with the Soviet foreign minister, V. Molotov, (I can't spell that first name, but it started with a "V"), on 23 August 1939. The purposes were that (1) Germany would not be attacked by the Soviets, and (2) the Soviets would get their "piece of the pie" when Poland was defeated. The treaty called for a division between their two countries of Romania, Poland, Lithuania, Latvia, Estonia, and Finland, comprising most of the smaller nations formed under the Treaty of Versailles. This treaty remained in force until Germany invaded the USSR in June of 1941. Russia still took control of sections of those countries. On the 17th of September, the USSR declared war on Poland, but the Poles were essentially beaten by then. After their declarations of war against Germany, Britain and France were still "mobilizing," but even on the 3rd of September the Polish had been fighting for 2 ½ days at a great disadvantage. Although they had a large standing army, it was disorganized and their munitions, air craft, weapons and materiel were vastly inferior to the enemy's. By the 8th of September, the German 4th Armored Division was within eyesight of Warsaw, having advanced along the Danzig Corridor. The German Navy faced Allied naval superiority, but clearly had air superiority with their Messerschmitts and particularly the Stukas, which were precision dive bombing aircraft, giving the Germans essentially flying artillery. This superiority was enhanced both by the obsolescence of Polish air assets as well as similar deficiencies in air power for either the British or French. Additionally, Germany had an elite Panzer force, and Poland had no real defense against it. After heavy shelling and bombing, Warsaw was pulverized, therefore Poland surrendered on 27 September 1939. Germany and the Soviet Union divided Poland along the Bug River, with Germany annexing directly West Prussia, Poznan, Upper Silesia, and the Free City of Danzig. The rest of German held Poland including Krakow, Radom, Lublin and Warsaw were placed under "general government control" headed by a Nazi lawyer. Germany was to

Dorothy A Adams

occupy Poland until the beginning of 1945.

Right after my graduation from Officer Candidate School, as a brand new 2LT, I was initially assigned to Elmendorf Field just outside Anchorage, Alaska Territory. It had just opened in 1940, and there was a strategic need for soldiers to be located within easy reach of the Aleutian Islands, due to the presence of Japanese elements in the region. Although I had been branched Infantry, at this US Army Air Force command, they made use of my previous background training as a medic, and I was put in charge of administration and logistics of the medical unit at Elmendorf. I was also to be on tap in case of Japanese attack from their positions in the Aleutians, with particular attention to Adak. The Aleutian Island Chain actually is a control point for the Pacific Great Circle Routes, and Gen Billy Mitchell had told Congress in 1935 that Alaska was the most important strategic place in the world, and that whomever holds it will hold the world. From Elmendorf Field, I was dispatched to many locations within Alaska, and the story told for public consumption was that we were there not because there was a danger of attack from Japan or Russia, but because we were supporting the construction of the Alcan Highway. Elmendorf Field in the Alaska Territory was to last from 1940-1945, after which it was transferred to the Alaskan Air Command and became Elmendorf Air Force Base, which my daughter told me is a transport stop when she is returning to the USA from one of her assignments in Asia.

Alaska is beautiful, and teaming with a wide variety of wildlife, and populated by Inuit tribes which have been there since time immemorial. They are fascinating people, friendly and very knowledgeable about their environment. I spent many hours of my off duty time chatting with them, and learning about the unique transportation methods by sled, ice conditions, chinooks, and the identity of plants which grow during the brief warm seasons. They were fascinated by my sketch books, and I gave away many of my drawings to various ones of them, which they treasured. They were at first put off my addiction to cameras, and didn't like to be photographed, but later came to realize that their spirits would not be captured in those small black box like instruments. They also appreciated it when I would treat some minor ailment for them, and would inundate me with small gifts, big smiles, and sometimes a warm meal, or advice about how to keep my ears and neck warm. I learned a great deal about surviving under such harsh conditions from them, and enjoyed their friendly nature. There was only one down turn during my stay there, which was the wreck of one of our ambulances. Since I was responsible for the equipment, and for safety of operators, I wound up paying for an ambulance which had been wrecked by one of my troops, who was drunker than the average skunk. The vehicle was totally destroyed and he was lucky to have been extracted before the tangled remains of it slid off into an icy oblivion. Fortunately for him, he was so limbered up by the alcohol that he received only minor injuries and I learned firsthand how to process a solider for a discharge under other than honorable conditions. It wasn't a task I enjoyed, but it had to be done. I then applied for a transfer, because I had served over a year there, and that incident negatively impacted my performance report and my paycheck. I was transferred to a small installation near White Horse, and was allowed a 14 day leave to go back to the USA for a visit.

    I visited my grandparents and mother in Elkhart, Indiana, and found that my Grandfather was quite weakened and almost immobile. John Crouch would not make it very much longer, and the strain on my Grandmother was apparent. But they were both cheerful and very glad that I had come to see them. The conversations were more personal during that visit, but they still had been keeping a sharp eye on what was happening in Europe, and they were not optimistic. They were very much aware that the

Alaskan Territory was in danger, and were hopeful that I would be transferred soon, but were fascinated by the photographs of the wildlife, and tales of the inhabitants I had met there. Of course, they were disappointed that I had not yet found a mate, and there not any great grandchildren on the way. Little did any of us know that while I was on leave, my transfer papers were being processed, and I would soon be a member of a stateside unit, or that I would soon meet the young woman who would become my wife. My sister and her husband were imminently to be parents, so they were comforted by the fact that there would be at least one great grandchild soon. They did bring up some of the policies that FDR had implemented, and they were not particularly impressed with him, though they listened to every radio broadcast he made. I was surprised, since the President was generally very popular.

After a few days, I took a quick trip to Champaign, Illinois to visit Grandpa Adams on his farm. He was getting very old by then, too, and it saddened me to realize that I wouldn't have any of them very much longer. When I got there, I was relieved to see that he still walked with a quick step, and his mind was as sharp as ever. He asked about Army pay, and what I thought about the change in uniforms. It seemed an odd thing to be curious about until he told me that he thought that the only reason it happened was because the morale had sunk so low, and that the strength was also pitifully low in both the Army and the Navy, should we have to engage in another global war. The new "wrappings" as he called it, were simply distractors in hopes that the true status of the military would go unnoticed. He was fairly critical of the British and French in their failure to assist Poland, and asked what I knew about that action. Then he said that we weren't much better than either of them, but he had a real case of heartburn over Neville Chamberlain, as well as the French inability to honor the French pledge, as well, to assist the Poles in defending themselves. Then he asked about equipment that the Army had on hand, like motor transport capability, artillery, infantry weapons and munitions, aircraft assets, and adequate clothing, food, medical capability, and dozens of other things. I hadn't really thought about it before in any detail, but realized that since the draft would be revving up, all of those were critically important for our troops. Then he asked if I knew that my father had remarried, as had my mother, and I simply shrugged my shoulders. He also asked what I thought about labor unions, and told me that my father had become a union activist. From the look on his face, it was obvious that he didn't approve.

At the end of my leave, as I was preparing to return to the Alaskan Territory, I received orders to report to a maneuver, which was to be held at the fairgrounds near a town, and in a county in Texas I had never heard of before. There was a small radar station near the location for the maneuver, and I was to report in there for further details of the exercise. I was surprised, but was transported by rail to a place called Lufkin, Texas, which had a small railroad depot, and was picked up by an Army sedan driven by a very young buck sergeant. I was taken to report in, received my assignment, and joined an Infantry Battalion, where I joined "F Troop," a company of approximately 200 men. They had not yet been assigned a new Company Commander, so the First Sergeant briefed me in as the interim CO. Our billets were tents, varying from GP mediums to GP large, but I was given a GP small, containing two cots, and just about nothing else. When I had gone on leave, I had not anticipated this chain of events, therefore had not brought appropriate gear, so the "First Shirt" took me over to draw what would be needed, and he continued to brief me in as we went. He asked if I had ever fired a 0.45, and I hadn't, but as for the M-1, I had been familiarized on it, but had more time on the old Springfield. I was informed that we would be conducting Record Fire, where troops are put on a firing line, with targets, and would be run through a drill for familiarization and marksmanship, and that for F Company, I would be "in charge," which translates into "responsible." That was to happen the day after my arrival, and he suggested that we hold an evening formation, both for introductions, and for announcing the training plan for the day. I asked him how long he had been in the Army, and I knew already that since he was what we called a "zebra-striper" he was definitely experienced. But I was still surprised to hear that he had been in since the latter part of WWI. He also said he felt really glad that he had been allowed to stay, because "experience definitely counts." I thought back to what Grandpa Alva had said about the dedicated core of enlisted men and officers that comprised the backbone of the Army, despite the continual diminution of the size of the force. Then he asked about me. He already knew that I had started out as an enlisted soldier and was trained as a medic before I went to OCS. He wanted to know exactly how much infantry experience I had, and why I was wearing cross-rifles on my uniform. I didn't pretend to know how the Army decides who will be branched into what career field, and admitted that I had done my best to learn as much as possible about the infantry from the Field Manuals, and limited interaction with the 6th Infantry, which was up in the Alaskan Territory. He grunted, and said that I was lucky to have an excellent NCO Corps, and that he was used to training young lieutenants. When we got back to the GP medium, which would be our headquarters, he familiarized me with the radio, land lines, field files, duty rosters, and handed me a clipboard as he pointed to a small field desk bearing an old manual typewriter. Then he asked if I could type. I thought it was an odd question, but answered in the affirmative, and I also asked about troop strength, supplies, mess capabilities, water sources, latrines, and the level of equipment, weapons, and general materiel to support the troops. His answers were crisp, quick, and he regarded me with a raised eyebrow, particularly since he saw I was quickly taking notes on the information given. Then slowly, he began to smile.

"You'll do, sir," he said. "I've scheduled a formation in 45 minutes to introduce you and the troops to each other. You can leave the clipboard on the desk until we get back."

Then I had to laugh, because there is an old saying in the Army that you can tell which one is the LT, because he will have a clipboard in his hand. And I replied "Right, 1st SGT. I will take my gear to my tent and meet you back here in five."

That was my first day to function in my branch, but it certainly wouldn't be the last. I look back on that fondly, and he was absolutely right about having an excellent NCO Corps. I was glad that they took the initiative to do all the drill and ceremonies training and they had that gaggle of young troops marching and responding to all the commands instantaneously. My job, as far as they were concerned, was to inspect things and people, attend the meetings at the "head shed," and see that the company had everything it needed to function. They didn't want minimum functionality, though. They wanted and demanded the best, and the troops gave it. There were zero disciplinary problems, and though they were driven hard, the morale of the unit continually improved. The new commander never did show up, so I became the commander of the unit, and my troops consistently made top marks in the maneuver actions. I could not take credit for it, nor did I attempt to do so. It was clear to me that the NCOs were the best in the business, they knew I thought that, and they took good care of me, and of the troops as well. That, too, was a valuable lesson.

Chapter Sixteen – World War II

The winds of war were sweeping in gusts of destruction across the weary world, and the call for death and destruction had their dark flags unfurled. It had been not one war in the now distant past, but the peace that was not peace that could never, ever last.

Just as the treaty originating in 1878, known as the Treaty of Berlin, signed at the Congress of Berlin, was hailed as the greatest achievement in peacemaking and stabilization, burst from embers into the raging conflict known as WWI, so would the smoldering disenchantment and disenfranchisement from the Treaty of Versailles burst once more into flames. Grandpa John, on one of my last times to see him alive, said that there was never an end to WWI. The new conflicts arising across the globe were merely a continuation of the same war, and he believed that this one would be even more destructive than WWI, because new and better ways had been devised to kill more people more quickly. He made some sharply derogatory remarks about the British and French, particularly about the latter, and about politicians, no matter where they infested civilization. After I received my new orders to join the maneuver in Texas, he commented that there was a large population of Germanic Americans in Texas, and said that they had integrated almost entirely to the local culture. Grandma Crouch laughed and said that the Irish were probably there first, and had integrated so completely that no one even noticed their lineal origins. It was always amusing to see them sparring again, and again, I had learned a great deal from them about what was going on in the world. They both assured me that the first battles of the ensuing world conflict would be the bloodiest because of the short sightedness of the political hierarchy. They also didn't think Hitler was stupid, but very, very cleverly sneaky. Germany had rearmed, and they did it with their usual efficiency in weapons development, training, transportation, and planning. They did think it was a mistake for Germany to depend on Italy for naval support in the Mediterranean, as well as control of the southern corridor through the Balkans, and dredged up the old saying "Fool me once, shame on you; fool me twice, shame on me." For some reason I didn't understand at the time, they thought North Africa would be part of the battle zone. I was reflect later on the wisdom of all their predictions, and was amazed at how they could be so accurate without having access to anything but their newspapers, radio programs, and what they called common sense. The irony is, it definitely is not common. I thought about it on the long ride to Texas after my young uncles, Clifford and Paul Crouch, took me to the train station. Indiana had been warm by comparison with Alaska, but Texas was even warmer than the Midwest, and I was dressed in my woolen uniform, sweat trickling down between my shoulder blades and dripping off my chin.

As described previously, I was quickly integrated into the unit(s) participating in the exercise, and began to adapt to the routine and requirement. The Battalion I was assigned to was at strength, but the Division was not. There were National Guardsmen intermixed with Army regulars, which was interesting, but at the company level, they congealed into coherent, cooperative units quickly. There was one Combat Engineer Company assigned to the Battalion, and they were very useful in many ways. We were instructed by the Battalion CO that we were not to damage the fairground, but that we would have to practice setting up defensive perimeters, complete with gun emplacements and foxholes…But the Engineers would cover up the holes we made each time the lines were shifted, and construct rope ladders for us across the multiple small streams if the order of the day required crossing them. There were no cliffs to climb, so they constructed a scaffold so soldiers could be taught both how to climb ropes and then rappel down a makeshift wall. Training went from 0700 to 2000 hours with reveille at 0500, followed by

Dorothy A Adams

Physical Training, hygiene, and Chow. It hasn't changed much over the years, and there were short breaks for lunch and dinner, which were done "by the numbers." Discipline problems were almost non-existent, because the 1st Shirt commented that tired, but well fed troops were obedient troops. I am sure that I learned as much as the average buck private, and our company, "F Troop," actually got frequent "kudos" for superior performance. At the end of the first two weeks of grueling training, limited liberty was permitted, and all of us were shocked to find out that Angelina County, Texas, where we were was a "dry county." That meant no bars, and no booze, but the food was good, and the people were friendly. We didn't have permission or transportation to go to a neighboring county to obtain alcoholic beverages, and didn't know any bootleggers, plus, we really didn't have the time to worry about it.

As I stood on a street corner in that tiny little town, a car pulled up, and a young man hailed me. He said there was someone in his car who wanted to meet me, and pointed to a very pretty young girl with reddish blonde hair and green, green eyes sitting next to him on the passenger side of the vehicle. The couple in the back seat giggled as I walked around to the passenger side of the car and introduced myself. Her name was Julienne LaGrone, and though I didn't know it at the time, she would be both my wife, and the love of my life. She suggested that we all go to a nearby restaurant, which we did, and I had to keep track of the time, because curfew was one of the things I dared not miss. I could tell she was annoyed that I kept looking at my watch, but was still obviously interested in me. From the way her escort, whom they called "Potsey," was literally hanging his head, I could tell he was definitely taken by her, too, just as I was. I had not ordered any food, just coffee, and when I knew I had to go or miss my transportation, I excused myself, and almost bolted for the door. As I double-timed it back to the departure point, I kept reviewing the information I had gathered, like name, address, telephone number, and what she was doing in town, or at home right now. She had said she was a college student. She looked young for that, but it was possible. She was studying "pre-med," so she could possibly get accepted to medical school and become a doctor. But supposedly, she was going to college at Louisiana State University, which definitely was not local. It was a puzzlement, but I had to scramble on to catch my ride back to the fairgrounds. Telephone. Poor people didn't have telephones. Neither did I, but I'd write it down as soon as I could. The address was local, but a rural route, which I later learned was north of Lufkin along something the locals called the "Nacogdoches Highway."

 I did manage to maintain contact with her, and met her family during whatever brief "Open Post" opportunities I had. It was a fascinating family, a product of North/South marriages, and diverse backgrounds. Both of her parents had college degrees, and her father, Ollie Clinton LaGrone, had been a lawyer and a judge, before he decided that the judicial field was simply too crooked for him to comfortably continue to function in it. He obtained a Master's Degree in Agriculture at Texas A&M, and became the County Agricultural Agent. He came from an extremely religious family, and two of his brothers were ministers, but his mother was a teacher, and his father was a Civil War veteran, whose forbearers had arrived in Texas by 1790 to take over their large Spanish land grant. They fought in the war of independence between Texas and Mexico. Raised on that large northeast Texas property, Ollie LaGrone was well versed in both agriculture and business. Their home in deep East Texas, just north of Lufkin, was a well-kept 2 ½ storied white house that was so large that locals referred to the house and spacious lawn as the LaGrone Hill. Mr. LaGrone, like his father before him, owned a sawmill which was a going concern, and he had a herd of experimental Jersey cattle. They had orchards, terraced fields, and large outbuildings, not to mention a clay tennis court for his children to play on. Julienne's full name was Helen Julienne LaGrone, and she was the oldest of five girls, and was just younger than one brother. Their mother, Helen Celestia Dawson, was a teacher, who had a degree in mathematics with a minor in astronomy. She was from North Dakota, and had a fascinating background, too. Her father had been with the New York units in the Civil War as an Indian Scout, though he was not a full blood Sioux, and had Scottish heritage, as well. Both of Julie's parents were as knowledgeable as my grandparents in the history and politics of the nation. Mrs. LaGrone was particularly astute, and had marched with the Suffragettes to secure voting rights for women. Her mother, Amanda Julienne Gray, had a music degree, and had been a concert pianist before her marriage to Ethan Allen Dawson. She had grown up in New York State near Massena, NY. She had died of pneumonia when her second daughter, Dorothy, was only 6 months old, and Helen was 10 years old. Though it was difficult for him, Mr. Dawson raised his daughters in the large house he had built for his wife, but was not supportive of a college education for them. He never remarried, ran and owned the only General Store in Bismarck, and though he was not a lawyer, I was later to be impressed by reading some of the contracts he drew up. They were as well and professionally written as any lawyer could have done. He took young Helen to hear the Cross of Gold speech when she was just a child. That is all I remember for now, but both sides of Julie's family, like mine, had been in what became the Continental United States since before the American Revolution. And Julienne was both highly intelligent and beautiful. I was entranced.

In the original orders, the exercise was only to last two weeks, but it stretched into a month. The training was intensive, and the previous closure of individual training centers was very apparent in the level of expertise exhibited in each echelon. Previous cuts to the military, all branches, had left it top heavy in rank, because there were limitations on how many at each level would be retained, and some high ranking NCOs and officers were offered reductions in rank in order to remain in the military. This was a severe morale issue, and the General Recruiting Command had been abolished as an "economic" issue. <u>In 1936 Congress authorized a new strength level of 165,000. The public began to fear German and Japanese militarism abroad.</u> Lower ranking soldiers didn't reenlist, and often left before their three years was up. Though the Recruiting Command had been authorized again, no funding was put forward to support it, and the military observation that it was easier to turn off recruiting than to turn it back on was absolutely accurate. Recruiters were deluged with demands that they recruit more soldiers, but in the mid to late 1930s, that was extremely difficult. The Adjutant General had set the recruiting levels for each Corps Recruiting Area at 1,500 per month. Recruiters balked at the new demands due to the prevailing social and economic conditions. The level of AWOL and outright desertions was at the highest level ever seen, near 8%, because the New Deal was actually having an effect on the perceived attractiveness of the military as opposed to higher paying civilian jobs. Many had joined because of the benefits offered at the time of their enlistment, but found that such enticements could disappear in a millisecond, if the attitude of the government swayed either toward economy (which was a false economy) or toward national security. Evidently, none of the members of Congress had ever seen the following quotation from John Steinbeck:

> *This is the law: The purpose of fighting is to win.*
> *There is no possible victory in defense. The*
> *sword is more important than the shield and skill*
> *is more important than either. The final weapon*
> *is the brain. All else is supplemental.*
> *John Steinbeck*

Perhaps he hadn't written it yet, but it is reflective of centuries of military philosophy. Training is essential. Melding a unit into a cohesive fighting or support team is essential. The will to win, regardless of the odds, is critical, and is honed to a sharp edge by training. The brain is the ultimate control panel of the body. A trained mind is essential. Adequate numbers are necessary, but bringing in large numbers of civilians without the means to train and support them does not build the comradery and respect that has made warriors brothers throughout the centuries. Training will ensure that they will succeed despite weapons or lack thereof, but appropriate weapons and training on how to effectively use them will make survival and success a more likely result. Treat the soldier right, and he/she will die for you willingly. Their families will support them, pray for them, and either welcome them home, or mourn their loss born of complete commitment. Our very first General said it best:

"My first wish would be that my military family, and the whole Army, should consider themselves as a band of brothers, willing and ready to die for each other."

General George Washington

His army won against incredible odds, and created this marvelous nation in which we are privileged to live due to the continued blood sacrifice of our dedicated soldiers and their families, who will forever hold them in their hearts as the eons roll by. Give them what they need, and honor them for the job they do, day in and day out, whether on the battlefield or as a deterrent against the next one. Strength is a deterrent; weakness is an invitation.

But what was happening in the government during these critical years? In 1934, FDR was busily implementing his policies through his press conferences, addresses, and "Fireside Chats," which gave him unprecedented prestige. He, personally, was far more popular than any of his Democrat associates, or even his legislative measures through which he promoted liberal measures to "better the lot" of the average citizen through government programs. Mrs. LaGrone rather pointedly said that creating a welfare state fostered an enduring dependency in certain strata of the society. She favored the two "I's" of Independence and Industry. I found that I agreed with her analysis, when I investigated the progression of the new programs. Government appointments and new agencies multiplied faster than the average barn cat could increase the feline population of the country. The Federal Government undertook direct intervention to provide direct relief of millions of unemployed and under privileged citizens while assaulting business interests. FDR undertook campaigning in the 1934 Congressional Elections with great vigor, to enhance support for the New Deal and retain unquestionable control of both houses of Congress in which the Democrats already held a significant majority. The Republicans at the time were badly split, and some of them also supported the New Deal. After the national elections in November, the Democrats indeed increased their majority in both houses of Congress, insuring that Roosevelt's programs would receive limited, if any, resistance. In other words, a strong, exuberant majority unchecked by a strong minority steamrolled its way to convert agencies created as emergency entities into permanent structures. Grandma Crouch wrote to say they, as well as new ones, were proliferating as fast as mold after a rain. That was an unattractive but accurate imagery. Bureaucracies and socialization of the Federal Government continued to concentrate power in Washington, D.C. By 1937, the number of federal employees had increased by over 250,000, and that didn't include personnel in legislative, judicial, and military branches of the government, as well as the CCC, and persons on relief. Many of the new "civil servants" had not been vetted by any sort of merit criteria, which had previously been required, and their raw numbers rose to almost a million. Ironically, unlike the military, this was not seen as an unnecessary economic burden. Plainly stated by an ancient philosopher, this sums it up:

> *"The Spartans do not enquire how many the enemy are, but where they are."*
> *Agis II, 427 B.C.*

At that time, in the United States, the enemy seemed to be within. However, world turmoil was roiling.

Chapter Seventeen – New Choices

Life spins the threads that become woven into the tapestry of our lives, and all that we experience becomes the pattern within that whole cloth. The family is the loom upon which it is woven.

During the last days of the exercise, I would sometimes sit at the field desk in the tent that was our headquarters, staring into space as though some great truth was written there, and I was obliged to keep trying to read it. Then, on the last day the First SGT came to fold even that and the camp stool up, because they were the last things to be uploaded for our departure.

"LT, don't you have some last minute business to attend to in town?" he asked, jolting me out of my reverie.

When I didn't answer, and just looked dazed, he let me know that he and the NCOs had everything in hand, and that transport to the train depot wouldn't be taking place until four hours later, so if I needed a few (three) hours to take care of anything else, I should get a move on. Then he smiled and said that the old dogs of war didn't need a green LT fussing around while they got everything finished up. He said it with a smile, and patted my shoulder. He pointed to the sedan, and let me know that I could use it, but they couldn't spare a driver. The telephone lines, even the land line, had been disconnected, so I couldn't call ahead to see if the LaGrone family was at home, but I didn't hesitate. I headed for their place, hoping that Julie would be there, and that I could convince her to write to me, whenever I got my new address confirmed. I would write to her to let her know exactly what it was. That was the plan, but plans oftime go awry. My eyes travelled to my duffle bag, and was then reassured that it would be on the loading dock at the train depot in Lufkin. I double timed it to the sedan, and found the keys already in it. I took off for the small farm north of Lufkin, along Highway 59, and noticed that my hands were sweating, and my perception of landmarks was heightened. I found the turn-off that led to the farm, and was relieved when I saw the tall white house as it hove into view. There were some farm vehicles parked to the south side of the house and one car in the driveway. At least someone was at home. I pulled up, killed the engine, and then paused for a second before going to knock on the large double door at the front of the building. When no one answered, I walked around the covered terrace to the side door, which I knew opened into the kitchen. It was a large room, and Mrs. LaGrone and her housekeeper, Maggie, were working busily preparing a lunch. They both smiled when they saw me at the door, after I had knocked on it. They pulled a chair up to a rather large, white porcelain covered table and asked me if I wanted some ice water, or anything to drink. I said that I was really looking for Julie, and the smiles seemed to recede into some unknown place.

"Please have a seat," Mrs. LaGrone said, nodding toward the chair. "She has gone back to school in Lousiana."

"Here, LT," Maggie said, placing a glass of cold water on the table. "It's warm with that uniform on," she said in her well-modulated voice. "I'll go in and set the table, with one more plate," she said as she bustled away.

"How long do you have," asked Mrs. LaGrone. "Mr. LaGrone will be here in a few minutes. I hope you have time for lunch," she said, as she took up some food from the stove into dishes on the counter.

"I will have to be at the train depot no later than ten to three," I replied, as I checked my watch. I was surprised that it had taken almost 30 minutes to get to the farm.

"Well, you will have time for lunch, barely," she said with a smile.

What Price Honor, Memoir of Eugene Adams

"The dining room is cooler than the kitchen, so you shouldn't be so uncomfortable."

I nodded, and thanked her, but was still decidedly uncomfortable, because my mission could not be accomplished as I had hoped. But as Maggie was moving the food dishes to the table in the next room, Mrs. LaGrone reached into her apron pocket, and handed me a folded piece of paper. She watched as I unfolded it and read it. It was Julie's address in Louisiana, and I was noticeably relieved. I would be able to write to her. She asked if I wanted to leave an address where I might receive mail, and I let her know that I was in the middle of a transfer, and would have to send a letter with that information as soon as I had the details. She smiled, and handed me another piece of paper. It had the address of the farm on it, and she let me know that she and Mr. LaGrone would be pleased to hear from me, too. Then she asked if it was likely that I would remain in Alaska, which at that time was an unknown. There had been the flights back in 1920 by some DE Havilland DH4s from Mitchell Field, New York to Nome, Alaska, which showed that the area could be reached by air, and she knew about General Mitchell's assessment of the strategic importance of Alaska, announced to Congress in 1935. There were other military flights to Alaska, one of them in 1934, led by LTC "Hap" Arnold, of some bombers from the D.C. area to locate potential sites for airfields and other installations. I was astounded that she would know such information, but this was early in our relationship, and I would come to realize that she and Mr. LaGrone were as astute about world political geography as my own grandparents had always been. I was reflecting on the strategic importance of those flights when Mr. LaGrone strolled in. During lunch, they discussed, to my utter amazement, the recent reinstatement of the 1939 funding for Alaskan bases, and the recommendation for air bases in six strategic locations. I was familiar with the locations of these installations, and of the location where Ladd Field, Ft.

Richardson, and Elmendorf were already under planning and construction. Later historical accounts would put those operations, as well as the smaller installations on the Aleutian Islands in 1941, and even later. They existed. It was 1940, and construction was ongoing, but they were already there... I had been there, but didn't really interject much into their discussions. Mostly, I was astounded at the depth of their awareness of the real threat of the Japanese in that area of the world. Then Mrs. LaGrone folded her napkin, looked at her watch, and raised those bright blue eyes to me, and without a need for words, I folded my napkin and asked to be excused from the table.

I now had only 34 minutes to make my departure time at the train depot. I was quickly ushered through the kitchen, said goodbye to Maggie, and ran for the sedan. I admit that I was praying that there be no traffic or delay problems on the highway back, but I knew the way to the depot. Then, as every soldier will, I began to worry about the sedan, and how was that to be handled, and wondering about the itinerary back to Alaska. Where would the stops be? How long would it take? The orders indicated that it would be at least 24 hours. I did make it back to the station with about 4 minutes to spare. The sedan was loaded up on a flatbed, along with other vehicular equipment, and that was done in no more than 5 minutes after I arrived. I retrieved my duffel bag, which was just as the First Shirt had said it would be. He came over, hand outstretched, and told me it had been a pleasure to serve with me, and he hoped we would meet again. I definitely felt the same way, and stood with him as our troops boarded the passenger cars. In my waning years, I have revisited this little scenario many times with fond memories of that snippet of time.

The passenger car seats back then were comfortable, and the resonance of the wheels as they clicked along the tracks were enough to induce narcolepsy. I had several changes of trains, but

What Price Honor, Memoir of Eugene Adams

was glad that during my tenure in Alaska, the Alaskan Railway had undergone many improvements, courtesy the US military and a forward looking Governor of the Alaskan Territory. It did, indeed, take 24 hours, and in my dozings, I reviewed the current status of US military power in the world; when I would awaken, I read newspapers from all over the USA. As we were pulling in to the last stop near Fairbanks, I was chuckling to myself over an old Mark Twain quote: "If you do not read the newspaper, you are uninformed. If you read the newspaper, you are misinformed." A wizened old man, who was my seatmate, stared at me quizzically, but quickly stepped over me to the aisle. I joined him, stretched, gathered my voluminous reading material, yawned several times, and rubbed the fatigue from my eyes.

That is not a trip I would ever want to make again. My feet weren't just asleep, and my legs had figuratively gone on vacation, plus my stomach was growling. I was met by a young E-3 driver, who kept repeating that I had to go right away to sign in, to which I responded that first I needed to take a piss. He looked bewildered for a moment and then reassured me that we could stop along the road on our way, and that it wasn't too cold for that kind of operation. Easy for him to say. I hadn't anticipated the differences in temperature between East Texas and Alaska in September, but we headed out. Amazingly enough, when we pulled in to the headquarters building and I reached the clerk's desk to sign in, I was told to report to the CO immediately. Still bleary from the long trip, I must have looked extremely confused, so the clerk came around to walk with me to the office. I didn't understand the urgency, and had a feeling of foreboding. When I entered the CO's office, came to attention and saluted, I noticed that he was smiling. He returned my salute and told me to take a seat.

"You are a lucky man, although the command will miss you. You are getting out of this deepfreeze, and you will be departing on the

0700 train. Have you ever been to Mississippi before?"

"No, sir, I have not," I answered, shaking my head in bewilderment. "Is it to an ID (Infantry Division)?"

"No, it is Training Command. Actually, it is the US Army Medical Corps facility in Mississippi. You will be teaching the incoming medics, and from the looks of things, there will be a lot of them. Have you been following the news lately?"

"To some extent," I replied. "I know that the Germans are rolling again, and have captured what are called the Lowlands, and that was over in Holland and then Belgium. That was in May. I learned a new name, Kesselring, and something named the Luftflotte II, and also that when Rotterdam, Holland's largest port, was blitzed, the Dutch gave up. Then there was the really novel use of glider paratroopers in Belgium, which worked very well for Germany."

"I'll miss the blow to blow update of world military news when you leave," he said smilingly, as he sat back in his chair. "Stay in touch. I have a feeling we will meet again. The clerk has your orders and itinerary. Good luck."

He nodded, tipped his head, and I stood, saluted, was dismissed, and went out in a semi-daze, wondering if my gluteus maximus could withstand the hours ahead in a train seat. I was given my orders, travel as well as assignment, and was shown to a transit quarters so I could at least get a shower. When I asked about the gear I had left behind to go on the maneuver, I was told that it had been packed in a foot locker, and would be brought to the transit quarters. I was told about the hours for chow, and then left to sort out my thoughts on these rather sudden shifts in my existence. Teaching? Medics? Mississippi? Well, at least it wouldn't be so damned cold. The day passed, then the night, and I woke up instantly when I heard Reveille being sounded. I gathered my gear, and wished that either the duffel bag or footlocker had wheels on it. I trudged out toward the chow hall, and the young driver from the day before hailed me with instructions on where the sedan was, and said that he would take my gear over there for me. I was amazed when he easily hefted a load that must have been almost his body weight, and marched away with it. I finished my breakfast, and was whisked away to the train station by this mighty marvel. Then I laughed to myself when he told me that he grew up on a farm in Indiana, and that my stuff was about the same weight as two bales of hay. When I listened to him talk, I could hear the Midwestern twang in his speech, and it was somehow comforting. Then we were there, and I was on my way for another tour of the United States on rail. I dozed off and on, and thought almost constantly. The President, FDR, and been requesting the draft, and the same old arguments about the economy still slithered through Congress, whispering about the utility of the peacetime military. I had been thinking about making the Army a career, and was taking advantage of the many educational opportunities available, as well as simply learning about soldiering from the bottom to the top. I began to recognize clearly that I would soon be in actual combat, because things certainly would not be getting better, particularly due to the shortsightedness of our government. The new assignment was a clear indicator that FDR would manage to get the draft reinstated, and I thought through the confusion that was bound to bring. The Wehrmacht was already on the move, and racking up successes consistently. The British and French were, as usual, bumfuzzled and somewhat angry that the Germans didn't attack where they had thought they would. I smiled to myself and thought "That is the absolute definition of surprise attacks." What intrigued me about the attack in Belgium was the use of gliders, which are silent, and virtually undetectable. It was both clandestine and extremely clever. Hitler may have only been a Corporal in WWI, but I doubted the continued assertions in the media that he was stupid. And he certainly had an excellent General Staff. Conflict in Europe was definitely not going to go away any time soon, and the time I had spent in the Alaskan Territory told me that the Japanese threat was certainly nothing to be ignored. There had also been Russian incursions in the frozen north, and as far as I could see, they were allied with Germany during the conquest of Poland, and there was no reason to believe that their alliance with the Nazi regime had ended.

I heard the squeal of the brakes as the train slowed down, slowly thundering to a stop, and the Conductor was walking down the aisle shouting "Hattiesburg, Mississippi! This is yore stop." Then when he looked down on me as I raised my bleary eyes up, he shouted "Sojurs! Camp Shelby is here. This is yore stop!" He smiled and kept on going down the long line of cars with his message of arrival at someplace with a truly strange name. Hattiesburg? Interesting. Very Southern. A fellow across the aisle turned to me and informed me that Camp Shelby was probably the biggest post in the US Army, and that it had been there since 1917, which I had not known before. He was a bewhiskered old gentleman, but had the growly voice that Command SGT Majors have always managed to cultivate. As the train jarred itself to a stop, he motioned to me to stand up, which I did, and I followed him out to the platform. He assured me that our luggage would be discharged shortly, and that I should scout around for a military vehicle that he was sure would be coming to pick me up. He absolutely had to be a veteran. As we stood there, he confirmed my thoughts on that subject. He had been in WWI, and had been a CSM when Pershing went to Europe. He treated me to a first-hand review of those operations, and how Black Jack was absolutely the best General ever to be born. He was just going over what he perceived as the idiocy of the current Congress, and the fools who could afford what he called frippery for government agencies, but thought that an Army and Navy were too expensive, when his rheumy but sharp eyes caught sight of a green sedan pulling up into the parking lot. He pointed at it, punched my shoulder, and waved to the driver, laughing and muttering about always having to take care of the lieutenants when they were still young. Then he turned to me and with a very knowing, and almost saddened look.

"Son, take good care of yourself and your troops. You won't be a young-un when you get back," he said, as he cuffed me gently and walked away.

I never saw him again, but I never forgot him, either. He was right about his prognostication, and every now and again, I can see him standing there, in that sultry climate, which is a Southern way of saying it was warm and humid. I never knew his name, but to me he will always be *the CSM.* The driver came over and helped me get my gear over to the sedan. He was a corporal, had a good military appearance, and was about six feet tall, with a good build, but I wondered if he was tongue-tied or something. Finally I found out that he was classified there as a "Yankee," because of the way he talked, so he just chose not to talk if he didn't have to. I asked where he was from, and when he didn't answer, I just asked what part of Brooklyn he came from. He actually laughed. Then he told me he had been assigned to come pick me up because I was to be one of the new instructors in "his" school. He was trained as a combat medic, and had finished the course with top honors, so had been kept as a training aide for the school. This was good to know. He would become my "right hand man" during my stay in Hattiesburg.

     We chatted about the organization of the classes, available equipment, and duration of each training class. Evidently, the training time had been cut from 2 months to 6 weeks, which puzzled me, but at least these soldiers would get some formal training, where for so long, new recruits had not. Then I suddenly remembered that during my long journey, one newspaper had announced that the draft had been reinstated, September of 1940, and that there was an ongoing controversy over training facilities, which would definitely have to be reopened PDQ (Army jargon for Pretty Damned Quick), because Congress was still balking over the expense of such action. At least FDR had gotten that one right. He had actually been trying to get the draft reinstated for the last couple of years. The first class I was to train was actually arriving, being assigned billets, and given training materials. The duty roster was already posted, and a nameplate for my door had been made and mounted. Door? An office? This amazed me, but I was more concerned about getting a look at the training materials being issued to the troops. Evidently, a set of them had already been placed on my desk, and according to my new assistant, we could go there first and pick them up before he delivered me to the BOQ (Bachelor Officer's Quarters). I simply nodded in assent, and struggled to keep my eyes open. It had been a long trip, and I was wondering how I would manage to go through the training material when my body was trying to shut itself down. But when I asked when was the first class to be taught, I was informed that on the next day at 0700, Orientation would begin, and I would be giving the first lecture. That little shocker jolted me wide awake, and I swallowed hard. He noticed, and said that he had been assigned to pick me for that first day, and would arrive at 0600 to take me to the "dining facility." I was amused at the new nomenclature, and wondered briefly what had happened to "Chow Hall," and he caught the smile. He let me know that for the school, officers ate at the Dining Facility, and soldiers ate at the Chow Hall. I instantly disliked that, but said nothing, as we were arriving at the training center.

    He volunteered to go get the training manuals and material for me, but I hopped out of the sedan and accompanied him into the building. We went quickly down a short corridor to a door that had my name on it. There, stacked neatly in the center of a desk, was an armload of manuals and a bradded packet of paper. That last item reminded me that I hadn't signed in yet, so instead of the BOQ, our next stop was to the Headquarters building of Camp Shelby, where I signed in and was handed a copy of the newest iteration of my orders. It appeared that I would be assigned to the School as the XO (Executive Officer), as well as an instructor. I was given the exact address where I would receive any mail that came to me, and an appointment slip for my in-briefing with my new commander. On the ride to the BOQ, my trusty driver informed me that there was a map in the packet of material we had picked up from the school headquarters, and that if I had any questions, I could ask him in the morning about locations. I was very grateful, but my eyes were beginning to involuntarily close. When I checked in and finally saw a bunk, I simply fell into it and didn't wake up until about 0400 the next morning. That was fortunate, because it meant that I could get to the shower before all the hot water was used up, and I would have time to organize my thoughts, read some of the material I had gathered, and mentally prepare myself for the day. It was clear that here I would be required to literally hit the ground running. By 0500, I was in uniform and quickly reading as much of the material in the bradded packet as I could. I found that it outlined the requirements for the troops, the uniform of the day, the length of the daily training period, and all other essential details which would be explicit in the full form of the training manual. That is one thing about the Army. They always produce excellent training manuals for each specialty. I was glad to see that the corpsmen would receive adequate training to enable them to function either in clinics, hospitals, or in the field retrieving injured soldiers, providing essential lifesaving measures, and seeing that the victims were safely transported to the nearest triage unit for further disposition. While the training requirements were very intensive, I was pleased to note that we actually HAD a training facility, because I was certain that their skills would soon be needed. I was turning that thought over in my mind when my morning ride arrived.

Breakfast was excellent, and both my gut and my brain were full. I was standing outside mulling that over when the sedan pulled up with my trusty driver. I asked him if he had had time to eat "chow," and he smiled. He said he had wolfed it down, including the grits, whereupon he expounded on his dislike for that particular dish, but admitted that it "stuck to the ribs." It was a productive day. I remembered from my own training in the not too distant past that the troops were to be marched in, stand beside their desk chairs at attention, and respond instantly to the command "Take Seats!" That part went quickly, as I introduced myself and my assistant. I then indicated that the packet of instructions for self-preparation, military discipline, military courtesy, attention to detail, and mandatory fulfillment of all training requirements were to be strictly adhered to the letter, as stated in the packet. They were instructed to remove the packet from their stack of material, open it, and for the following 20 minutes, they were to read and absorb the information therein. Suddenly, my aid snapped to attention, and called the classroom to attention. Some of the greenest troops didn't quite know what to make of that, so everyone sprang to their feet, and assumed the position of attention next to their desk chairs, as best they could. I also stood at attention, turned to face the approaching officer, saluted and gave the command "Present Arms" to the troops, some of whom were confused, but most saluted as well. When my salute was returned, I gave the command "Order Arms, Take Seats. At Ease." The troops did a credible job of it, and I was pleased.

Then a gruff voice, somewhere beneath my direct line of vision said "LT, they don't have arms to present, and are not going to be allowed to carry them. You Infantry Guys are all alike." He glanced up at me and said "At Ease, LT. Welcome to Camp Shelby and to the school. By the way, I am down here." There was a tittering in the classroom, as some of the troops tried to stifle their laughter, but I put that to rest with a steely, sweeping gaze.

Then looking eye to eye with my new commander, I noticed that he was a full Major with a chest full of medals, which surprised me a bit, but not as much as my paltry 1LT rank surprised him. He turned to the class, introduced himself, let them know that discipline problems would not be tolerated, that AWOL would be severely dealt with, and he, himself, a WWI vet, would be in the search mission to bring them back, and it would be an unpleasant capture, return, and punishment. However, good behavior and study habits would be rewarded. He instructed them to take a blank piece of paper, write their name, rank, serial number, religious preference, and their three preferred assignment locations on it, then date it, sign their names, and hand it forward immediately. As always happens, one troop raised his hand.

"Your question, son," the MAJ fairly barked.

"Sir, are we 'sposed to print that stuff?" the gangly youngster asked.

"Good question. You damned straight. Print everything except your signature. The signature is your full name as it appears on your dog tag, in case you forgot what it is, in long hand. If you don't know what that is, then sign it just like you would sign a check or other legal document."

While they busied themselves completing that task, he motioned me aside and said that I was to continue with the class, NMT (no more than) 50 minutes long, with a 15 minute break, because it was their first day. During that break, I was to come to his office. I did not know what I was going to lecture on, but I suspected that he would be there listening. I looked up at the clock on the rear wall. I suspect that every army classroom from every army that has ever existed had some timepiece at the back of the classroom, or a sundial when classes were given outside, going back before the Roman Legion. I decided to lecture on the responsibility of the medical corpsman, and rolled on through the full 50 minutes. They were attentive, and I released them precisely at the end of 50 minutes, and my attendant herded them to a shady area that had a water fountain, and some butt cans. They looked numb, and clustered around him, asking as many questions as they could conjure up. They were going to be a good class. I smiled for the first time since I had arrived in the BOQ last night. The CO was brief, complimented me on the lecture, and asked where I found it. There was a twinkle in his eye, and when I didn't sound off immediately, he answered for me that I would be given a typewriter, and would commit it to paper as soon as possible before I forgot the extemporaneous remarks. I must have cocked an eyebrow when he used a fifty cent word, and he grinned almost from ear to ear.

"I think we'll get along well, and that you'll be a fine instructor. Get back and conduct the next class, as soon as you figure out what it is supposed to be about," he said, ending with a guffaw, and a curt dismissal.

We did get along well, and the days seemed to fly by. I hadn't realized that these troops were to undergo weapons training, even though they were to be denied issue of one. Surprisingly enough, they did quite well, especially some of the troops from the Midwest and South, and the others learned quickly. The marksmen could be seen answering questions for their mates as they waited for firing position. The bonding was happening, and it made me mildly sad that they would definitely be split up when the training was over. But bonding is a skill that can be used over and over, and pretty soon, they would feel a kin to anything military, provided it was on our side. There were some of them who already knew a great deal of biology and some smattering of medicine, and they taught the old adage to the others "Cooperate to Graduate." I wonder if the Greeks said the same thing in their training classes, over a thousand years ago. There were no AWOLS. There were no discipline problems. They adapted amazingly fast, and the six weeks was almost over when I was called in to be told by the CO that I would be going on Emergency Leave. My father had been fatally shot on Saturday, 3 May 1941, and I was to go immediately to Elkhart, Indiana. The Clerk was preparing the paperwork, and the Transportation Officer was scheduling my transportation. My assistant would take over the class until I returned, since it was mostly about stretcher bearing, different types of single carry of injured soldiers, low crawling to get to injured soldiers on the battle field, splinting broken limbs, emergency care of wounds in the field, emergency establishment of an airway, and instruction on administration of injections…which I wanted them to do on tomatoes first, but I wouldn't be there. I started to ask if I could just continue to teach, and nearly said that my father and I had not been close, but the direct, steady gaze of the CO made me swallow those words.

"He may have been a swabbie, but he was a veteran. Go put him to rest, and console his parents and your mother. Go gather your gear. You're leaving today," he said in even tones. I almost asked how he knew my father had been a sailor, but he answered before I could say anything. "I'm from Benton Harbor, and I knew Fred. We weren't friends, but I knew him. I also knew you were his son the first time I set eyes on you. Go, be safe and get back in one piece. Be sure to keep an eye on Alva, and give him my regards. He's tough as a cob, but older than Methuselah. Go. Go now to the Clerk and to the S-4."

Dorothy A Adams

    That was the first time I realized down deep in the marrow of my bones that vets are all of one family. It reminded me of an old poem, Thanatosis, by William Cullen Bryant. Particularly of the last stanza. I had read it at Alva's house as a child, and he had patiently gone over it with me. That last verse is particularly important to the soldier.

> *"So live, that when thy summons comes to join*
> *The innumerable caravan, which moves*
> *To that mysterious realm, where each shall take*
> *His chamber in the silent halls of death,*
> *Thou go not, like the quarry-slave at night,*
> *Scourged to his dungeon, but, sustained and soothed*
> *By an unfaltering trust, approach thy grave*
> *Like one who wraps the drapery of his couch*
> *About him, and lies down to pleasant dreams."*

Chapter Eighteen – Life Change

The passing of the torch from one generation to the next comes at a time when the recipient could hardly expect to hold that gilded trust as high as in the past, and know that its brilliant beauty must last and last, and last.

Somehow, I find it most difficult to think about 1940, even though at Christmas of that year, I was to marry the woman whom I loved and will always love. How it has come to pass is that we are divorced after more than 16 years of marriage, and that occurred more than another 16 years ago. I had not told my new commander anything of my marriage, because at the time, the military discouraged marriage for the enlisted men and lower ranking officers. She had run away from college to meet me in Elkhart, Indiana, when I mentioned in a letter that I would have a short leave for Christmas, and that I would go visit my family for the holiday. I included the address and telephone number of my grandmother, and was shocked when I arrived to find that she was already there, and had enchanted my family, as she had me. Back then it was unusual for young women to travel alone on such a long journey, but I was to learn that it was not unusual for Julie to do exactly what she wanted to do, when she wanted to do it. We were married on Christmas Day, and for a while, I was deliriously happy, though ill at ease because of the suddenness of it, and the fact that it might negatively impact my military career. It is easier, here in the twilight of my life to recount the multitudinous events that were surrounding us in a myriad of changes that would forever entangle us all. I was and am caught in that vortex and feel an obligation to catalogue the events that affected our lives then and continue to impact us today.

Though heralded by many as the salvation of our nation, the New Deal formulated by FDR in the years leading up to our entry into WWII altered irrevocably social conditions that persist to damage our society today, some 50 years hence. But it is time to discuss the thick, treacherous destructive, progressive tresses of that Medusa that wound themselves throughout the world. There was the imminent defeat of France, coupled with the ongoing political upheavals after the fall of the Lowlands to Germany, and continuous insurgencies of German troops into an ill-prepared, scantily mobilized or militarized France. That country clearly lay in the shadow of disaster. One major problem was that structurally, within the French forces, excellent fighting units were often in close juxtaposition with very poor units. The quality of the active divisions and reserve divisions was extraordinarily different, and there was little cross integration. There were two Polish divisions and one composed of Belgian troops, which had escaped when their countries were defeated, and they fought admirably for France. Though there was assistance from Britain, it was quite clear that there wasn't that element of dedicated mutual support which in warfare is essential to success. British military organization was also lacking. The Somme was again the focus of defense for the beleaguered French and that was poorly orchestrated, though the French soldiers fought valiantly. We hear now about de Gaulle, but little about Weygand, who actually fought the Battle of France against tremendous odds. Nothing was safe from the bombing by the Stukas, and French lines were spread too thinly due to lack of manpower. The idea of cutting off the advance of the Panzers was certainly a good one, but Weygand didn't have the armor or artillery, nor antitank or antipersonnel mines to augment the infantry effort. It was simply a lack of adequate assets, and not one of strategic incompetence or temerity of the troops.

De Gaulle, a newly promoted General, and an astute politician, sent a message that Weygand should form two large armored units of 1200 tanks and attack the flanks of German units which managed to break through – except that France didn't have anywhere near 1200 tanks, and certainly not 2400 of them. The French Premier Reynaud had requested help from Britain, particularly from the RAF, because of the continual bombing of the French by the Germans. It was refused, probably because Churchill envisioned the need to reserve it against German Luftwaffe assault on Britain. At the time of the request there was only one British (the 56th) and one Canadian division in France. France fought essentially alone, and though there was a grandiose offer from Britain to comingle their countries in a grand alliance whereby a citizen of France would automatically be a citizen of Britain, and vice versa. This sat with the citizens of both countries like sour milk in an empty stomach, but through such an arrangement, France would have the right to support as part of the British Union. Those negotiations, however, would be lengthy, and the need for support was immediate in the ongoing onslaught of the German juggernaut. Additionally, the French partisans, as well as the citizens of the British Empire certainly viewed it with jaundiced eyes. In the interim, the troops on the ground were covering front lines of 280 miles or more, and with no depth to sustain them, and inadequate materiel to withstand the rolling thunder of the extremely efficient Panzers and the constant drumming by the Stukas, which were essentially flying artillery. France had almost no air power, and the battles were raging too far away for the excellent French Fleet to be able to assist them, though the Fleet did hold back the Italians in the Mediterranean.

At the time, there was "trouble at the top," politically, in the French government, and ultimately Prime Minister Reynaud would step down. Marshal Petain of WWI fame was rising in the government as well. France was in agony and though under General Weygand they had fought valiantly, especially the 14th Division, but by June, 1940, the French had lost approximately half of their divisions, so by mid-June it looked to be nigh unto impossible for them to defend Paris from the thunderous German onslaught. There was a civilian mass exodus, though it has been described as a huge party of eating, drinking, and socializing. The French have always been a puzzlement to me.

In June,1940, Italy under the Fascist Mussolini was entering the war, even though he had sent in 1939 a non-belligerence pact to France. That most likely had to do with the Allied blockade of Italy, which was announced by London and Paris if Italy remained neutral. The Allies did seize all shipments to and from Germany, and especially German coal for the Italian industries. However, Mussolini had a long time fascination and admiration for Hitler, plus a desire for the fame, grandeur, and worldwide exultation he believed a close alliance with Hitler would bring to him and to Rome. Unfortunately, there were huge military deficiencies, as well as industrial lack of essentials, such as nickel, required for production of armaments and ammunition. While Mussolini was delighted at becoming a military leader of his country in time of war, he was blind to those inherent deficiencies and of the degree to which he was held in total disrespect by the majority of the German citizenry. Hitler was his only friend there.

The Germans drove on to Paris, but informed the French Government that a decisive breakthrough could come at any moment. Weygand had hoped to hold on with British help, which was never to come. By mid-June, General Hering and his forces became the Army of Paris. Reynaud and his cabinet were trying to decide how to cease hostilities. A prior agreement with Britain had pledged both countries were not to make any peace treaty or armistice with Germany without the agreement of the other country. Churchill had already refused to release France from that agreement. The question still remained "Should France surrender?" There was quibbling over whether France was required to abide by the prior agreement with Britain, but the situation was literally impossible for France. They had to renounce the previous agreement and decide between armistice or capitulation. Reynaud wanted to keep the alliance with Britain, and continue to fight Germany, but instead the French in essence surrendered to Germany, and to occupation by both the Italians and Germany. Within days, Reynaud was replaced by Marshal Petain. That was hard enough for me to wrap my mind around, because Germany now controlled the vast majority of Europe, and even more difficult because my new wife kept nearly incessant outpourings about her French heritage. I was later to find out that it was actually minimal, but she was very proud of it, and insisted that the French would somehow win in the end. I held my tongue, because as far as I could see, France had already "ended." The government of France had removed itself to Bordeaux in late March, later to be called the Vichy government, and France was occupied primarily by Germany. Britain was simply waiting in trepidation for the Reich to turn its way.

As always, there were meetings, and Weygand had completely rejected formal surrender, refusing to dishonor the army by sending envoys to ask for terms from the Germans. Before stepping down, Reynaud even offered to give the General formal written orders to do so, but he didn't want absolution from the ignominious surrender, which he believed dishonored his troops. He refused and resigned. De Gaulle made political hay from it, because though he had been willing to surrender, the armistice was then the only choice. Therefore, he is quoted as having said "France has lost a battle! But France has not lost a war!" So armistice negotiations resulted in what was nominally a "Free France," but was in reality a conquered France. The Axis was actually persuaded to allow French rearmament in North Africa. Another twist was the Navy, which was a very different matter. Admiral Darlan, at the announcement of a separate armistice by France with Germany, in accordance with a private conversation with Churchill, he insisted that even if he received orders to turn over the fleet to either Germany or Italy, he would refuse to carry out that order. He was determined to sail the entire French Fleet, and all auxiliary supply and support vessels to the nearest British port they could reach. Though aware of all that was going on, FDR in my own country seemed far more focused on elections, and on creating more and more agencies to the detriment of the ever growing national debt. There did not seem to be any inclination to aid France or try to limit the German onslaughts throughout Europe.

Our own economic problems were rapidly growing, and the US dollar had fallen in actual value to fifty cents. My paycheck, with the new marital responsibilities, certainly didn't stretch as far, so personal considerations began to insert themselves over concerns with the world situation. Julie didn't adjust well to living in reduced circumstances, since she was raised in a 12 bedroom house with a full maid's quarters, as well as having been accustomed to a housekeeper and maid in the home. It was a beautiful, stately place, and though she would bemoan how "poor" they were, during the Great Depression, they had a car, clothing, plenty of food, and her father had taken one of the large farm buildings and renovated it into apartments for those who had lost everything. The families who were allowed to move in had plenty of food, warmth, shelter, and worked on the large farm until the economic situation allowed them to find jobs and move on with their lives. Mr. LaGrone was loved, as was his wife, who was a teacher. They also took in children of some relatives who were having financial reverses, and saw to it that they continued school, and were well cared for. Mr. LaGrone had been a judge, but had decided it wasn't for him, so, when he made his rounds as the County Agricultural Agent, the children would run along the fences shouting "Here come da Judge, here come da Judge." There is a comedian who now uses that line, but I heard it first from those children, when I went on one of his rounds with him, just to discuss why he left the legal profession. That is another story. He would go to vaccinate their animals, or provide whatever help he could give to the poor farmers, and always when they couldn't pay for the vaccines, or the materials he gave them, he would just shake his head and say that it was fine. Some would insist on paying him with some jars of canned goods, or a bushel of turnips, or something of the sort. Then, when he was preparing to leave, he would often leave a bag or two of groceries on their door stoop. Kindness just came naturally to him.

    My new in-laws weren't critical of me, and welcomed my entry into their family, but they saw the future better than I did. I was told clearly that if the United States entered the war raging throughout Europe, Julie could come home, and perhaps then she would finish college while I was gone. That did remove a niggling worry I had, though my own family would have welcomed her, too. It was definitely a different time back then, and even though money was short, our apartment was very small and inelegant, and I worked long hours, we were happy. That was colored by the fatal shooting of my father, Fred Dewey Adams, on 3 May 1941, so we went to the funeral in Elkhart, Indiana. He was only 42 years old, and was shot and killed by a Merchant Policeman who worked for the railroad, who mistook an habitual gesture for a potential drawing of a weapon. Oddly enough, that motion, pushing back his coat and putting his hands on his hips frightened the policeman, who had been patrolling the tracks. When I thought about it, I realized that I, too, had almost a reflexive habit of throwing my shoulders back and putting my hands on my hips, as does my son and one of my daughters. But it spooked the hired policeman. My father, Fred Dewey Adams, died an hour after arriving at Elkhart General Hospital, and ironically, my mother was the nurse assigned to monitor his vital signs and report his time of death to the attending physician. She was very withdrawn, and didn't think it appropriate for her to go to the funeral, since he had remarried, and his widow would be there. But I knew she was devastated, and Julie seemed to sense it, too, and volunteered to stay with her. I called my sister, who did attend the funeral, bringing her baby daughter and husband with her. We stayed until the 7th of May, and then returned to Mississippi. Coincidentally, we were blessed with a baby daughter almost exactly nine months later. I always thought it odd that one life ended, and another seemed to begin virtually synchronously.

There was a hearing, after we left, and a Grand Jury heard testimony from witnesses on the case. The shooting was finally dismissed as accidental, but the railroad did promise to pay for educations for me, my sister, and our offspring. Fred had been working for them in some capacity concerning the labor unions. I didn't need the scholarship, and my sister, Mary Ellen, wasn't interested. We really hadn't known our father very well. I had been born while he was serving a tour of duty in the Navy at the end of WWI, and she was four years younger than I was. Our parents had divorced when she was a toddler. Divorce was frowned upon back then, and neither set of grandparents was pleased about it, but it was what it was.

Chapter Nineteen – Conflagration Begins

The advice about changing horses in the midst of a great conflict was touted to change the course of history, and when history changes, it is not always for the better. Sometimes it is necessary to change both the horses and the chariot, when the wheels have come off the conveyance and the horses are mired in mud.

    In 1941, I was busy with the coursework for my budding saviors of life in the midst of conflict, and with the prospect of becoming a father, having been caught off guard by the death of my own. The elections of 1938 and 1940 had highlighted the continuing difficulties both with labor and the economy in general. Unions proliferated, and their strength grew, but at that time, they were largely run by the workers themselves, and Congress was becoming more receptive to their demands. There was a Wagner Wages and Hours Act, placing a ceiling over hours and a floor under wages, as its author described it. The Act called for a 40 hour work week, and a minimum wage of forty cents per hour, and the name of the Committee for Industrial Organizations, under John L. Lewis was changed to the Congress of Industrial Organizations (CIO). They claimed that the governmental regulations and restrictions had caused the severe recession of 1937, and with the AFL under William Green, established a new method for dealing with the government. Agriculture was affected by the Agricultural Adjustment Act, which was supposed to "keep our granaries full" in lean years by forbidding the release of surpluses to the world market. There were subsidies, but not sufficient to offset the losses to the farmer from the difference between what they could have earned on the world market, and what the government was willing to pay them. In addition, the government had placed quotas on what specific crops could be produced, and though there were monetary rewards for abiding by this control of productivity, it was another government seizure of control over matters which had hither-to-fore been inherent in freedom of enterprise.

By the end of 1938, although the severe recession was essentially over, due to the excellent work of Cordel Hull, FDR had been experiencing increasing conservative pressure to alter his policies. During the latter days of the recession, Congress had given him power to reorganize the Federal departments of government in the interest of economy and efficiency. However, he began to experience opposition both in and out of Congress to several key measures of the "new" New Deal. Five years of spending and debt accumulation found the country still in relief mode, with no foreseeable possibility of a balanced budget. Even his Democrat Party was badly split, with a significant number of them collaborating with the Republicans to defeat some key measures he wanted to institute. What he did then was try to attack and weed the opponents out of his party, using some of the same tactics he had used to pack the Supreme Court in his favor. Just as the latter had backfired on him, so did the attempts to pack Congress. The conservatives won many governorships and more than doubled their seats in Congress. But FDR was always resilient, and though his popularity had suffered among his colleagues in the government, he was still extremely popular with the general public. Fireside Chats were listened to as millions sat by their radios to hear the President. He was re-elected in 1940, as the world churned into chaos. The AXIS, a term developed by Mussolini as the line formed from Rome to Berlin which he said was the axis upon which the world would turn, was fast gobbling up Europe, and American eyes were focused there. Japan would later join the AXIS powers.

Americans still clung to isolationism, and were still disenchanted with the results of WWI, so they were reluctant to be drawn into another war. The disarmament, peace, and democratic style governments to cover the face of the earth that they had hoped for, had not arisen in that postwar era. What had materialized was constant quarreling among the European powers, tariff wars, and failures of those nations to reduce armaments to the levels imposed on Germany and Congressionally mandated in the US military. Furthermore, the League of Nations had utterly failed as a true instrument of peace. The League had failed to halt the aggressions of Germany, Italy, and Japan in the 1935-1937-time frame. In Russia, a Comintern, which is an organization for the proliferation of Communism throughout the world, had been formed by the Communist Party. The League was virtually oblivious to that fact. WWI war debts had not been repaid to the US by foreign governments, with the notable exception of Finland and Germany, which had negatively affected the US economy. Pacifism instead of involvement seemed to the young of the nation to be the better course of action. Relationships with Japan were becoming very tense and extremely complicated by 1941. Although many Americans still believed that the Atlantic and Pacific oceans were sufficient to protect the United States from attack, even if the evolving aggressions were to crush all opposition in Europe and Asia. It was also believed that Latin America was another safeguard, particularly after the formation of the Pan American Union. Also in 1935-1937 Congress had passed a number of neutrality acts, as a result of Mussolini's unprovoked attack on Ethiopia, of Spain's civil war, or continued German and Japanese aggression. As pointed out previously, the US was actively supporting Chiang Kai Shek of China in the struggle with Japan. The subtle underpinnings of the neutrality laws withdrew the neutrality of the seas, restricted civilian international travel, and limited what commodities could and could not be sold to belligerents by American citizens or businesses. Yet the restrictions didn't limit the government from providing both munitions, hardware, materiel, and military expertise to Nationalist China in their continuing conflict with Japan. This had been a possible trigger for combat with Japan in Alaska, in what came to be the 'forgotten conflict,' with over 500 dead American soldiers, sailors and airmen in an undeclared war. I didn't forget it, because I knew some of the dead and injured personally.

Though negotiations continued to go on between the US and Japan, the neutrality laws made it more difficult to aid victims of aggression, the aid to China continued. The 1937 Panay Incident, which was the Japanese aerial bombing, strafing, and sinking of the gunboat USS Panay and three oil tankers on the Yangtze River, was literally swept under the rug. It did draw a "sharp note" from Secretary of State Hull to the Japanese government, even though Americans were killed or wounded. Hull demanded an apology, compensation and a promise that nothing like that was to happen again. Japan complied.

During the summer and fall of 1940, the US continued to prepare for its own defense. Congress passed the Alien Registration Act, which also made it illegal for anyone in the United States to advocate the overthrow of government by force or to belong to any organization advocating violent overthrow of government. Previously, FDR had extended the Monroe Doctrine to include Canada, and frequent meetings of the newly formed Pan American Union were conducted to insure hemispheric security. But the arms embargo had been lifted, and as a response to the Battle of Britain, FDR transferred 50 old but serviceable destroyers to Great Britain in recognition of the British need to attenuate the threat of a cross-channel incursion. Other munitions, ammunition and materiel was made available to the British, as it had been to China in their resistance to the Japanese in the Pacific Theater. In return, the Americans were permitted to establish installations in the British possessions in the Caribbean and on Newfoundland. As Britain became financially exhausted and the results of Neville Chamberlain's ill- fated pact with Germany was recognized as an abject failure, a Lend Lease program was instituted, and FDR announced in his Fireside Chat that "Our country is going to be what our country has always proclaimed it to be – the arsenal of democracy." Roosevelt reinstated the draft in September of 1940 when he signed the bill for all male citizens between 21 and 35 years of age to register and be required to undergo 1 year of mandatory military training under the Burke-Wadsworth Act. The US also vastly increased the production of all kinds of military equipment and even extended availability to the USSR when their mutual non-aggression pact with Germany was violated. Isolationists recognized fearfully that these measures were drawing the US closer and closer to involvement in the global conflagration. It was apparent to even the most casual observer. Canada and the US had several meetings to insure the security of the northern hemisphere.

By July of 1941, Japanese/US relationships were strained to the breaking point, and while negotiations were still going on, no resolution was apparent. The Japanese continued to push forward and occupied French Indo-China, so FDR froze all Japanese assets in the US, and Japanese bank balances in the US were blocked, even against expenditures within the US. An embargo was placed on shipment to Japan of essentials like gasoline, oil, machine tools, and even scrap metals and steel. The Japanese retaliated by freezing American assets wherever it could, and ended trade with the US. As if to add insult to injury, the US then sent a Lend Lease mission to China in August of 1941. Japan sent a demand to the US in November to unfreeze Japanese assets and allow trade in gasoline and oil to meet their needs, and for the US to stop all aid to China. The US refused, and by mid-November, negotiations ended. The Japanese, under leaders like Yamamoto, had already been putting together a contingency plan to attack the US, but that had been held back until negotiations ended. So on 7 December 1941, they attacked at Pearl Harbor, where at FDR's direction, virtually the entire Pacific Fleet lay snug in the harbor, and aircraft at Hickham Field were parked wing tip to wing tip to prevent sabotage from Hawaiians, known to have a large Japanese American component. Also hit were Wheeler Field, and Bellows Field. I'm not sure where the latter one is, but all three airfields were badly damaged. In a few short hours, thousands were killed or wounded, six battleships were sunk, all eight were damaged and 70% of the aircraft destroyed or severely damaged. A total of 18 ships were sunk or run aground, so the attack was an extremely successful military strike. General Billy Mitchell had previously warned about this possibility, but was ignored. Yamamoto wanted to continue the assault to take out fuel, ammo and repair capability to insure that the Pacific Fleet would remain disabled. Permission to do so was denied, and therefore probably lost for them the war FDR declared against Japan next day. Even though Japan had not completed its paperwork on a declaration of war, such a declaration was claimed to have been made by them in their newspapers on 8 December 1941.

What was evidently not realized, or certainly not widely publicized, were the simultaneous Japanese attacks against the Philippines, Malaya, Wake Island, Guam, Singapore, and Hong Kong, the oil rich sources in the Pacific. Japan launched these six other devastating attacks, and obtained access to logistical necessities, including gasoline, oil and rubber, for them to continue their war against China. Immediately after the declaration of war by the US against Japan, Japanese America citizens in the United States were rounded up and placed into internment camps. These citizens lost their homes, businesses, and for a time, their identity as Americans. Though there were outcries against the injustice of this, they were muted, and no one seemed to remember similar treatment of American citizens of German heritage during WWI. The action against Americans of Japanese heritage remained in force until the end of WWII, and very little was done in reparation for the damage done to them by denial of their civil rights, but I have heard very little bitterness from them, or from the soldiers of Japanese heritage I have met since WWII. I was very uncomfortable with it, but understood the security measure some thought necessary during the conflict.

I received new orders to report to Ellington Field near Houston, Texas to participate in an experiment on understanding g-forces which would be experienced by pilots and crew in the newer aircraft. The test apparatus was called The Human Centrifuge. Julienne was of mixed emotions over this situation, and by now was visibly pregnant and exhibiting all the emotions some people told me were common for a woman in that physical state. While to me, it seemed logical for her to remain in Hattiesburg for the short time (six weeks) that I would be on temporary duty at Ellington Field, she seemed frantic to go with me. She didn't want to be alone, and since she had not integrated well into the society of the military wives, she had no close friends there at Camp Shelby. I suggested that she could go stay with my mother, who was a nurse, or with my grandmother, who would definitely be willing to welcome and help her, but she was adamant that she would not go to Indiana. She began bouts of crying, and it sounded like her very soul was a fatally wounded entity. I couldn't seem to comfort her, so we agreed that she would go to stay with her parents just outside Lufkin, Texas while I was at Ellington Field. It would be closer, and if there were any complications with her pregnancy, she would have help. She seemed to brighten up after that and went into a frenzy packing for the trip. I found it amazing that the sorrow was turned into joyful energy, but decided that part of her misery had been from just being afraid of the upcoming birth, and homesick to boot. The trip went well, as did the assignment. It was interesting, and I briefly toyed with the idea of applying for flight training, because the US Army Air Force was short of pilots. But the Army and personal events had other items on my dance card.

When I wasn't busy with the experiment, the world was busy coming apart at the seams. I developed a close association with the telephone, and though my wife was only about 120 miles away, there was no way I could do much visiting. Then, in early February, just as my assignment was ending, I received a call that Julie had gone into labor. Also, I had orders in my hand to report to Ft. Benjamin Harrison. I put in for an emergency leave, and by the time I got to Lufkin, my daughter had been born. I didn't get much positive reception when I got to Lufkin because I made the remark about the newborn baby that didn't sit well with Julie. The little one had red hair, was wrinkled, and small. I said that she had to be G.I. issue, because her skin didn't fit. She had been born on the 7th of February, and I got there on the 8th. She grabbed my hand with her little fist, and hung on to it, wiggling and squirming, and making soft little noises, and looked up at me with big, blue eyes. At that moment, I had the uncanny sense that there was definitely someone in that little skull, and that she already knew me. Whenever I held her, there was something possessive about the way she would cling to me, and I was a very proud father. Julie had been so convinced that she was going to be a boy that she had made a bet with her sister, Dorothy, that if the baby was a girl, Dorothy could name her. There was an argument going on between the sisters when I got there, because Julie had not chosen any names for a female child, but was going to renig on the bet. I listened for a while, but told Julie that a bet was a bet, so Dorothy named the baby Dorothy Ann Adams. When asked why she had named the baby after herself, she smiled and her dark eyes danced with mischief. She simply said that she couldn't think of anybody else she'd rather name her after, then laughed with that musical soft laugh of hers as she held the wriggling baby. Mr. and Mrs. LaGrone were very pleased that things had worked out so that they would get to see their first grandchild immediately, and their youngest daughter, Farah, who was only nine years old, was obviously thrilled. The other sisters, Idell and Ollie, were very attentive, too, and giggled as they took turns to hold the little one. Julie's best friend, Jane Colmorgen, was also omnipresent. It was obvious that I didn't have to worry about mother and child. I called my family to let them know about the new arrival, but my grandmother said that she couldn't come down, and that my mother was visiting my sister, who had a new baby boy, about six months old. Grandma Crouch did say that I was to take good care of them and get them up to visit as soon as possible, but severely warned me that my future was in God's Hands, and that if I needed to, I could bring my family there "for the duration of the war," as she put it. I was instructed to send pictures, because she knew I would have a camera with me.

    I didn't have much time, and Julie wasn't well enough to travel right then, but I wanted to have the baby baptized. I was Roman Catholic, and worried a little about it as I made my way to report in. When I called back a few days later to check on my growing family, I was told that it had been taken care of, but didn't know for a long time that Julie had taken her to the Baptist Church to a friend who was a pastor there. But for the moment, baptism was baptism, and I didn't argue about it. God would take care of the details. I just told her that I had packed up our gear and processed out at Camp Shelby, and that I would get a leave to come back to get her and our daughter as soon as I possibly could. The war was past the smoldering point and had burst into flames, as the Battle of Britain and conflict in North Africa had insured that the jaws of war were devouring more and more of the surface of the globe.

Dorothy A Adams

Headlines were ominous everywhere, and I was distinctly uneasy.

*"From Vanquished to Vassals: 20 Nations
Gobbled Up By Nazis," published in
Newsweek September 7, 1942.*

Chapter Twenty – Prelude II

When the winds of war are gales of speed and strength, when the pain then comes in torrents, mankind will rise to flex its muscles, as much as destruction warrants.

1942 was to be a gut-wrenching slide into the jaws of war, though I was given a brief reprieve at an assignment to Biloxi, Mississippi to recruit more troops. Unlike the prelude to WWI, American public opinion in 1941 had moved to favor US involvement, and the disaster of Pearl Harbor had heightened a grim determination with unanimity never before seen. The populace was committed to making every sacrifice necessary to winning the war, without the usual fanfare that precedes armed conflict. Throughout the country, a pattern of total war was adopted, with civilian responsibilities and obligations equal to those necessarily imposed on the military. The hysteria over foreign born persons, either naturalized or un-naturalized was lessened, and even of those of Japanese heritage, fully half were released. Of those, many of the young men of American birth went on to serve admirably in the US military. In fact, many as yet un-naturalized Italian and German young men entered our forces and provided us with added strength, both with weapons, and with their knowledge of language. The contributions of these soldiers in the American intelligence service was nothing short of outstanding. The FBI under J. Edgar Hoover was also incredibly effective in ferreting out any subversive activities, disloyalty, and indiscretions in the civilian population. They were so effective that there was virtually no sabotage or serious interference with the conduct of war from that theater. Even so, Congress, early on, enacted very stringent anti-sedition law, though there was little occasion to use it.

However, Roosevelt did believe, after Pearl Harbor, that some restrictions on freedom of speech were warranted. He appointed an "executive editor" of the Associated Press, as head of a new bureaucracy to censor the press, cables, and both ingoing and outgoing mail. I am continually astounded at how few people were (and are) unaware of this. The measure was established in February 1942 by Executive Order, and required even cabinet members, undersecretaries, and Federal administrators to submit proposed speeches to it. There was also a Committee on War Information set up to supervise release of war information to the public. Later, it expanded to include broadcasts in multiple languages across the world.

Wars have to be financed, and Congress finally realized the necessity of funding in order to ship men and goods to the 4 corners of the world. Actually, Congress came to believe that it would be less expensive overall to fight the war where the enemy was, instead of waiting until the US was attacked and forced to fight on her own turf against the enemy's terrible weapons of destruction. To keep the enemies from the homeland, an effort as yet unsurpassed in the history of the world, was mounted. Instead of quibbling over the figurative nickels and dimes, Congress made mind boggling appropriations, and the people, in response to the perceived need, looked past the rapid increase in their tax burden and the explosion of the national debt. The debt would rise from forty-nine billion to 272 billion by 1946. The government met most of its expenditures by borrowing – through the sales of bonds and savings stamps, which were sold to citizens in nationwide drives. Everyone also became accustomed to ration stamps, saving any scrap of metal, oil, and the scarcity of rubber for use in the civilian population. With the increase of funding from Congress, the military could immediately be massively expanded under the peacetime Selective Service from 1940, administered through Draft Boards. At first, they registered all men between 18 and 65, and exempted those needed for critical skills in industry, research and development, or agriculture to support the war effort.

What Price Honor, Memoir of Eugene Adams

Late in 1942, the Navy began to use the draft instead of relying solely on volunteers, and about simultaneously, the Army stopped accepting volunteer enlistment. Few men over 38 years of age were called up, and emphasis shifted to youth.

General George C. Marshall was the Army Chief of Staff, and he and Admiral Ernest King, Navy Commander in Chief did an amazing job of orchestrating and coordinating this huge program to rapidly expand the military to more than 14 million souls under arms. They were efficiently assigned to bases set up in up to 50 different countries. All of these bases were intricately linked to the US by a network of supply and communication lines to enable them to exert their effective operations where ever they might be. This took extraordinary planning and timely execution. To hold this together for operational effectiveness, detailed, accurate planning had to be in place, and cooperation amongst all branches of the service was essential. Lengthy supply lines were essentially maintained by the Navy and USAAF.

After being called up, men were put into basic training according to the needs of the service to which they were assigned, and in some instances, assignments were made in accordance with their previous professional expertise. When time permitted, they attended further intensive specialized training. For those with a high school education, which was over half of them, some received specialized training at over 200 US colleges and universities for advanced work. This benefitted the schools financially, as well as the individuals educated as well as the services to which they were assigned. We fielded a better equipped and better educated force than any ever raised before. Women were also encouraged to join the services to fill non-combat roles, entering by voluntary enlistment, as clerks, technicians, telephone and radio operators, cooks, and even pilots to ferry planes. Their numbers reached over 200,000, and their presence released men for combat duty. Also,

50,000 Merchant Marines were recruited and placed under the War Shipping Administration's cargo ships authority, so there was a steady flow of cargo to US troops overseas, plus lend-lease base supplies to Allies.

On the home front, millions of citizens had semi-military responsibilities under the Office of Civilian Defense. We were waging a war over 3,000 to 4,000 miles from home, and we were a major logistics arm for the Allies, as well. I was soon to get an up-front and personal taste of what that meant.

Chapter Twenty – One – Axis Expands

War will take all hands and hearts to push beyond the bounds of death's consuming maw of heinous sights and sounds.

The contributions of the home front to the demands of the greedy jaws of war exceeded all expectations. America's total mobilization in industry, transportation, agriculture, and ingenuity demonstrated the capability to participate in unanimity beyond any rational expectation. It was a war of production, planning, and of machines, which were provided to the armed forces in superb logistic effectiveness despite the colossal obstacles to doing so. It required intricate planning, but overall, the right materials were delivered to the right places at the right times, in most instances, and in the right quantities. The home front came through, and my younger sister even became a truck mechanic, though she was so small that she had to have a ladder to get to the engines, and some of the wrenches were almost as big as her little arms. She was a mother and wife at night, and a warrior in her own right by day. Transportation by rail, road and water was essential to the phenomenal success of the US logistical support for our troops, and for that of the Allies.

By the end of 1941, the Axis powers had overrun most of Europe, and though they had stopped before Leningrad and Moscow, they were pushing eastward through southern Russia. The non-aggression pact between Germany and Russia had obviously been violated, which would unalterably change the alignment of combatants and the future of the post war era. England had pushed the Italians out of Ethiopia, Eritea, and were hoping against German reinforcements for Rommel, who was heading for Egypt, intent upon taking the Suez Canal. Reinforcements were not to come. This was late in October 1942, and my chance to know the desert, far more intimately than I had ever wished, was imminent. I had been reassigned, and found myself on a troop ship, the Augusta, I think, landing in French North Africa. We were to stop Rommel and his Afrika Korps from reaching Cairo and taking the Suez Canal. We were to fight alongside the British 8th Army, which was commanded by Gen Sir Bernard L. Montgomery. It was based at el Alamein, inside Egypt.

It had been a chaotic few weeks, and Julie had refused to take our child and go home to Texas. She insisted that she could get a job and stay in our little apartment until I got back. I couldn't convince her that I might be gone a very long time. The worst parts were here tears and the way she would turn away from me, with those beautiful green eyes downcast and running rivulets down her cheeks. The more I tried to encourage her to go home, the worse it got. As I slept on the troop ship, I was worried and couldn't quite put aside the vision of her aura of misery, but steeled, as she was, with determination. The last night before shipping out, I slept with little Dorothy on my chest, her soft red-blonde hair tickling my cheek. She was only 9 months old, but had begun to walk and talk already. She would be a handful for a working mother alone in a rickety apartment. Though I knew Julie would be furious with me, I called her father, just after receiving my travel orders. He assured me that he and Mrs. Helen would go fetch my little family back to their wartime house of safety. Still, it was hard to sleep on the troop ship, and the crossing had taken 10 days, with another stop at Gibraltar. I prayed that night, and it wouldn't be the last time.

The USS Augusta had loaded up with ammunition in preparation for landings in French North Africa. There were other troop ships in our convoy, with 2,000 to 3,000 men on each one, and most of them were American. It was thought that the French would be less offended if they thought the operation was to be American, and these were mostly US Army Rangers. We were to land at a place called Oran, but we entered the Mediterranean and

What Price Honor, Memoir of Eugene Adams

sailed on past, as if bound for Alexandria. The subterfuge was to give the Afrika Korps the idea that the invasion wasn't going to be in French North Africa…but under the cover of darkness, we turned around and made for the port of Oran. There was some resistance, and some troops were lost, but we got in, sinking one of the 3 French destroyers guarding the port, grounding another and silencing the coastal defense fire. We unloaded with wave after wave of landing craft. We had a couple of essentially free days in town, but that was not to last. Within that first three days, an armada of 850 warships and transports had landed on the coast of Morocco, and the Allies, under Gen Dwight D. Eisenhower had control of French Morocco and Algeria, all the way to the border of Tunisia. Admiral Darlan of the French Vichy cabinet, went over to the Allies, which went a long way to lessen the resistance we met in North Africa. We had arrived a bare two weeks after the British 8th Army attack against Rommel at el Alamein, in which Montgomery had air superiority and used the American Sherman tanks to great advantage, inflicting great losses on the retreating Germans. Realizing the treachery of Darlan, Hitler ordered the complete occupation of France – but as the Germans approached Toulon, where the majority of the French Fleet was based, the bulk of the French naval officers skuttled most of the French Fleet and refused to join the Axis.

Unfortunately, our supply lines had not yet been fully established, so in the ensuing days, Rommel, the Desert Fox, with the infusion by Hitler of a large army by air and sea, seized Bizerte and Tunis before we could get there. We suffered massive casualties, and were forced to retreat. That still gives me nightmares. It took weeks before the debacle of supplies could be overcome, and my battalion, in which I had been made the S-4, was negatively impacted. Flies are a tremendous problem there, and I am certain that the "national bird" of Morocco is the great fly, who can fly next to you in a 30 knot wind, watching you with its large eyes, and then at the slightest reduction of wind, will quickly land on your face. The mouth and eyes are preferred targets. I remember that I had several times gone through the arduous task of quadruplicate and octopulate order forms to get fly paper for our mess tent, along with the other essentials we required. I was excited when one day when a large carton was unloaded near the mess tent. But upon opening it, I found it was full of Kotex. Dejectedly, I walked back to check the rest of the shipment, and as I was passing by, my CO called me into his tent.

He was a professor in his civilian life, and smiling and while puffing on his pipe, he asked "What's wrong, LT?" Then he listened to my story.

Smiling again, he asked, "Well, instead of feeling sorry for yourself, who do you think runs the supply operation for the Germans?"

"Oh, the Italians, I suppose," I responded

"And how do you think the German S-4 feels every day?"

I could feel a smile threatening to break out, and replied "Not very good, sir."

Taking another long draw on the pipe, and slowly releasing the smoke he grinned at me, saying "Now, you just go feel sorry for those nurses who got the fly paper! Dismissed."

I had to laugh as I left him, and filled out another set of requests in quadruplicate for our fly paper. We did finally get it.

There is a battle I cannot yet force myself to commit to paper. It still haunts me, and I am told that I often wake up screaming in the night when it intrudes in my sleep. Let me tell about a great success. We were to be in the desert until Bizerte and Tunis fell to the British and Free French under Montgomery, pushing from the south, and British-American armies from the west, pushing the German-Italian forces back further and further. Rommel had been replaced by then with Gen von Arnim, and on 12 May, 1943, he surrendered 16 Axis Generals, and 300,000 men to the Allies. That opened the way to a very short direct route through the Suez Canal for the Allies to take the war straight to Italy. It didn't take much imagination to see where I would land next.

By this time, more than two million men had been shipped overseas, and an even more enormous army was being trained for combat. The US factories were churning out immense quantities of the lethal war materiel, and offensives were in progress literally all over the world, but not on the North American continent. That thought comforted me, and I had sporadically received some letters from home. Anyone who has never served can never really understand how much that means to each soldier, sailor, marine, or airman. I was still a little dejected over the two battles of Kasserine Pass, but remembered the quotation from another famous military giant:

"Victory is reserved for those who are willing to pay its price." Sun Tzu

We had paid a horribly heavy price, but in the end, we won. It unearths memories of the desert, the ubiquitous sand, and the winds, which will sweep into howling schmalls cloaking everything in brown grit, with force enough to remove skin from your hide, and paint from vehicles. It invades every crevice, every pore, and even hides advancing forces, for it dulls the sound of moving threats, as it shrieks in unimaginable fury. I will mention it, because such sacrifice should be lauded, not hidden. On Valentine's Day in 1943, Afrika Korps under Rommel ambushed the 1st Armored Corps under the cover of such camouflage and darkness, through two mountain passes near a little village called Sidi Bou Zid, and the results were disastrous. This is known as the

Battle of Kasserine Pass. Two battles were fought there, and we lost the first one, but not the second. I will give a brief accounting of that horrific effort, as best I can. It will be brief, as I cannot afford to dwell on it, even now, these many years hence.

First, it is worth noting that Monty's operation in El Alamein, where he told his troops that they were to fight for as long as they had breath in their body, had in 200 days run Afrika Korps out of Egypt. His personal message to the Eighth Army contained that very verbiage, as well as "and let no man surrender so long as he is unwounded and can fight." His losses were great, but in that short time, the Eighth had covered over a thousand miles, using their air superiority, and pushed the German-Italian divisions westward to Tunisia. They had then occupied Tripoli. The Germans had lost nearly 40,000 troops, but the British had lost about 30,000. The British forces, comprised of British, Australian, and New Zealand units, were in agreement that Monty was indomitable in defeat, but in victory, insufferable. They had a standing joke that God once had St. Peter call a psychiatrist for him and after the consultation, the psychiatrist told St. Peter that God was just not feeling well, because he now thought he was Monty. In the early morning of 23 October, the Eighth attacked Rommel in Libya, swept the Axis air forces from the skies, and by November, the Nazi Army was sent running helter-skelter in defeat for hundreds of miles.

It was due to some political maneuvering going on among the American Commander in Chief (CINC) Eisenhower, and French Gen de Gaulle behind the scenes that gave Germany's Gen von Arnim time to organize his forces in Tunisia. The allied sweep across Tunisia was to be accomplished by the 8th pushing from the east, and the Allies fighting against the German western flank. However, of all the American Armored Divisions, the US First Armored Division was the only one that had absolutely no desert training, although they did have some experienced tank crews.

What Price Honor, Memoir of Eugene Adams

The infantry, artillery, and 168th Regimental Combat Team, which was ordered forward at the Kasserine Pass, had virtually no desert training, insufficient training overall, and zero combat experience. There were no terrain maps, the II Corps commander had never been to the front lines, and so it was America's first blood, with green troops, being led by the blind, against the seasoned desert fighters of Afrika Korps. Gen Eisenhower had been to Sidi Bou Zid only a few hours before this debacle began, to inspect, but the II Corps commander just transmitted orders without ever having been there to look at the terrain or the battle positions. The Germans attacked and pushed their panzers through two passes and into Sidi Bou Zid. The Afrika Korps skirted around the soldiers at the Allied rear, cutting them off, and punched through the 1st Armored Division front at a critical point along the thinly armed 60mile front. The command tanks didn't even have maps, coordination among the radios was poor, and they did not receive air support. In the first fight, the engaged Battalion lost 44 of its 50 tanks, and caused only a minor delay for the Germans. The whole thing went downhill from there. The Germans certainly had air support, and the Stukas were merciless with their airborne artillery. Being familiar with the terrain, the Germans had the maneuverability to get to Sidi Bou Zid, leaving a desolation of destroyed tanks sending plumes of flames into the air, while the crews screamed as they were immolated, and dead bodies spilling their blood into the thirsty desert. The Germans put their anti-tank guns, artillery and machine guns on available elevated ground, making the Americans easy targets. They also used the wadis, buildings, walls, and outcroppings to their advantage. Roughly a full hundred tanks were lost, as were most of the experienced tank crews. Tank destroyers were disabled, and lay in mangled masses of steel. Of the 2,000 soldiers marooned in the rear by the passing Germans, only a few were able to get away. The rest were taken by the Germans as POWs, and it was a miserable retreat of the scraps and shards of the 1st Armored Division. Some of the division infantry survived so they and the walking wounded joined the few of the 168th that had escaped from captivity earlier. I came across a dead medic, and picked up his pack. It came in handy, because I treated as many of the wounded as I could as I made the long trek back, ignoring the shrapnel in my face and legs. God must have known that I would need that medical training someday. When I ran out of supplies, I just did the best I could with whatever was available, and tried not to retch at some of the wounds of some of the not yet dead who could not be effectively helped. The burns were the worst, and the smell of burning flesh is carved deep into my memory. I gave what comfort I could to those for whom there was no hope, and it seemed that I took down endless numbers of names on a pad I always had with me. I collected dog tags, and just kept moving along for hours. I didn't black out until I finally reached a rally point, which had an aid station. I don't know how many miles I walked, but I do know that I sometimes used my weapon like a cane, because one leg had swollen badly, and I had lost copious amounts of blood.

The first thing I remembered after I woke up was a voice with a very Southern accent saying "Wouldja look at this? I ain't never seen no LT medic before. The Army shore is puzzlin' sometimes." Then he cut my trousers so he could begin picking the shrapnel out of my legs and dropping it with a ping into a can. I bit down on that pad I had been writing on and did my best not to move, but he finally noticed that I was awake and asked if I needed some anesthetic. I told him no, but a good swig of whiskey would certainly help a lot. When he said that wasn't an anesthetic, I told him it certainly was, and was classified as a transesophageal anesthetic, used by a large percentage of discombooberated or hurt American soldiers. He eyed me for a minute or two, and then started laughing. He told me he reckoned I wasn't going to die, because most smart asses were mostly stubborn as the average mule. He had good hands, and was even gentle with the shards he took out of my face. He shot me up with antibiotic, and then tried to radio to my unit, because he didn't think I should try to walk back. He got a young CPT to come talk to me about all the names and dog tags, and blessedly, one troop brought me a cup of strong black coffee. I asked the CPT what was going to be done about all those soldiers who had been surrounded and cut off from the Armored Division by the Germans, and he said he didn't know, but would ask for me. A little later, he came back to tell me that they had been just abandoned, and I felt sicker about that than about my wounds. I noticed then that I couldn't see very well out of my right eye, but didn't mention it, because I wanted to get back to my unit. The radios still weren't well synchronized, but he said that the battalion was sending someone, with a uniform, to pick me up.

A few years ago, a piece of shrapnel worked its way out from under my right cheek bone, and the VA doctor said that he thought that it must have been pushing against the optic nerve on that side for all those years. He assured me that I was very lucky, because it could have worked its way into my brain, instead of finally working its way out. Lucky. I guess I was, but I felt the rage again, at the miserable way so many untrained troops were used as cannon fodder, and though we did win the next battle, that II Corps commander, whose name I still refuse to say, was removed, and we got some actual leadership which included Patton for a while, and Bradley. Gen Marshall, the Chief of Staff, made that happen. The Brits were very blunt about what they thought about American soldiers for a long time, and it still, in the vernacular I learned in the Army, pisses me off. We "Yanks" were no longer green, and we were angry. That perceived lack of military prowess was a direct result of years of whittling away our standing military forces for bogus economic reasons. I've seen it happening again, and have come to believe that a prerequisite for being in Congress should be at least one hitch in the military. The same is true for the Executive Branch. Possibly then there would be a greater understanding of the danger in skeletonizing our armed forces.

Chapter Twenty – Two – Competition Among Allies

As the spinning wheel of Fate spills out our thread of life, it never fails to incorporate the joys as well as strife.

I was later to learn, as we were licking our wounds, that for the second battle for that bloody, noisome pass, at first, the British wanted to exclude the American units from action on the front lines. To avoid adding insult to injury, confident that our ire would strengthen our prowess, Eisenhower and Patton prevailed upon Gen Marshall. The bitter fact was that in about a week, American losses had amounted to about 20% of those from all the engaged forces, as well as having suffered high losses in materiel and equipment. We were hurting, and we didn't need to have our prestige savaged as well.

Gen Eisenhower insisted that "Our people from the very highest to the very lowest have learned that this is not a child's game, and are ready and eager to get down to the fundamental business of profiting by the lessons they have learned…"

More than that, we had not only learned, we were madder than Hell, and being more aggressive than before was not going to be a problem. We were spoiling for a fight. We were conducting ourselves well, and Eisenhower knew this; but he also wanted the leadership problem corrected immediately if not sooner. The II Corps Commander was removed, and Patton was named to assume the command in early March. It was clear that as soon as Patton got the kinks out of II Corps, leadership at all levels and the entire force was to be groomed to go to Sicily. Patton named Gen Omar Bradley as his deputy, with the understanding that he would succeed to Corps Command soon. The lost ground at the Kasserine Pass had been regained, and Americans were on the attack. Though British Gen Alexander had wanted American units relegated to the non-combat and tactical positions, which Patton "patently" rejected, a position hotly backed by Bradley, they finally got Ike's and Marshall's backing on the issue. The 34th Division had been particularly targeted by Alexander, but it and the other three American divisions remained in line for the rest of the campaign.

There were multitudinous military/political games going on in the background, as usual. As Plato once pointed out, he who says politics is not his business, has no business. Also, the press continued to denigrate us to the American public, and across Europe as well. It was mercifully only intermittently made known to us, but my Grandmother, as always, would get some information to me. I could tell that the letters had been opened, and from what she wrote, that articles had been removed from them before I received them. I managed to scribble some short notes to her, and to my wife, from time to time. I knew full well that the next stop was Sicily, but couldn't directly say so. I could only bemoan the fact that I would not be going home any time soon. I was also aware that the operation was to be under the overall authority of Monty, and that this didn't sit well with Patton, or with us. But at least, it wasn't the worst place to be fighting; we wouldn't be in Leningrad or the Philippines. We had all adjusted to the Mediterranean climate, and would be happy to get out of the sandbox. Around the world, Japan still held lots of real estate, though she had lost Guadalcanal and Papua, plus Americans were landing on the Attu Island in Alaska to drive the Japanese out. The U-boat action in the North Sea had been blunted significantly, relieving logistic pressure on Great Britain in the English Channel. While we "snuffies" were occupied with staying alive, living in sand infested with sand fleas, and breathing the air full of flies, other changes were going on. Due to international cooperation, things in the multinational military/political background had given birth to a new entity. As we were preparing to move to the next objective, we heard of that new player called the United Nations.

It had been born in January of 1942 when 26 nations had come together to pledge mutual support. There had been tremendous cooperation among those united in purpose to stop the aggressors who were spreading misery and death across the globe. The new UN formalized the cooperation and promised to:

1. Give full cooperation in the war effort,
2. Members agreed not to make a separate peace,
3. Endorsed the war aims of the Atlantic Charter.*

A statement of war aims crafted by Churchill and FDR in August of 1941 pledged the UN to work for an aggression free world in which every nation, large or small, could adopt its own form of government. Once aggressors were crushed all nations were to work together to free all men from fear and war.

In their struggle for survival, the Allied Powers worked as a team. The USA continued to support this mutual mission both logistically and militarily for as long as necessary. Eventually, more nations joined the UN, and in 1945, it became a permanent international organization.

But Sicily was the next step in which I would be personally involved, though not the last.

The strategic advantage gained by the victories in North Africa, as mentioned previously, gave control of Mediterranean air and sea to the Allies, so their ships would be protected by air support from airfields along the North African coast, and the sea lanes would be free for logistics. As mentioned previously, the Suez Canal was also under Allied control for the first time since 1941. That saved two months sailing time for convoys out of Britain to India, since they wouldn't have to circumnavigate Africa. Also, from these air fields, Sicily and Italy were subject to literally merciless bombing, which softened the target for the invasion in July of 1943. The Sicilians offered little resistance, and the crack German troops were greatly outnumbered by the British, Canadian, and American troops invading the island. Also in July, Mussolini fell from power, so the supply lines not only from the Mediterranean, but from Italy, were cut. The radio broadcasts tended to minimize the competition and near hostility between Monty and Patton in this campaign, but lauded the UN to the people at home. The seasoned German troops fought well and hard, but were overwhelmed by the large Allied forces and loss of their supply lines.

But why Sicily? Prime Minister Churchill had traveled to Washington, DC to meet with FDR, and in his not to be denied fashion, had argued against the US military experts, including Gen Marshall, for striking at what Churchill believed was the soft underbelly of the Axis. He had arrived with a large retinue of more than 100 generals, admirals, clerks, bodyguards, detectives, and Royal Marines. The US military experts and planners had recommended a Cross Channel attack to enter the European continent on the West while Hitler was occupied on the East. FDR went to meet Churchill's train, chauffeured in a limousine down streets lined with Secret Service. As the train squealed to a stop, FDR was lifted from the limousine into a wheelchair. His obvious pallor and outwardly stressed visage was transformed as Churchill tramped down the gangplank. FDR looked forward to the conference which he felt would lead to a mutually acceptable winning strategy to end the war in victory. This was in May of 1943. The next day, they met in the Oval Office along with ten members of the Combined Chiefs. As mentioned before, American planners had previously determined, after careful scrutiny of portals to the European Continent that the best route was across the English Channel. But FDR had a history of being susceptible to Churchill's persuasive powers. No one was more troubled by this than Gen George C. Marshall, who with the Joint

Chiefs had been arguing ardently for the Channel crossing. Churchill kept referring to the need to grasp the "fruits of success" in North Africa and quickly striking "the soft underbelly" of the Axis, because he believed that Italy was "ripe for the plucking." He wanted to start with Sicily, never mind that there were about 25 Allied Divisions with 15,000 men each who would be on the small island in the Mediterranean at the end of the operation, which was code named Husky. Marshall, in particular was against it, because he foresaw the logistic inadvisability of creating a vacuum in the Mediterranean, because the next British step would be invasion of Italy, creating a vacuum which would suck troops away from the Channel crossing or any other European action. Furthermore, he fully believed that the value of Mediterranean operations was highly speculative as a strategy to end the war. Eliminating Italy from the war would actually materially benefit the Germans, who would no longer have to supply coal to Rome, could remove their rolling stock support, and other actions to supply food and goods to Italy. The US would then have to feed and supply the civilian Italian population, and to top it all off, there were insufficient adequate landing sites in the toe of the Italian boot to permit ease of invasion. The Joint Chiefs concluded in their memo, submitted to FDR and the Brits that "It is the opinion of the US Chiefs of Staff that a Cross Channel invasion of Europe is necessary to an early conclusion of the war with Germany."

After a brief sortie around Washington, DC, and Williamsburg, VA, FDR retired with Churchill and his staff to Shangri La (later to be renamed Camp David). The deadlock continued for several days, but one of the Brits mentioned that the President "must be thinking," but hadn't been saying much of anything. He was then told by First Lady Eleanor Roosevelt that "The President never thinks! He decides." And he would, since the Joint Chiefs of Staff from either side remained deadlocked, the decision lay with him and with Churchill. It was a compromise of sorts, with operations to be scheduled for crossing of the English Channel, after the conclusion of Operation Husky and invasion of Italy, in no more than 55 weeks (1 May 1944). The susceptibility of FDR to Churchill was clearly demonstrated. Sicily was to be the frosting, but the cake was Italy. Churchill meant to have it – and his private physician, Lord Moran, once said of the PM that "He is so taken with his ideas that he is not interested in what other people think."

Most of this information came to me after we had been victorious in North Africa, because I received frequent letters from both my grandmother, and the LaGrones, but also was in multiple military briefings. I also received some pictures of my daughter, which made me a little sad because I had missed her first birthday, and letters from my wife, which made me very happy. I had been made a Company Commander, and had made many other military contacts by the, but I am as gifted as FDR at hiding in my own mind. I had dragged some of my Black's Law Books to North Africa in my footlocker, and spent much of my free time studying law. I heard the scuttlebutt about Sicily, but found it exceedingly difficult to address the necessity of the attack on that island that had been besieged since about 300 BC, and had remnants from the Bronze Age to the Hellenistic and Byzantine times littering the landscape. Though it was only two miles from the Italian boot at one point, it still didn't seem as strategically important, even to me, an unimportant Lieutenant. It wasn't nearly as strategically important as crossing the English Channel, which was a much shorter path to Europe and would stop aerial attacks on the British Isles. Also it occurred to me that Italy is much easier to attack by land from the north than from the south by sea, and amphibious operations are even tough for those experienced in that methodology. I knew full well that the US units were not experienced in, nor trained for amphibious landings, and my mind periodically wandered back to the lack of sufficient training that had hamstrung us before. I was also worried about logistics for any such venture, but tried to enjoy the brief interlude we American warriors had in Algiers and Tunisia while those in much higher pay grades than mine decided what would happen. It was comforting to know that Patton would lead us, whatever our assignment was, even though many soldiers groused about the fact that the General would exact a $25 fine from any soldier he saw who was out of uniform. Failing in military courtesy, like saluting properly at the appropriate time, was even worse. Convoys now stretched from Algeria to Tunisia. There were literally tons of all sorts of supplies, LSTs, LCTs, small craft including submarines, bustling around the huge battleships, cruisers, aircraft carriers, tankers, and anything in the Navy inventory. The planning for casualties had received particular attention, and it was assumed that the operation would last two months with casualty rates at about 15% in the initial assault. The medics and corpsmen received some intensive training for this eventuality. Since invading armies have the responsibility for civilian populations as well, medics were provided with vaccines for tetanus, smallpox, and typhus, plus additional supplies for non-fatal injuries, or illnesses. I was pleased by that, and by the casualty and graves registration program plus materials and markers for graves. It showed attention to detail and careful planning.

There were considerable fireworks between Eisenhower and Montgomery over the plan of attack, because Monty demanded it be done his way, and only his way, plus he wanted Patton's 7th Army under his command. That didn't sit well with Ike OR Patton, so it didn't happen, but the invasion spun off in one of the worst gales I ever hope to see – and we Americans were to land three assault divisions on the southwestern part of the island at the Gulf of Gela, with Montgomery's units landing on the southeastern portion.

In the center, the 1st Division was to take the town of Gela, with the 3rd Division on our left and the 45th on our right. There was a terrible storm raging in the Mediterranean, but the winds miraculously died down enough to allow us to get some of the landing craft (LSTs) to the beach under the cover of darkness on D-Day, 10 July. Oddly enough, I changed my mind about only God being able to sail and land an LST; the Navy did a pretty good job. The other odd thing was that beyond the sandy beaches, the land seemed to be on fire. We later discovered that it was wheat stubble burning, and before us was that limestone hillock where the Greeks had founded Gela in late 600 BC. Virgil wrote about it in the Aeneid, and about the fertile fields surrounding it. There was something called a Yellow Line about 10 to 20 miles inland which we were to fight to reach, but Patton hadn't been given any orders beyond that. I had told my men to wrap their dog tags in friction tape to keep them from rattling, but as the Navy began firing before our feet hit the ground beyond some large swells, the sound was deafening, and it lit up the night more beautifully than any fireworks I had ever seen, in white and golden flashes, with attendant smoke rings floating above us in the air. Dog tags rattling under those circumstances would have been irrelevant.

Patton had planned well, and about 3,000 paratroopers (4 Battalions) were supposed to be dropped at critical road junctions beyond the beaches to prevent German repulsion of our landing. That was to have taken place on the 9th and 10th of July. It was the mission of the 82nd Airborne under Gavin, and would be their first night time jump, which wasn't easy. They were on the C-47 Dakotas, 226 of them, which were the workhorse airframes at the time, but the wind was twice the recommended level for jumping. It was about a 3-hour flight, and in the heavy wind, many of the planes got lost. The paratroopers also jumped in those heavy winds, but some had to jump at about twice the altitude and at high speed of the aircraft. Before it was over, nobody knew where they were, including those who had made it to the ground alive. Despite the careful planning, many were as much as 65 miles from the drop target, and over three hundred were casualties. Eight planes were lost, and not to enemy fire. We didn't arrive at 0300 hrs without multiple SNAFUs either. Some ground soldiers jumped out or were told to jump out of the landing craft where the water was too deep, and with packs weighing over eighty pounds, they sank and drowned. The beach was mined, as were the exits through the dunes, and many died within inches of the water, or from enemy fire which was directed down at them from pill boxes on the hill. One saving grace was the DUKWs which was a "deuce and a half" truck with flotation tanks and twin propellers, which could ferry howitzers and ammunition, plus the gun crew, or a rifle platoon to the shore, slowly but efficiently. Then it could move along a road smartly, carrying other loads of much needed equipment. Unfortunately, a good many of them got blown up by mines, so we truly treasured those that weren't destroyed. The tanks didn't make it in at first, and the LCTs carrying them were moored off shore. The beach quickly became a catastrophe of strewn wreckage, bodies, supplies and equipment, plus we were 50 minutes late, which is a Patton "no, no." Fate had played her hand in the early hours of Husky. With dawn, we experienced an additional horror – enemy air strikes. The Navy got the brunt of that, and one ship was sunk. We could see the light from the beach when her powder magazine detonated. We weaved in and out of burned DUKWs and debris east of Gela. Darby's Rangers took Gela, and we moved on as Navy barrages also pounded the northwest side of the town. A column of French made Italian tanks was wiped out by a combination of the paratroopers, salvos from a Navy cruiser, and the 16th Infantry.

    Ernie Pyle was with us and wrote about the American Landings, losses and life. He had a much better way with words than I do – and I can't describe much of the campaign because it comes back full force, complete with the smoke, sulfur, blood, and the cacophony of screaming shells intertwined with the screams of dying or wounded men. I find myself there again, and it is difficult sometimes to disengage. But sometimes, I see the small children coming out of hiding, shy smiles on their faces, and arms held up in a "V" for victory. I had learned a lot of Italian in Chicago, and sometimes it got me a hug from some of them. I met a lot of people, some famous, like Gen Truscott of the 3rd Division on our left flank, Gen Ted Roosevelt, and some whose names I do not remember, but whose faces are indelibly etched in my brain. I remember the Italians streaming out of their pill boxes when the brush and grass camouflaging their position caught fire and smoked them out. They were the most terrified human beings I have ever seen. The 45th Division suffered more than we did, because of the swells of the windswept sea, which were challenging to the 3rd and 1st, but worse at the 45th's landing site, but as the the day rose up to meet us, we were ashore. My company had suffered casualties, but they weren't as bad as I had anticipated. The Yellow Line seemed like a dream, reached through a nightmare, but to be reached, none-the-less. Thousands of us had landed and thousands were waiting offshore to join the fray.

Oddly, we had not seen a single Panzer or any German soldiers, but that, too, was to come. There were hundreds of Dago prisoners, but not one Kraut, as my First SGT observed.

Chapter Twenty – Three – Unprepared but Undefeated

When clouds high overhead seem not to know the struggles of human kind, so far away below, the beams of a kindly sun can find the weary, bleeding hands, striving to do the very best that honor now demands.

Operation Husky was successful. Gen Hans Hube, initially the German Commander in Chief in Sicily was a tanker by trade and training, and when the German High Command had realized the next Allied attack would be to the south, (as Churchill had insisted), Hube and additional forces were sent post haste to Sicily. But that would be too little, too late. It is clear that Fate, not a mortal enemy, or stealth, is the undiscriminating enemy. The weather for D-day, and better planning and training prior to that, could have saved lives. The paratroopers, glider pilots, and pilots of the airframes for the 8th Army could have been trained better. The pilots flying them at night, under forbidding weather conditions had little experience in night flying; neither did the paratroopers or glider pilots have requisite pre-operation night training. But it did convince me to refuse glider training and elect to remain a "ground pounder," when that opportunity presented itself later in the war. The 8th Army had their part of the invasion, and we had ours, and I did not regret it.

We were later to learn that the Germans had their own communications and manpower distribution problems, which blunted their initial responses. Field Marshall Albert Kesselring was to shake off the ostensible subordination of Italian authority, to become a fierce, able opponent. He had few equals in any army, and was completely loyal to Hitler. He was "underwhelmed" with the capability and dedication to duty of the Italians, and saw the danger to the Fatherland. He knew that the entirety of Italy was defensible IF the Italians would fight, but he believed that they were not soldiers from a fundamental heartfelt passion. He realized that Germans must strike before the Allies could consolidate their forces from their separate beachheads. He took over command of German forces in Sicily, and ordered the most tactically positioned unit, the Herman Goring Panzers, to attack Gela at daybreak on 11 July to drive the invaders into the sea. The Panzer Grenadier Division was too far away over very bad roads.

Gen Ted Roosevelt, was a WWI veteran, who had been with the Big Red One back then. He was gassed at Cantigny and wounded at Soissons, then decorated for valor in that war, and had come ashore with us on the 10th, stomping up and down on his thin, putty-wrapped legs, waving his cane and bellowing in his fog-horn voice, directing troops at the very edge of the water. It reminded me of a Bantam Rooster, or a little fighting cock. He had come back to the Army to serve as Assistant Division Commander of the 1st, and he seemed oblivious to any danger to himself as he moved undaunted in his determination to get the beachhead secured and the soldiers moving on to the objective. Patton viewed him overall as weak on discipline and training, but as a fine battle commander, and so he was. The pugnacious warrior was said to have been born for combat, and the troops loved him. He was angry that the LCTs with the tanks were still offshore, as were men and other essential equipment. If he had thought he could, he would have swum out and pulled it all in by himself. Roosevelt had moved forward by dawn, established a 1st Division Command Post, monitored a 6-mile front, and was enduring with mounting impatience the unnerving, fragmenting radio messages that were coming in. German Panzers were moving south from Ponte Olivo, southwest from Nicemi, and west from Biscari. The Italians had massed further west for attack on Gela. Most of this intelligence came in bits and pieces over the radios, but much of it from his binoculars and sharp assessment of the impending battlefield situation. He and the Sergeant assisting

What Price Honor, Memoir of Eugene Adams

him (another WWI vet), had placed several calls to Gen Terry Allen, the Division Commander to have tanks, howitzers, mortars, and other relevant weaponry moved forward and immediately call in air support. He fumed when he finally was informed that the tanks still weren't on shore, nor were the other assets needed to repulse a Panzer attack. Air cover was being given to the Navy, and wasn't available to the 1st Division. That sent him out with his gamecock stride, and waving cane to get the riflemen into position, and it is reported that he yelled at them "These guys can't hit me! They've been trying through two world wars, and if they can't hit an old grandfather like me, they sure as hell can't hurt you!" More calls flew between the command post and Gen Allen, and from Allen to HHQ. The few antitank weapons had been used by the Battalions in contact, but against 40 tanks and associated infantry, the 16th Regiment's 2nd Bn had held on for two hours. The 3rd Bn was finally pushed back by 30 Panzers, after losing six of their nine antitank guns and a commander. I was with them, and it was ugly. It got worse when the Italian dive bombers came in. I managed to climb up on a dune, high enough to see more of the battlefield, and it was aflame with burning tanks, bursting shells, debris, and total confusion. The few artillery pieces that had made it to shore were firing away, but I knew that there wouldn't be enough power for them for long. There were some junior grade officers who were desperately even firing into the viewing slits of the Panzers with their 0.45s, and I couldn't look any more. I got my troops dug in, and I can't think about this part of the action any more. While in my foxhole, I took a stub of a pencil out and scribbled out a poem, ignoring the whistle of the bullets going by, and knowing that my field of fire wasn't active at that moment. I found that little ditty many years later…

> I am the man who can do everything,
> Who lives through life without a care.
> I am the man who can do everything,

Dorothy A Adams

As I sit rocking in my chair.

Yes, I am the man who can do everything,
No matter when, no matter where.
I could have conquered Rommel and Kesselring,
But alone, I did not dare.

It brought a tear to my eye, because I was there where those opponents were, and after Sicily, we all three would "still be there," except that Rommel would be murdered before all was said and done. All of us, the warriors, would bear the indelible marks, some of which cannot be seen from the outside.

I remember that on day 2 ½ on Sicily, as we were taking blows, and Gen Allen was experiencing tremendous frustration trying to get us assistance, amidst a complicated telecommunications snarl, something nearly miraculous happened. It will make me a devoted admirer of the irascible general who would lead us to victory against Germany and to defeat them in Sicily. George S. Patton came ashore, at about 09:30, on Sunday, 11 July 1943, and as a Roman Catholic, like General Allen, I felt it was an answer to my prayers. As some grizzled old SGT had once told me, there are no atheists in foxholes, and he was undeniably right. Patton went into Gela and up onto a rooftop, where he could see for himself what was going on. It was only about 30 hours since we had made a beachhead, and now were embroiled in the staving off of a German counterattack, or being driven back into the sea. Patton, in his inimitable way, called in naval bombardment, and I must turn away now from the smells of cordite, phosphor, and burning flesh. I can smell them even now. We got supporting fire from the Navy and one hideous memory still boils up of dead enemy soldiers hanging from the trees, burning. The shells from the USS Boise, and then the USS Savannah, screamed overhead, later supported by some destroyers, who pulled in and also began shelling the enemy. The white phosphorus came from mortar shells, which heralded the landing of our much needed artillery assets. The Germans, many of whom had been screaming as their tanks were burning, with crews trapped inside, pulled back, and by mid-afternoon, picked up speed in their retreat. The Italians had been stopped dead in their tracks, and the counterattack had been successfully stopped. In response to Patton's full throated demands, which probably didn't need a radio, we had tanks, artillery, ammo, and other assets ashore, and were happy to obey the order to "get our asses off the beach." We had an Artillery General, whose nickname I only remember was "Mr. Chips," strolling along among about four or five battalions of artillery, pointing out targets, and now I must simply describe what happened after Patton departed in late afternoon, with Allen at the command post insisting that we continue to hit the Germans so they couldn't reorganize for an additional counterattack. I reorganized my unit, counted casualties, and pressed forward. Memories between that and Palermo are sketchy and extremely painful, but we had won the day. Ultimately, we would win in Sicily, as would Montgomery and his 8th Army.

That's another whole story, though it happened literally within 38 days, believe me, it was a lifetime. On the 12th of July, the most horrific example of death by friendly fire occurred. Communications again failed miserably, and the USAAF sorties arrived to relieve the US Army on the beach head and provide cover for the Navy. It was an unmitigated disaster. Having survived an intensive attack from German aircraft only shortly before the USAAF carrying US paratroopers arrived, Americans were understandably jumpy. They fired on their own, and Patton's order to inform them of the impending arrival of friendly forces failed miserably. The most horrible of all experiences a soldier can have is to know they have killed their own, and the losses were significant. For five months before Husky began, Patton had been trying to get the USAAF commanders to participate in the operational strategic planning, but those commanders strongly resisted efforts from both Army and Navy to produce a unified air plan. That led to losses to all three arms of the US forces. On the morning of the 12th, Patton had issued an order that all ground troops were to be expecting and on the look-out for US air frames and paratroopers. That message was not decoded and issued until nightfall, and Gen Ridgeway, commander of the 82nd Airborne, whose headquarters was near Gen Allen's Command Post, personally checked to see if his ground troops knew about the inbound Allied Parachute Infantry from Tunisia, with 2300 men and 144 planes, due before midnight. Five of his 6 antiaircraft batteries had heard, but the 6th had not, until Gen Ridgeway told them. But the thousands on the ground and in the sea hadn't gotten the word. The planes initially flew over the 45th Division position, the first place where they would reach land, and the Division had not received any notification of the impending arrival. Far too late to get the word out, Patton had tried to abort the mission (about 20:00 Hrs), but to no avail. Ridgeway had been warning about the possibility of such a catastrophe for months, and he was watching as the first stick of paratroopers jumped to be slaughtered by machine gun fire from a bunch of frightened soldiers, unable to identify the DC-47s overhead as "friendly." It went downhill from there. Planes began to tumble out of the air, both over the fleet and the beach, before the firing stopped.

When Eisenhower visited Patton on his barge the day after the disaster, he was provided with the excuse he (Ike) had been wanting for a long time. He wanted to replace Patton as 7th Army Commander with Gen Omar Bradley, but wasn't aware of it until later. Patton didn't tell Gen Eisenhower about the disaster, but instead informed him that the "Yellow Line" had been crossed by one division, and the other two would shortly follow as the 7th Army pushed on. We did push on, through the heat and dust, and I remember the colors of the landscape and sky, as we drove the

Germans along the pre-planned path. I refuse to remember some of it, but the smells come back vividly when I can't block them out. Montgomery, small in physical stature, but gigantic in ego, was to confound us when we were only about ½ mile from the road to Messina by deviating from the original plan and receiving permission to do so from Eisenhower and Alexander, though his forces were much further away at the time. It also gave the Germans a better chance to execute their exit strategy, and they took advantage of it. But Patton brilliantly diverted us to Palermo, which we took. A pleasant memory floats up now, of a basement in a semi-gutted building in Palermo, where I found a case of very good red wine. My 1SGT and I buried it in the dirt floor there, after we shared a bottle of it, and it is probably still there. I doubt that I can go back there any way but in a memory now, but the wine blunted the serious business of counting our losses and requesting reinforcements. We tried to ignore the scuttlebutt about the II Corps Cdr, Gen Bradley, fuming over the fact that Patton didn't prevent Montgomery's power move, as well as shutting out the sweet smell of honeysuckle rising over the odor of blood, manure, and rotting bodies that seemed omnipresent. I was later to reflect that Montgomery simply wanted to get to Messina first, the better to humiliate the Americans and emphasize the supposed superiority of the British 8th Army. I also remember how I hate the smell of honeysuckle and jasmine. I always shall.

The Germans were in almost full retreat by then, and under the shrewd guidance of Gen Hans Hube, were rapidly moving materiel and assets across to Italy while Kesselring adeptly protected their rear and prepared to defend in Italy. By the time the 7th and 8th Armies met in Messina to congratulate themselves on their victorious success in Operation Husky, fully two thirds of the German forces and tanks had escaped destruction. Gen Hube is said to have been the last German to leave Sicily, after he had gotten his beloved Tiger Tanks and their crews off the island. II

Corps Commander, Gen Bradley, besieged by personal and health problems, hadn't come ashore at first, but his dislike of Gen Patton continued to intensify after he got over his initial sea sickness and established a command post. His biggest problem was the multitudinous throng of Italian prisoners of war, who surrendered in seemingly unending but festive hordes as they were herded to the LSTs which carried them away. But even though he was knocking heads with Patton, he was absolutely infuriated when Montgomery got that approval from Ike and Alexander to cut in front of the American advance along two critical points along a highway leading to Messina. He would never forgive Patton for not refusing the plan, and was correct in pointing out that the move allowed the Germans to save a great deal more equipment and experienced forces than they would otherwise have been able to, had the original plan been honored. Also, the Americans were to be again denied the honor they had earned at such a high price.

The Italian air force had been completely impotent, and under Mussolini's personal command, they were not allowed to move further than specified distances from their airports. Likewise, the naval assets of Italy were not effective because of similar restrictions. In other words, they were essentially useless in the struggle for Sicily, ill-conceived as it was from the beginning due to pressure from the British led by Churchill. However, the Italian Navy would not have been equal to a struggle against Admiral Cunningham's Armada of over 2,590 ships of all classifications, which had been dedicated to Operation Husky. Mussolini was in the process of being deposed, and King Victor-Emmanuel III was dithering over whether or not to change sides in the conflict, because there was fear that the Germans would exact retribution, but there was also pressure from political powers within Italy to seize the opportunity to defect. On 17 August 1943, the Sicilian Campaign was over, at least for those on the ground, falling from the air, or under fire at sea. I was certain that some of us would have occasion to return from time to time, in spirit, if not in fact. But my tenure in the confines of Italy was not yet done. Salerno would be the next objective, which was anticipated by Germany, as was the fall of Mussolini. Rommel was on his way into the vacuum created for the Axis by the southern attack. Although Mussolini would be forcibly put back into place for a short time by Hitler's agents, the Fascist control of Italy was teetering and would fall. But in the field with my soldiers, I was less concerned with these geopolitical machinations than with getting the letters written to families of fallen soldiers, and making sure that their personal belongings were collected for possible later shipment. It had been my first command position as an Infantryman, and I had probably aged a couple of decades in less than two months. For that brief interlude, we had an overwhelming number of troops in the 15th Army Group, and the wheels were turning, on and on, and the grinding could be heard. The axles would be greased with gallons upon gallons of blood.

Chapter Twenty – Four – Another Sortie

Cheers for the victors will ring out, no matter who they are, whether they be native sons, or came there from afar. The will to change anything is beaten into dust, and everywhere the people know, survive this time, they must.

 At Catania, it had been hard to tell the dead from the dying, except that flies walked in faces of the dead, and medics moved among the fallen bodies, injecting morphine into those who lay dying. The Germans had held the high ground, and the terrain was a labyrinth of foliage and structures most amenable to concealment from our approaching attack. Casualties had been massive. Though history books may never acknowledge it, Patton and not Montgomery had saved the day, and at the end of the Sicilian campaign, American forces held more than twice as much territory than the 8th Army. But Monty was still adored by the press, so Montgomery was awarded the victory and the Americans were considered "also rans." We, in what was left of the 7th Army were hopeful that Alexander would be moved aside, and Eisenhower would turn Patton loose, because we now would face both Rommel and Kesselring in Italy. We had soldiers like the physically tiny, but giant in bravery and combat, like Audie Murphy among us, but leadership we craved. We American warriors wanted American leadership. That way we would not again be fettered by British elitists.

 The Trident Conference, I was later to find out, is what sealed our fate in the further prosecution of the Italian Campaign, because agreement between Churchill and FDR dictated to Eisenhower that "no objective could be complete without the capture of Rome." Churchill also advocated invasion and capture of as much of the Italian boot as possible, to push the Germans back to the Balkans and southern France. He was uncomplimentary to and about the American forces, to put it mildly, and insisted on British oversight of operations in Italy, with 5th Army Commander, Gen Mark W. Clark subordinate to the British. This was a recipe for disaster entailing far greater suffering and death of Americans, as it had been before, but Eisenhower acquiesced. I was transferred out of the 7th into the 5th Army after our beachhead. The British landed in Italy on the 1st of September, and we battle weary members of the 7th Army mounted a beach head at the Gulf of Salerno, near Naples, to link up with the 5th Army on the 8th of September. We were not so fortunate as the British, and again, the Germans held high ground, and due to their withdrawal from Sicily, had forces and assets in excess of our four divisions. In addition, they had been reinforced from the north, and were occupying Rome with Panzer Groups, paratroopers, Panzergrenadier units, Infantry and Mechanized Infantry, plus an intact logistic chain. The vacuum predicted by our military planners if an attack on Italy was made from the south were coming true in vibrant colors of exploding shells and splashing blood, as these assets under the control of the two best German generals ever born were sucked down into Italy and thrown against us. Hitler was as determined that Rome would not be captured as Churchill was demanding that it should and would be. What we did have was excellent naval support, as well as Gen Clark's bulldogged determination, plus the sparring of Rommel and Kesselring in the background.

The operation was code-named AVALANCHE, and we were given only three divisions instead of the four that Gen Clark considered minimally sufficient. The 82nd Airborne under Gen Ridgeway was taken away from us, too. The Prime Minister had demanded withdrawal of seven British and American divisions to England, and again, he got his way. Though Gen Marshall was very leery of an attack against the Italian mainland instead of the planned invasion of Sardinia, again, Eisenhower acquiesced. It was a recipe for disaster, and we attacked through a bay that was thoroughly mined, necessitating disembarking from the troop ships on LSTs 12 miles out to reach an incredibly beautiful, but completely lethal beachhead ringed by mountains. Some troops were not issued even rifles before they disembarked from North Africa, and they landed the same way, unarmed. The beachhead reminded me of a giant cup, and the Germans occupied the high ground. The Gulf of Salerno, was just barely in the range of the Spitfires, allowing only about ten minutes of combat time before they had to return for refueling. We had adequate naval support, but it had to be held out away from the gulf due to the mines, potential long range artillery in the mountains, and inadequate air cover against the Luftwaffe. Kesselring had anticipated the point of attack, and I have read afterwards with burning anger the newspaper accounts of how the British under Montgomery suffered much greater resistance at their point of attack than the Americans at Salerno. The plan was for us to land at Salerno, seize Naples, then establish air bases. There would be three American divisions against six German divisions, and their first 40,000 would grow to 100,000 within 4 days. Of the American divisions, some units within them had never before participated in an amphibious operation. Eisenhower had asked for bombers, but was denied diversion of any of the B17s bombing Germany from Britain. 12 miles off shore, at the 100 fathom line, the captains stopped the engines on the vessels just before midnight, so anchors, chains, and winches were in tune with the hissing of water. Then there was gold and crimson tracer fire from the distant shore, which told us the enemy knew we were there. Kesselring activated his plan, developed when he anticipated the point of attack. The sea was calm, and the soldiers began loading into the LSTs. The Allied plan was to have us 4,000 or more yards inland immediately after the beach head, which was a wish dream. Someone forgot about the fact that the Germans held the high ground when the operation kicked off at about 0300 to 0330 AM.

What Price Honor, Memoir of Eugene Adams

Salerno is difficult for me to remember as clearly as the two major conflicts I had previously engaged in. I was growing battle weary, and had had no R & R since departing for North Africa, which seemed like an eon ago. The battles at Salerno, then at Anzio, were no more horrible than North Africa or Sicily, but I was increasingly impacted by being on edge for 24 hours a day, 7 days a week, without interruption or decompression from the sounds, smells, and egregious scenes of battle. I was also developing a deep-seated anger mixed with disgust over the result of poor training, planning, and political interference (insertion of British authority lines over American forces), exacerbated by partisan media coverage. I will always admire Mark Clark for his tenacity, and his bucking of the afore noted impediments. There was also an underestimation of the two German Generals (Rommel and Kesselring) whom we faced on our bloody, costly climb up the Italian boot. The only solace I have when I think about it is that the Axis was beginning to internally suffer both politically and economically. There was also dissention between Rommel and Kesselring, but their leadership was undeniably superb. Clark had to make this attack with only three divisions, against their initial four, due to the demand for American, Canadian and Australian forces to support European action. Back in July, Mussolini was deposed, and Italy, under the rule of Victor Emanuel III, surrendered unconditionally, although el Duce would be rescued by Germany, temporarily. Essentially, he was done, and the Mediterranean was completely under Allied control. The German generals were not particularly concerned about the loss of Italian combatants, because they considered them almost useless, in any case. Russia was moving westward, and the Allies were bombing Germany from the east. The loss of Russia as an ally to the Axis powers was more strategically important, as was the internal conflict among the German military hierarchy over the Fuhrer's leadership in this death struggle of their nation. The British General (Alexander) placed in command over Operation Avalanche was a battle hardened WWI vet who had gone "over the top" in that conflict over 30 times, and was wounded during the war. He was no fool, but was constrained to follow the orders given, and certainly understood the hardship the operation would meet, and frustrated by being powerless to attenuate it. The landings were disastrous, and wave after wave of our landings were met with flares to highlight us as targets, steady machine gun fire, mortar fire, and 88mm barrages, illuminated in flight by bright light, and trailed by amber flaming tails before they hit the beach or the landing craft, or the DUKWs, hauling artillery and crews. Our casualties were practically incalculable initially, but later, the medics lined up the bodies with their feet showing out from under blankets or tarps, neatly in row after row. By about 0600, the German Luftwaffe hit, and the driving objective was to find cover, and find it fast. It had been the longest three hours of my life, and though we had run straight into the teeth of resistance, scrounging ammo from the fallen as we went, it was certainly not a walk in the park, and we were only about 400 yards inland at the farthest point.

Finally, Admiral Hewitt was able to move the fleet in, thanks to the excellence of the minesweepers, and could lay down more effective supportive fire. I wasn't particularly fond of the smoke shells fired to help obscure the landing craft and troops. It made no difference, really, to the German machine gun and artillery fire, because that just swept from side to side, mowing down anyone unlucky enough to be in its path. We were able to advance after the carnage, and it was rumored that Clark moved to block a pincer movement to cut the American forces off from the British. By the 11th, we were about 11 miles inland, and we heard that Gen Clark stopped the Germans by throwing everything he had into battle, including cooks, admin personnel, a band, orderlies, and his two artillery battalions into a pitched battle, slowing and eventually stopping the Germans. We got Ridgeway and the 82nd Airborne back by the 13th. The conflict between Rommel and Kesselring kept the release of the 24th Panzer Division for Kesselring to use against us on the 9th, which might have turned the tables at a critical point in the American beach head and inland advance. After the final defeat of the German Army at Salerno, and the threat that it posed to his rear induced Kesselring to disengage by 16 September. Rommel and Kesselring were still at odds, because Rommel wanted to abandon Rome. Kesselring did not. Neither did Hitler. Hitler relieved Rommel, promoting Kesselring to complete command in Italy. Hitler also moved two divisions to the Eastern Front and Kesselring moved units to Southern Italy.

Sometimes when I think about that particular ten days of unremitting Hell, I can smell the greasy smoke of a tank burning, and hear the screams of the German soldiers dying in Hell inside them, as well as my own wounded either calling out for help or uttering that shattering death moan as they gave up the ghost. At other times, I visualize again the enormous castle of over a thousand rooms, built in about 170 BC, where the Allied Headquarters was established. Every now and again, someone would drop one of those heavy porcelain plates on the stone floor, and it sounded like a gunshot, so everyone of us who had been in combat would dive for cover. I remember clearly that after another seven days in Hell, I was weary, miserable, and oblivious to the charm of what was left of the beautiful countryside. I just wanted to go home, at least for a rest, or even anywhere there was no smoke, no explosions, no whistle of incoming rounds, and no more blood pouring on the thirsty ground. My fog was punctuated by the necessity of writing up the casualty lists, preparing the notifications for the families, and getting the wounded in line for either evacuation or sufficient treatment to return to duty. I still can hear things in my mind, like Highway 18, Tobacco Factory, or see the flaming packs, set afire from tracers, as the desperate soldiers shed them to avoid being burned to death, the smoke pots sending up their choking attempt at shielding the troops from the view of the well situated, pre-placed German vantage points, the clouds of smoke from the destroyers, sent to shore in the same futile attempt, the smell of burning flesh, images of the long shallow graves dug for those who would never go home, and the little tags, call "52s" by the medics, attached to the wounded by little metal clips. The worst image is sometimes having to follow my troops into battle, threatening to shoot them myself if they ran.

Dorothy A Adams

It was then that I remembered the poem by Henley called Invictus. I played over and over in my mind to distract me from more morose thoughts. I still do it, even as time and distance has separated me from that and subsequent battlefields.

Invictus

By William Henley

Black as the night that covers me,
Black as the Pit from pole to pole,
I thank whatever gods may be
For my unconquerable soul.

In the fell clutch of circumstance
I have not winced nor cried aloud.
Under the bludgeonings of chance
My head is bloody, but unbowed.

Beyond this place of wrath and tears
Looms but the Horror of the shade,
And yet the menace of the years
Finds, and shall find, me unafraid.

It matters not how strait the gate,
How charged with punishments the scroll.
I am the master of my fate:
I am the captain of my soul.

It's too long to be chiseled on a headstone, but just right to be etched on a heart. It brings me great comfort, as it did then, just as the hope and confidence of the troops could salve my own conflicted mind. At future battles, I would recite it to my troops before we engaged in battle, and some of them even scribbled it down to keep with them. Every little scrap of hope and every prayer is important when embarking on an unknown, unpredictable journey, unlike you have ever known before, or ever will again in its scope and finite detail, along paths prowled by the ever present specter of the Grim Reaper. As I have said before, Salerno is very hard for me to think about, because the injuries I received there cannot be seen. Only felt.

But my trial was yet to end. I would go away from the city of Naples, from the beautiful, sometimes purple shape of Mount Vesuvius, and from the vision of the Italian people, confused, tearful, and terrified, to another bloodbath in another scenic, beautiful creation of the Almighty, to see it desecrated by the yawning maw of mankind's inhumanity to man. Someday, I thought, I will go home, but in a sense, I will never return.

Chapter Twenty – Five – News from Home

No matter where the road may lead, follow it, you must, toward the final tolling bell that turns you back into dust. Every footfall along that road moves to the drummer's beat, accompanied in strength and cadence, by millions of marching feet.

 The hands of the clock were relentlessly moving, and occasionally I would receive some letters from family and friends. I kept the tattered bits of them until this last, final evolution of the downward spiral of my life. My little daughter was walking and talking, and I received a picture of her with her maternal grandparents in a letter from my wife. I learned that one of the young men I had met through my wife's family, who would later become a brother in law, Wallace Scott Patterson, (Scottie), was a navigator-bombardier on the Flying Fortresses bombing Germany, and another, "Junie" Yates, (which stood for Junior), was a gunner on one of the same birds. Another future brother in law was in the Army artillery, but there weren't many details about that. The LaGrone daughters, including my wife Julienne, were finishing their college degrees. My grandmother was still living on Rice Street in Elkhart, Indiana, and I could tell that much of her coded messages had been redacted by those concerned with security. I wasn't sure whose security was in question, but many of her intended messages got through in her letters because I knew her so well. My young uncle Clifford was doing well, and supporting us in the civilian sector, though there weren't many details about that, and my also young Uncle Paul was a fighter pilot in the USAAF. My tiny little sister was still a truck mechanic, and her husband, a tool and die maker, was also supporting us in the civilian sector. Like any other soldier, I was enthralled with the very fact that I had letters from home. One of my cousins was headed my way to 5th Army, and I was unsure if that was good or bad news at that point in time. We were later to be reunited at Anzio, which hadn't happened yet. The Army creates abundant paperwork, and any lull in the combat operations was taken up with getting all the requisite pieces of papers completed, with the required number of copies, and either delivering or having it delivered to the correct offices within or near the required time limit. That, I am sure, has not changed, but may even have become more complex, as the bureaucracies have grown while the number of trained, armed troops have been shrunk again as I record my observations from a now long ago time. Some of the news I received was wonderful, but mostly it renewed the determination in my very soul to keep fighting, as they were, in their own ways, for our nation, our flag, our way of life. The completion of paperwork was punctuated by re-reading my letters, and training and integrating the reinforcements to my company, for our work was not done, and 1943 was almost over.

On the 16th of January, 1944, Gen mark Clark continued attack on Cassino against the 14th Panzercorp, but that is a little ahead of the story. Behind Cassino, at Anzio, Americans made a surprise landing to force Kesselring to bring in reinforcements from around Rome to strengthen his front. Gen Alexander, Commanding Officer of the 15th Army Group saw this operation as one to secure the beachhead and to cut off the German main communication center at Colli Laziali southeast of Rome, at the rear of Kesselring's 14th Corps. Clark directed Gen Lucas to seize, secure Anzio, and advance to Colli Laziali, which was short of Gen Alexander's intent. His intent had been to seize, secure and advance, in that order. Patton heard about it and was furious, but unable to intervene. It was fraught with lack of accurate strategic analysis and knowledge of the terrain or distances. Mountains dominate that landscape. But Gen Clark's approach might have been a result of his feeling that 5th Army had fought so long and so hard, that they deserved to take Rome, and at times he seemed somewhat possessive of it. But there were many more than the already almost 40,000 men to be killed or injured before he walked on the Appian Way, begun in Rome over 300 years before the birth of Christ. He was thought to be a very tough commander, and from his height might have seemed to look down on the members of his staff, with whom he was often impatient, but he also was seen frequently at the front, talking with the soldiers, encouraging and inspiring them. I thought at the time that it must be lonely with all those stars on his shoulder, knowing that to achieve the objectives we must achieve, many young men would die or be maimed for life. I was convinced that I would not like to carry that burden. My cousin, nicknamed Killer Crouch, because of his way with the ladies, had been made my 1st SGT, and we were on that beachhead at Anzio. Later I was to learn that the PT boat Gen Clark was on was shot up, and that Clark himself helped the helmsman get it out of harm's way, and got the wounded offloaded. Then he heard that the LST and other navy assets, in large numbers were to be moved out of the Mediterranean. That was certainly an ill wind in a burgeoning storm, because Kesselring was moving in reinforcements, and at the time had air superiority. One truly great event that I remember from that time was that during an air assault roughly a mile above the beachhead by German, a miracle occurred. A flight of American fighters waded in and shot down at least a dozen of the enemy aircraft that had been strafing our troops. Later on, they would become known as the Tuskeegee Airmen, but on that day, they were God's avenging angels, and I still don't give a damn what color they were. They put up one hell of a fight, as we were to go forth against about 70,000 battle tested Germans. Gen Truscott was with us, as were Darby's Rangers. Truscott refused to stay down after his leg was injured with shrapnel, which he simply had tweezed out, the leg bound, and then he hobbled about taking care of business. Names like Conca and Cisterna float into my memory when I remember those late days of January, along with the victories and setbacks. By January 30th, we had about 1,500 casualties, the Rangers and Truscott's infantry having been almost decimated.

    We were then moved to Cassino. Monte Cassino. That is one part of my war experience that haunts me, perhaps more intensely than any of the others. The Germans had fortified the huge monastery high on a steep precipice, where the abbey had been founded by St. Benedict centuries before. At first, we learned, the Benedictine monks had managed to get the invaders to let them remove much of the irreplaceable artifacts and art work to safety, facilitated by a German LTC, who had been an art historian in civilian life, although a significant portion of it was stolen along the way to Rome. The monks were at first allowed to retain a small portion of the first floor of the abbey, a chapel where they prayed almost constantly, and to shelter many terrified refugees for a time. Then Hitler ordered that the Germans would occupy the abbey itself, and nothing but the building could remain, so it became the pivotal point of the Gustav Line. It wasn't the first time it had been occupied, or even razed in its 15 century existence. Though St. Benedict's and his sister, Scholastica's bones may still be in their tomb, little was left to identify the abbey as a holy site by mid-February. It was a well-fortified command post with a commanding position, and German engineers had even leveled some farmhouses and outbuildings to provide better fields of fire. Pits for riflemen, bunkers, observation posts and nests for machine gunners were carved out around and in the heavy stone walls. Mortars were set up, along with other artillery, with steel shielding around them. Full preparation was made to make our lives even more miserable than they had already been the month before. The French were making some progress against other points in the Gustav Line, though their casualties were virtually astronomical. A couple of other strategically important sites at high elevations had been taken, but Monte Cassino still remained.

Dorothy A Adams

I cannot continue to describe the ordeal in great detail, as my hands are sweating, and my heart is thundering in my chest. The shortest this time is perhaps the best. Killer (my 1st SGT and cousin) and I were pinned down as we and our company inched up that ill-fated slope, but our company was following faithfully, and some of them dying hideously. I can hear their screams now, but above it all, I can hear Killer shrilling in that unmistakable death cry in my mind, as he did when he was literally cut in two by machinegun fire, and I could not even move to try to help him. From the time he was hit until he died was probably only seconds, and not long after that, the fountains of blood that had spewed up and spattered all over me stopped after covering the stock of my carbine with a red, slick, sticky, glistening coating. I was finally able to wriggle over close enough to check for a pulse, I think I found the carotid, and there was nothing. Then I heard my men crying out, asking what to do. There was a very slight lull in the firing, then a shell hit the machine gun nest that had us pinned down, so I ordered them to follow me, as I rose and began to run, about 200 yards, directly toward the abbey. They followed, but by then, about half of them lay dead or dying. Always at this point of remembering, I hear the words "cannon fodder" echoing in my mind, as it did then, and it is hard to make it stop. To make a long and bloody story short, we were the first to arrive at the entrance of the abbey, and by then, it had been pounded almost into rubble, corpses of their fallen mingled with our own, and the smell of blood, death and destruction hung in the air like a thick fog. I was amazed as a staggered to my feet and approached the open doorway to encounter a German officer, hands in the air, surrendering to me. My men fanned out, arms ready, but the German took me back to a sort of atrium where his men immediately put their hands on top of their heads, and I could see their weapons and "potato mashers," (grenades) stacked neatly to the sides. I ordered my men to round them up to go outside, and form a line of 2 x 2, and hold them there until I returned. I then herded the officer back into the small room we had passed just moments before. I drew my 0.45, and he immediately fell to his knees, took out his wallet, and began showing me pictures of his family, and begging, in perfect English that I spare him. I had intended to do so, but the sound of a gunshot outside, and blood on my hand from the holster of my side arm blacked out that thought, an evil rage took me in its grip, and I shot him between the eyes. I watched dispassionately as he crumpled and fell, gripping a cross he wore around his neck as he fell, spilling the contents of his wallet like a deck of cards on the floor at my feet. I went out, and we marched our prisoners down, down, down. They actually outnumbered us, but walked with heads down and shoulders slumping in the traditional aspect of the defeated, never turning their eyes toward me as I paced up and down the column to make sure that no one made a threatening move. As we went down, the medics were busily checking and tagging the fallen. It was many hours later, but during the short time after transferring the prisoners to be taken to a POW camp, I was numb, just doing things by the numbers, then retracing my steps to Killer's body, I sank down and just sobbed. I had left an NCO in charge, because I had no more lieutenants and had had the troops fall out, before I went to that place of everlasting misery, where I also prayed for the man whose life I had just brutally taken in one of the holiest places in Italy. I can never brush it away, nor expect that even the ever merciful God in Heaven will forgive me for that mortal sin, nor will I ever forgive myself, for the memory lives on with me, to be silenced only on the day I die. It had shattered that little place of peace I had in my soul, where I had always gone in times of extreme distress, which remains in disarray to this very day. I didn't even realize that I, too, had been wounded, but could not see the shrapnel embedded in my forehead, one piece of which had lodged up under my cheekbone, pressing against my optic nerve. That would not be discovered until many years later, when it finally worked its way down and out of my cheek, but I did know I was blinded in my right eye. The medics came and tagged me, too, and slammed Killer's dog tag into his teeth as the corpse would be removed later. I was later dragged away, treated, and sent to the US to pick up another company.

Later, I would make up stories about having Killer with me when my new company was formed and trained. He was, in a very real sense. I heard that we had actually broken the Gustav Line by taking Monte Cassino, but that only brought faint, fleeting relief. My grandmother sent me a letter saying that notification of Killer's death had been received and that I had signed it. I do not remember having filled out the paperwork, but I must have done. His gear had been sent home, and my Aunt and Uncle were devastated by the loss. Somehow she had found out that I would be returning stateside, and hoped that I might be able to visit, or might be kept in the United States for the remainder of the war. I knew that Kesselring had essentially closed out the Gustave Line, and had moved his assets to the east, below the Po River Valley, and near Rome, but at the time, I simply didn't care any more. I did briefly wonder if anyone had collected the German LTC's belongings, and if his family had been notified of his death. But only briefly. I spent a couple of weeks being treated for my physical wounds, but nothing was or could be done about the emotional trauma, or the battle fatigue which sapped my emotional and spiritual strength. I would never be the same person again, and the only living soul I would ever tell this tragic story of irrational ferocity to would be my daughter when she was about 11 years old. She held me and comforted me as I cried even then, and with a wisdom far beyond her years, told me that the prisoners might not have been so docile while being marched away if their leader had been present, even trussed up. She may have been right; that was years after the incident, and no such thoughts had entered my mind as I irrationally and inhumanely murdered another warrior, who had fought for his country, his family, and been concerned for the welfare of his own troops. Forgiveness didn't come, even in face of that rationalization. It never will.

Chapter Twenty – Six – Cannon Fodder

The injuries we can see will spill the body's blood as it pools, encrusts, and dries, but the tearing of the soul can be seen only in the eyes of those who have done or seen the battles that are not yet won. Perhaps they never will be as time just travels on.

I arrived at Ft. Benning, GA, and was informed that I would be commander of a unit composed of "lifers" from prison, who had been promised that if they served honorably in the US Army, and survived to come home, they would be pardoned and freed. That may seem shocking, but it was mildly jarring after all the experiences of war had gnawed away at my sensitivity to any such disjunctures. I would do my duty. The training and preparation to rejoin the battles ahead was to last approximately six weeks, and in private, I held a handful of soil up, reverently praying in thanks that I had gotten to see it again. The reddish color of it reminded me of East Texas, where I had the things most precious in the world to me, my wife and daughter. She would find a way to come visit me, and bring my little toddler with her. That would ultimately result in my only son, whom I would not see until after the war was over.

Training hardened criminals for battle was very different from training raw recruits, and in some respects, it was easier. They were afraid of snakes and completely distrustful of armadillos, panicked at the sound of wild turkeys squawking at the early morning runs, confused by the thought of polishing boots, but delighted at the "comfortable" bunks and beautiful (temporary construction) barracks buildings. They excelled at hand to hand combat, physical training, and many were excellent marksmen. Discipline improved rapidly when they found out that their commander (me) had for five years been the middle weight 5th Army boxing champion, but also was familiar with standard street fighting. When I had a disciplinary problem with one of them, I would simply take them out behind a building or in a sheltered area by the Chattahoochee River, with witnesses, take off my rank, and tell them "take your best shot, then I will kick the living shit out of you." It only took a few times, and I won all of them, for the word to get through that it was best to obey orders, keep their noses clean, and get on with becoming the best infantrymen in the Army. They were spooked when they heard that I had been offered glider pilot training, but noticeably relieved when I refused and chose to stay with them. Training equipment back then was in short supply, but we were very inventive with it. My wife during her visit was not impressed with soldiers popping out of the brush with broomsticks and mop handles shouting "Bang, bang, you're dead!" But my little one supposedly thought that wearing a sign saying "I am a tank," and running down the road was not only funny, but something to which she should aspire. I never heard how that panned out, but I certainly heard about it from my wife, to which I replied that it was OK, because some day she would be a soldier, and maybe even a tanker. When I would return to the Guest House, tired, grubby, and grumpy, she would do the unspeakable of taking a wash cloth and wiping down my boots, dusting off my brass and clothing, and making a general mess of "cleaning up Daddy," then asking me in a pleading tone if I really had to go spend the night with all those soldiers, because they were already "grow-ups." I would wait until she fell asleep before slipping out the door to return to our area to check on the troops. Sometimes, I would slip back to spend some time with my wife, but was back on duty by Reveille, for formation, the morning run, PT, and chow. I always ate with my troops, and somehow that made a difference, too. Many of them were blacks, and they were nothing short of amazed that I would sit at the same table with them, or answer questions they asked as we were seated. Of course they would always complain that when I had finished my food, I would call the table to attention and have the nearest NCO march them out to wait in formation until the entire company was present for duty.

Then we went to training, all day, every day. Then I went back to Italy with them, but received orders to keep them in leg irons until we were past the 9-mile limit at sea. When the troops were informed of this, one big fellow asked why that was, and all eyes were upon me when I answered that it was being done to insure that they didn't desert and try to escape. One young troop erupted in indignation, saying it was the best food and bed he had ever had, and this time when he was shot at, he could damn sure shoot back and hit what he aimed at. Another said that he didn't need leg irons, because he couldn't "swim a lick." I knew this to be close to the truth, since we'd had to fish him out of the Chattahoochee several times during training exercises where soldiers had to swim with their gear and packs on their backs. My 1st SGT let them all know that there weren't many people on earth that could swim nine miles in the Atlantic Ocean, and not get washed up on the shore dead as a door nail, even without leg irons. I waited for some one of them to ask how door nails got dead, but they passed on that one, but wanted to know if they would ever get a day off. A smart aleck veteran, Platoon SGT, who, like me, had been reassigned to this unit after being at Monte Cassino, gave an appropriate reply:

"When they stop shooting and trying their best to kill your ass, or the tanks run out of gas, you might get a few minutes off."

Memories were triggered by his remarks, and for a few uncomfortable moments, I was back in Anzio. Things I had been busy burying in my memory, like Hell's Half Acre and the Valley of Death, from that beachhead. In later years, it would be called many things, but it was my first experience with that retrograde reality, foisted into my consciousness. It lasted only minutes, but it was terrifying, and I regained my composure by forcing my thoughts to facts as I came to know them later on. The battle for Italy was the longest and most difficult of the entire war for the

Allies, and much of that was because of the incredibly long supply lines, and the division of it to support other operations. In addition, the terrain and bad weather seemed to favor the Germans, though they had to shift forces of their battle hardened troops to replace the Italians when Italy had unconditionally surrendered on 8 September 1943, and Naples had fallen on the 1st of October. Anzio began on 22 January 1944, only 25 miles from Rome. The Allied armies finally entered Rome on 4 June 1944, leaving behind thousands of dead and wounded, with the Nazis fighting desperately to halt the advance and cut us off from Rome. This is all now suppressed in my weary mind, and only rears its ugly head when triggered by a chance remark or fleeting vision. I could instantaneously smell the smoke, sulfur, and almost unbreathable dust clogged air, hear the artillery, the machine gun fire, and remember the leaflets that the USAAF had dropped on that stately, enormous, ancient abbey before it was bombed into heaps of rubble. I brushed it away, as I could not let that haunting domination which arose in that smoldering crucible that had flared to the very hottest, glowing, ravenous inferno of Hell take possession of me. It burned away my moral compass, my integrity, and so charred my very soul that I had done the unspeakable in that never to be forgotten instant at Monte Casino, but I had other responsibilities with the new assignment, the new troops, the new battles to win. I will always try to suppress it, with varying success for the remainder of my existence.

 From Rome, the Allies would slowly move northward, and the composition of that polyglot concoction of troops from all over the world, called by some news moguls "the fighting men of the UN" would move forward. To call them multinational would be an understatement. There were even Brazilians, and a Jewish Brigade from Palestine. Though the Allies fought long and hard in a literal uphill battle, the victory we were to attain there was critical to the overall effort, and my company fought valiantly, being well and frequently used as cannon fodder. But we weren't at the Po River Valley yet. The ocean crossing was difficult, and it took 12 days, that voyage to their ultimate trial. It was a troop ship, and the seas were not kind. There was no roll stabilization to prevent the anger of the Atlantic during our passage. I spent much of my time down in the hold with my men, and the sea sickness was rampant, to say the least. The air was foul, and the floors were slick from vomit, but we made it across, despite the remnants of the U-boat infestation, which had essentially been wiped out by the end of 1943, but there were still "lone wolves" occasionally found in the sea lanes. Improvements in radar had helped detect them, as well as spotting enemy planes. The new American and British submarines as well as battle ships now rolling off the production lines of shipyards provided us better protection than had been possible earlier. That crucial freeing of the logistic lines in the Atlantic, marked by tremendous positive impact of the massive US support in materiel and manpower was critical to the European Theater. It ultimately provided bases from which air assault against Germany could be ferociously mounted. Even so, the fighting in Italy continued to the last few months of the war in Europe. From all those days of brutal, fierce fighting, only nine of my company of lifers survived to return home. I was yet to be released, but discovered that on their repatriation, they were returned to their prison cells, from combat all the way through the Po River Valley.

Knowledge of that turn of events probably was the beginning of the end of my military career, because I began to intensively review both military and civil law. I had gained my law degree over the course of my chaotic life, but now studied at every possible instant with a vigor I had never had before. In the last gasps of the war, I noted the constant push by the Russians on what the Germans would call the "Eastern Front, and the major campaigns of bombing ground operations then closing in an ever tightening vice on Germany made me very uneasy. However, I was intellectually and emotionally consumed by my search for ways to correct the injustice to my warriors, most of whom gave the last ounce of strength and effort to each mission we were assigned. I submitted paperwork to transfer to the JAG Corps, and though I knew it would take an inordinately long time to be approved, I knew I had work to do. Even before leaving the Theater, I was sent on various missions, because of my skill with a camera, to include an 8mm Bell& Howell movie camera, to record the results of events in that war ravaged countryside. That included some brief episodes with the Navy and Marines at their specific sites, selected areas of the Pacific which were still heavily embattled, and Eastern Europe, into which the Russians under Stalin were rapidly advancing. I think they would now place that under the Civil Affairs branch, but then it was just "Gene, get your cameras. You're going to "_____(designated destination)." It was on one of those jaunts that I learned that back in Anzio, when the Luftwaffe took out the 95th Field Evacuation Hospital, a number of the medics I had once trained, it seemed like a lifetime ago, in Mississippi, were casualties. Briefly I tallied up the casualties from the Italian Campaign in my tortured thoughts, and it seemed to me that we lost about 75,000, and the Germans lost about 75,000. It was essentially a generation of young men in each country, and didn't even count those lost in the Pacific or the rest of Europe. It was devastation that defied all, even twisted logic, and would torment all of us who were still above ground until our final journey into eternity. During that interim, I researched how to get justice for my few remaining soldiers with whom a solemn bargain and promise upon fulfillment had been made. It would take me a year after I was repatriated, and later RIF'd to get the pardons officially issued to eight of the nine survivors. The ninth one died in jail. It was a travesty, but I did what I could, and at least, I thought, if another major conflict broke out, I wouldn't be an Infantry Officer any more. I was deathly tired of beachheads,

Dorothy A Adams

foxholes, the scream of artillery shells, the hum of attacking aircraft, the smell of blood, the horrid wails of the wounded or dying, and lines upon lines upon lines of shallow graves from which some would never be returned home, and perhaps not even be identified. I noticed that I had sprouted some silver gray hair, sprinkled among the black, and looked at the world through eyes under a furrowed and scarred brow. I thought of Thanatopsis, that old poem, and wondered if when I dawned my robe to begin the journey down that long corridor into the silent halls of death, if I would meet the throngs of warriors from both sides of a near genocide of the human race. As I prayed that night on the troop ship which would carry me home, I asked God to forgive us all, and could I please not have to spend eternity in purgatory, or go into the extinction of Hell, where I probably belonged.

Chapter Twenty – Seven – Home at Last

Sometimes there is no way home, if home ever existed, for all the paths you've trod have become completely twisted. There are no road signs within your mind that point the way to what you left behind...left as one thing, transformed to another, because fate is a fickle mother.

Home. I did get a leave. I did get to meet with other members of the family into which I had married. I did get to contact and later visit my grandmother and mother in Indiana. There was joy in the arrival in Lufkin, Texas, and virtual ecstasy in the welcome we all received. We were met at a house on 3rd Street in Lufkin, where our loved ones waited with open, eager arms. We had travelled in uniform, so it was a mutual celebration of the ended conflict, and we didn't care if our brass got mussed or gig lines were askew. We just accepted all the hugs and kisses, and returned the same. It was almost unlimited joy. My heart swelled in my chest, and at that moment, all the horrible memories I had just gathered, like nests of anguish in my mind, were banished in the unbelievable tsunami of both pride and relief at this homecoming it had often been doubtful that I would ever experience. This is what we had fought for, and it was certainly well worth it.

My mother in law had moved the household into town due to the tragic illness of Mr. LaGrone, who was still suffering from the effects of a catastrophic stroke. He, however, held his head up high, and welcomed all of us home, all the warmth of the world reflected in his eyes. Though it was a shock to see how his debilitating illness had transformed his body, it was clear that the strong, highly intelligent mind was still intact. He could not speak in that sonorous, powerful voice of his any more, but his words were well chosen, and emanated from a body twisted and painfully transformed into a pajama clad prison. I reflected that it was a punishment that I could not wish on my worst enemy, but he was cheerful and reflected the gladness that we had all returned home. Present were Joel Parrott, a brother-in-law, Scott Patterson, soon to be a brother-in-law, and the undauntable, tiny powerhouse, Aunt May. It was a parade of green into the arms of those who had served, too, in their unflinching support for us during the war. The LaGrone daughters, all of them, were beautiful, but none more lovely than Mrs. LaGrone, who stood quietly by, her competent hands folded into her apron, a smile lighting up her face. My little wife was tugging at my arm for me to see my son, who had been born while I was gone, and my 3 ½ year old daughter who had scribbled notes to me, most of which would not reach me until the military postal service finally caught them up to me.

John. My son, John was the result of that brief visit I had made when I came back to train and pick up my new troops, it seemed like an eon ago. He was still an infant, and had been placed on a bed in a lower bedroom, with his sister. When I went into the room, he was peeking around from behind his sister, with great, round, blue eyes. She didn't make a move, except to put an arm back to protect the little golden haired boy, and her eyes regarded me with both curiosity and obvious wariness. I knelt down beside the bed, and held my arms out to her, but she scooted back just an inch or two, shoving her brother behind her.

"You were kissing my mother," she said sharply, looking into my eyes with an accusation in hers.

"Yes, my sweetheart. I am your Daddy," I said, with joy in every word.

"No," she snapped. "You are not my Daddy, because my Daddy doesn't have any gray hair. His hair is black!"

I sat back on my haunches and swallowed hard to hide my shock. Then I remembered that there were now a few scattered

What Price Honor, Memoir of Eugene Adams

silver hairs in my hair. I felt the sting of tears, as they flowed out of my eyes and down my cheeks, watching as she crawled forward on that pink chenille bedspread, and reached out to me.

"Please don't cry. My Daddy is a soldier fighting in the war. You are a soldier, and soldiers don't cry," she asserted, full of confidence as she shook her head full of blonde curls, and stared at me in sorrow. Little John crawled up to her, and again peeked out to see what was going on. He was blonde, too, with the same color hair as my mother had. It was golden, and very straight. He looked sturdy and was very curious, but not particularly brave at that moment. Little did I know that one day he would be taller than I am, and would join the Navy as a common seaman, after he told me that he didn't want the appointment to West Point I had worked so hard to get for him. Both of them would serve, and both would live to tell about it. In that moment, though, all I knew is that there were more trials ahead of us all.

Then, I simply rolled up on my knees, then onto my feet, sweeping them both into my arms as I did so. Once I had them, one on each side of my body, she wrinkled her little pug nose, then buried her face in my neck.

"You are my Daddy," she exclaimed. "You smell like him. Most of your hair is black. I'm sorry, Daddy. I love you."

As she did this, little John continued to look at me, but regarded my brass with possessive little hands, then smiled as he planted a very wet kiss on my cheek.

That was the hardest part of coming home, and at the same time, the best. I have wondered over the years how often a similar scenario played out as we all came back from the far corners of the world. For a few moments, I remembered some smells from my own lifetime, and realized that it is a sensitive, highly accurate part of our memory system. My mind spun back to my own childhood, and I could smell again the delicious aromas of my grandmother baking bread, my grandfather Adams' farm with the sweet, heavy smell of the ploughed earth, my mother and some sweet smells of perfume, and many, many more things that I could not consciously forget. When I turned, little Farah, the youngest of the LaGrone daughters, was standing in the doorway, staring with her large, dark eyes and twisting a long dark braid with one hand. Suddenly, Aunt May pushed by her, and demanded her time with the little ones. I reluctantly released them to her, and watched as they headed on their way to the living room, the young girl carrying my son, and my daughter bouncing along with "Ever May," informing her that her "Daddy Gene" had come home. It wouldn't be long until there would be more babies in that family, and I would have two more daughters to add to that tribe. That was the future, and my war experiences were the past, as were all the days I had been away from my family. It was difficult to get acquainted with the present which presented itself to me.

Aunt May, who was a tiny dynamo, was in the living room, letting my daughter comb her hair. It was absolutely hilarious, because the little one was babbling about giving her Great Aunt an Atom Bomb hairdo, which consisted of combing those dark locks up in wisps, sticking out as far as possible. The strangest thing was to hear a very young child prattle on about one of the most controversial events in that time. I didn't know that much about the conflict in the far east, to include the Philippines, but I had heard of the massive destruction wrought by the dropping of two "atomic bombs" on two cities in Japan, to bring the Japanese to their knees. It would be debated for years, but from my standpoint, it brought the Japanese to the surrender they might never have willingly accepted, and the cost would have been as much as a million lives on either side…two million lives lost with the ultimate result of an eventual surrender by the Japanese at the end.

What Price Honor, Memoir of Eugene Adams

The totals of casualties, mostly civilian, had yet to come out, and I tucked back my silent thoughts about how much had been lost already, in both the Pacific and European campaigns. It was staggering, and this homecoming was no place in which to be staggered. I needed desperately just to enjoy it, and hopefully not see any more action where brutality and blood ran together in the self-destruction of mankind. It flickered through my mind then that the only reason that casualties had not been as great in the conflicts of the past, with the possible exception of the Civil War, was that we now had the capability to kill more efficiently, with the frightening prospect of continued advances in exterminating large numbers of human beings. I said a small prayer that it would not happen, but definitely didn't have any confidence that my prayer would be answered. Strange. Standing there in a safe environment, still in uniform, I wondered about the possibility of ensuing conflicts and involuntarily shuddered as I brushed the thought away.

My reverie had been interrupted by a loud, angry little voice. My daughter drew back her arm and threw something at Aunt May, and it hit her squarely in the forehead, then fell into her lap. She threw back her head and laughed, while little Dorothy stomped her foot in anger.

"I said a quarter," the little girl said angrily, while stomping her small foot. "That is not a quarter, and I don't want it!" she fumed.

I strode toward the small combatant, and Aunt May intervened. "No, Gene. She is right, it wasn't a quarter. It was a silver dollar I was going to give her for my hair-do." She chortled some more and held her arms out to the little termagant, saying "Come here, DA. I will give you that quarter now. My mistake, sweetheart."

When I looked at May's hair, which was a complete mess, I almost laughed, until I saw the red mark on her forehead. It was a perfect imprint of a silver dollar, and the impact must have been painful as well as unexpected. May looked up at me and laughed again, looking at me and nodding to the little imp in her lap. When I looked down, DA, as she would be called for years, had one eyebrow raised and her head cocked slightly to one side and was staring intently at her great Aunt. It was a shock to my system to realize that I, too, had an eyebrow cocked in exactly the same way.

"Like father, like daughter," Ever May said, as she fished out a quarter from her purse, handing it over to DA, whose face erupted into an angelic smile, and whose little arms wrapped themselves tightly around her benefactor's neck. May responded with "Shoo, little angel. I have to go change clothes now. I want to get out of this uniform for a while. It's hot."

The little one fairly danced, taking the good Sgt's hand and piping up with "Can I have it, Aunt May? Can I have the uniform? It won't take me long to be big enough to wear it. May I please have it?"

"In good time, my little friend. In good time, but right now, I need to go quickly, and you need to visit with all these other soldiers who have just come home. I will be back down in a few minutes, after I hang up my uniform."

I didn't really know how prophetic her words would be about DA becoming a soldier at some distant time for some unanticipated conflict, but somehow as I stored it in my mind, I knew deep down that it was true. So I swept her up quickly and headed for the kitchen. The kitchen back then was always the central meeting place for families, and it was already noisy and crowded.

"Can I really, Daddy? Can I really have a uniform? I want to be a soldier, too. How big do I have to be?"

"Well," I replied, we will have to see. Right now we have to talk to these other soldiers. This is your chance to learn."

She was only slightly mollified, but turned her attention to the group of smiling handsome people gathered there, and it is an understatement that her ears were definitely tuned in. She squirmed away from me and went to stand by her Aunt Dorothy, who was listening intently, too. Then she went to her grandfather's side, next to that rocking chair he liked to sit in, and held his withered hand. I later realized those were two of her three places of comfort. The third was her Grandmother LaGrone, who also stood listening and periodically refreshing the iced tea being drunk by those raising the cacophony of excited voices, missing nothing, from the words spoken to the body language of the members of that group.

Julie, my wife, who sat nearby, cradling Little John, was the breathtaking image of maternal strength and beauty. Her light henna curls fell around her shoulders, and her beautiful green eyes flickered between the members of the crowd and the baby in her arms. She, too, was listening, making no comment, but nodding from time to time. It took a while before I could catch her eye, and when I did, I virtually melted into a heap of both pride and affection. Yes, this is what we had fought for, and would fight again if it was necessary to do so. I did not know then what lay ahead, but was totally enamored with what was, then, in that precious and now elusive time. We had both changed, and would continue to do so, and so had the nation. Our President Franklin Delano Roosevelt, the only president in the history of our nation to serve more than two terms, had died, and Harry S. Truman was the President of the United States now. He became my favorite president of all times, because he fought for us, the people of the nation, and was not fooled by Stalin in the least. Nor was he enamored of Churchill, or of MacArthur, who would continue to agitate for the foreseeable future. He objected strongly to the almost instantaneous move by Congress to begin chopping the military, all branches, and to the abrupt discharge of so many troops, who were returning for an unimaginably horrific experience to no jobs. I listened to the conversation around the table, and found that not all in that gathering agreed with me, but no matter. I had things to do and people to see, and I believed then that my military career was not over. I took an extended leave, enjoyed my family, and did some farming at the old LaGrone farm. That was a cleansing experience, punctuated by getting on with a duty I would accomplish with great difficulty for my last troops.

Then came the shock. I was informed that I would be RIF'd, which means caught in the Reduction In Force mandated by Congress. It was 1948, and already so many soldiers, sailors, airmen, and marines had been summarily received a "welcome home, and we don't need you anymore, so goodbye." I talked to everybody I could think of who had any pull with the military to at least let me stay on, even as an enlisted man. I finally got my wish, and I think that it took Vinegar Joe Stillwell's recommendation to keep me on, if I would accept an assignment to the Occupation Forces in Germany, and bring my cameras along. Little Dorothy was already 6 years old, and in the second grade already. She had been going to a school called St. Anne's, and had done amazingly well. She was absolutely worshipful of her school Principal, a Father Julien. I found out that Fr. Julien had been a POW of the Japanese in the Philippines, and had narrowly escaped death as a result, but had returned weighing only about 50 lbs, yet still had a great love for humanity. When I had met him, a small man in black robes, it seemed to me that there was a halo of light around him, moving along and surrounding him as he walked. He had a soft voice, and snow white hair. Dorothy's other favorite was Sister Nicholas, whom she often mentioned, talking about the musical voice and the beautiful hands Sister had. They both were concerned when I told them that I would be taking my family to

Germany with me in the near future, but wished us all a safe journey, and promised to pray for us. They recommended that I keep my daughter in a Catholic school, telling me that there were many in Germany, which I later found to be true. I felt lucky that I could still stay in the Army, and that there would be some continuity for the education of my precocious daughter. When I told my mother-in-law about their recommendations, as well as my concern about putting Dorothy into a German Catholic school, because she wouldn't be able to understand anything due to a language barrier, Mrs. LaGrone laughed. She called Dorothy into the kitchen, and began speaking to her in German. Dorothy answered in German, smiling up at her grandmother. I was astounded, but Mrs. LaGrone assured me that even if we were transferred to France or Italy, the little curmudgeon would have very little difficulty with language. She told me that the way she had met Mr. LaGrone was that he was searching for a tutor for German, which was a requirement for his degree program, so she had become his tutor and later his wife. Later on, I found that my daughter not only spoke German, but easily passed for German as well, probably because she is such a duke's mixture of blood lines, as most Americans are.

Chapter Twenty – Eight – The RIF Effects

There is an old Irish ballad called "When Johnny Comes Marching Home Again," which is supposed to be nearly 500 years old. However, things are no different now, nor will they be in the future…

I wasn't as unfortunate as so very many of my fellow soldiers, because when I reported in to Ft. Benning, I was informed that I had been reduced in rank to E-7 with diamond device…First Sergeant. It would later be increased to E-8, still with the diamond device. That was so much better than many of us who returned from battle, with spirits high from the victory knocked into the dust by the brutal demilitarization which was dictated by Congress. But there was at least a mission for me. I would proceed to in processing, while my family would be in family housing undergoing medical evaluation and updating of their immunizations prior to embarkation. Things were moving very fast.

My wife and children were following, and the housing we were assigned was in a series of small trailer houses up on a hill. It definitely wasn't anything my wife was used to, and there were some problems with it. I did manage to get her and the children moved down to guest housing on post, which was better, but certainly not elegant. I continued my in-briefings on the mission I was assigned to, and also the information on our impending transport to Germany.

I was to join the Occupation Forces in Bremen, Germany, which is about 17 km from the port of Bremerhaven, and along the Weser River. I was to learn later that Bremen and Bremerhaven are actually considered the same city, and "Bremerhaven" means harbor of Bremen. But that is a detail. There was one regiment, among other units sent over to occupy Germany, which was stationed in Bremen, and I belonged to that regiment. Housing was quite adequate, as I remember it, and we were provided with a housekeeper due to the fact that my wife was ill by the time we arrived. She had come from Texas by train, with our four children, to Ft. Benning, and from there, would join me on the troop ship to go to Germany. Her youngest sister had accompanied her to help with the little ones, the youngest of which was six months old during that journey. We were at Benning for about another six months before we boarded a troop ship to go to Germany, and Julie didn't do well during that voyage. It takes nine to ten days on one of those ships to make a trans-Atlantic crossing, and she and the three little ones were seasick most of the time. However, Dorothy was neither seasick nor easily contained in the cabin they were in. She would get out and roam the vessel, asking questions of the sailors, and generally making a pest of herself, as many six year old children will do. But the sailors were generally amused, and taught her what a stern and a keel were, and what kinds of knots they were tying, but they did worry about her being washed overboard, because she was absolutely fearless. It wasn't really anything brought to my attention, because I had been spending most of my time during duty hours down with the troops who were being transported with us, and we did have a pretty bad storm when we were mid-Atlantic. During the storm, the hulk of a ship which had been sunk, or partially so, was seen about 250 yards from our sea lane, and everyone was crowding around to see it, even with the rough seas and high waves. Little Dorothy decided that since there were so many adults crowding around the railings, she couldn't see, so she took her little brother, went up the stairs to where the Captain was viewing the ship through field glasses, and asked to see through his "glasses," too. He did let her do that, but demanded that I be brought up to get her and her brother. She had given him my name, rank and serial number, so that day I got a chewing out about children wandering unsupervised on a ship during rough seas, but he smiled and said that she wasn't much trouble, but other children and adults might try to follow her example. When she looked up at me, with question marks in those eyes, she merely commented that she didn't know what kind of ship got "burped" up out of the ocean. The Captain ruffled her hair and said that it was a Merchant Marine ship, and gave me that look of "take this kid and get out of here."

I took my errant offspring back down to the cabin where my family was quartered during the voyage. When we got to the door, she pulled back, shielding her brother behind her. She begged that they not be put in there, and said it was "stinky." I was a little impatient with them, and opened the door anyway, and was almost knocked down by the stench. The ship was still pitching as we inched through the storm, and Little John was clutching his stomach.

"Don't barf, Johnny. Please swallow hard," came a little voice behind me, and I saw Dorothy pull him closer to her in protective arms.

I told them to stay there and not to move, as I entered the cabin. There were some containers, I was later told were "emesis basins" sitting around, and they had not been emptied. There was evidence of where the vomitus had missed any kind of container at all. I emptied the emesis basins in the toilet, rinsed them, and turned them upside down in the sink to finish draining. I looked, but there was no disinfectant, or any rags to clean up the mess. I went back out and took the little ones with me to find someone who might get me something to clean up the cabin, and one sailor just told me not to worry. He'd see that it got done, and that he knew my wife was very seasick most of the time. He told me where to go to get the medic to give me something to help her. I went back to collect my children, and then on to that mission for some meds. While we were going along the causeway, my daughter told me that the reason she would leave the cabin is that she couldn't stand all the vomiting, and quizzed me on why some people did that and others didn't. She was still questioning the matter when we got to the medic, and he took over the explanation, obviously pleased with the questions of the little termagant. He told me to bring my wife to him so he could explain about the medicine and about the necessity to remain hydrated, but I knew that would be a tough sell with Julie. I agreed to bring her at the first opportunity, and Dorothy said that she would tell her mother, too. I gritted my teeth, and hoped that she wouldn't, because Julie would probably get angry and slap her. I got her aside when we got back to the cabin, and the sailor was just leaving the cabin when we got there. I thanked him, and was grateful that the smell coming out of the door was more of the green soap we used to use back then, instead of the stench of vomit. He let me know he had opened one of the portholes so there would be some air in the cabin for a while, and that I should shut it in about half an hour.

He smiled and looked down at Miss Blue Eyes, as he called her. "Are you gonna come out for your walk with me in the morning?" he asked.

"Yes, indeedy," she responded cheerfully, as she hugged him around the knees. "Thank you, thank you, Jake. You are my favorite sailor."

He patted her on the back, and said "And you are my favorite passenger, short stuff," as he headed away from us. I was thanking him profusely as long as I thought he was within earshot.

As I circulated among the troops that night, I knew I would have to go back and see if I could get the Ship's Doctor to dispense something for many of them, as well, because there is something about a ship without roll stabilizers and ground troops that just isn't compatible. It worked even better than I had hoped, because the Doc came down to the hold where the troops were, and walked among them to find out how many were badly afflicted with seasickness. He was very helpful, and during our chats, he wanted to know how I knew so much about pharmacology and medical terminology. I had to laugh, and told him that I had once been a medic. I stopped laughing when he said that if we came under fire, and he needed me, he'd know where to find me. We talked about that for a while, because as far as I knew, we had cleared the sea lanes of enemies, and he countered with the stupidity of the government for cutting the strength of all the forces as fast as they could. I had to agree, because in 1945, as near as I could remember, we had about 8 million soldiers in the Army and Army Air Force, with many of us arriving home to receive our discharge orders. We decided that the force strength of all forces had been cut to about 1/8th or less almost immediately. I didn't say anything about having been demoted from 1LT to enlisted ranks, but also realized that I had a guardian angel someplace that had let me remain on Active Duty. I even retained my officer rank in the Army Reserve, which accompanied my demotion and assignment for Active Duty. Even the Occupation Forces numbers had been significantly reduced, and I was lucky to have an assignment at all. One brother-in-law had gratefully accepted his discharge, and went on to work as a petroleum engineer at Conoco for the rest of his working life. Another was retained, with his rank, and remained in the USAAF for the Korean Conflict, and in the USAF when the branch split away. We weren't having the Korean Conflict when I was on that ship headed for Bremerhaven, but it was clear that with the reduction in forces, there would be another upheaval.

Strength is critically important in world political geography, but our Congress never seems to get the message. The Doc said he was being allowed to stay, because there weren't that many doctors who would even consider it after all the carnage they had seen. I felt my own stomach clench, and that may have been my first flashback. He asked if I had seen much gangrene during the war, and I had answered that I only saw a lot of blood and death from soldiers bleeding out before anyone could get to them to put a tourniquet on a severed limb or staunch a wound. For a moment, I could see some of those beachheads, and he reached out to pat my shoulder, apologizing for bringing back those memories. He did say that there were some things he had discovered for helping soldiers with gangrene, and something about a Navy Diving Chamber, because the bacterium that causes gangrene can't tolerate oxygen. I couldn't take it in, but was glad to hear that there were some cures being worked on.

What Price Honor, Memoir of Eugene Adams

Occupation. I was hoping that the punishment of Germany wouldn't be as brutal as it had been after WWI. I was soon to find out about it from the inside this time. In June of 1945, a conference held with England, the US, Russia, and France resulted in a signed declaration giving them supreme authority in Germany. Germany was divided into four zones in each of which one of those countries held jurisdiction. The US had the central southwestern portion of Germany and part of Austria, and forces were allocated to occupy their quarter, forming an American Military Government to denazify and demilitarize the inhabitants. There was to be no fraternization with the Germans, but no abuse of them, either. And as usual, the Army published a literal ton of new manuals on every aspect of the job ahead. Soldiers just recently released from combat were not ordinarily assigned to the Occupation forces, but in the beginning, it was a difficult transition of the Germans from enemy to subjugated people, some of whom had lost literally everything. It was also a strange transmogrification for the American soldiers assigned this duty. I gave some serious thought to what had been negotiated at the Yalta Conference, shortly after which, FDR had died. Harry S. "Give 'em Hell" Truman was in charge now. By the time I and my family were headed to Germany, Hiroshima and Nagasaki had literally ceased to exist, Japan had surrendered, and things with Soviet Union were becoming uncomfortable. I gave this some serious thought, but had to turn my attention to the troops, who were growing uneasy on that eighth day of the voyage, with a million questions on their minds. They had already been briefed that there would be no fraternization, but some of the young pups didn't really understand what that was and wasn't, so it was my job to inform them. Some were really saddened when I told them that they were not only to leave the Frauleins alone, but they were not to interact with the children except tangentially. I had to agree with the very young troop who didn't understand what on earth was wrong with being nice to youngsters, but rules are rules. This would be an interesting assignment.

Chapter Twenty – Nine – Wounded Warriors

> *Though life goes on for some, for most, some live*
> *with confusion or perhaps a ghost of what*
> *happened back on a distant coast, where it seems*
> *our memories hang on a, ragged, piercing post;*
> *there are things of which we cannot boast.*

    I am growing very weary now, and perhaps I must hasten to complete this tome, which will likely gather thick layers of dust, my archive of a life which had more twists and turns than the trail of the average snake. Although the manpower and some of the confusion of the occupation areas of influence had shrunk before we arrived, the geopolitical landscape was no less torturous. Neither was the home life which became unwieldy. My wife was ill, though I now wonder if it was more spiritual than physical, and my career in the Army now had taken an odd twist. At least, I wasn't cashiered out on the point system that had been developed to effect demobilization. At least friends, other combat veterans, had spoken up for me, and though I served there in Germany as an enlisted man, it was at a senior rank. There was more for me to do. I was allowed to keep my officer rank in the Reserves, but served on Active Duty. I know that my time now is also limited, and I must complete these recollections, because the Army is going through the same tortuous changes that it faced after WWI. It seemed that the government hadn't learned from past mistakes, and the cuts to the military were drastic. Millions of confused warriors returned home, or if they were lucky, to new and different duties in the post-war era. Many families were shattered, perhaps more then than during active combat in a war we had clearly won. In odd moments, I would hum or whistle the old tune "When Johnny Comes Marching Home," and dreams troubled my sleep, but I kept putting one foot in front of another, and watching the political developments unfold.

What Price Honor, Memoir of Eugene Adams

I thought about the Yalta Conference, which one of several conferences the "Big Three" had attended. Yalta is in Crimea, Stalin's turf, and was the last one FDR would attend. At the time, Japan had not surrendered, and it didn't really look like they intended to do so. It took place in early February, 1945, and it was decided then that the Big Three plus France would occupy Germany, but what they didn't tell the world was that in return for Russia to declare war on Japan, which had not surrendered, the Russians would receive the Kurile Islands, southern Sakhalin Island in Korea, and the right to dominate Outer Mongolia and Manchuria. Chiang Kai Sheck was not in attendance at that meeting, or the deal might not have gone through. However, by the 19th of February, the hideously costly attack on Iwo Jima by the US Marines was mounted, costing 20,000 Americans killed or wounded, though they did gain control of some strategically important airfields. The Japanese did not surrender. A few weeks later, a landing was made at Okinawa, within 300 miles of Japan, and although the Japanese resistance was fierce, it was taken by June. The fanaticism of the Japanese warriors was obvious, and another event would change the course of history. FDR died of a massive heart attack in April of 1945, and although Japan was suffering increasing damage, she still had both the blockheaded determination, suicidal airmen, and large numbers of troops, and refused to end the war. Next was the Potsdam Ultimatum, coming from newly sworn in "Give 'em Hell, Harry" Truman, Joseph Stalin, and the new British Prime Minister, Clemet Atlee, who meet in Potsdam, Germany. They demanded an unconditional surrender from Japan, which Japan refused equally unconditionally. That July 29th refusal would unleash a new kind of warfare.

On the morning of August 6th, one lone plane crossed high over and bombed the Japanese city of Hiroshima. It was the first use of an atomic bomb in the history of warfare, and half of the

245 to 250,000 Japanese men, women and children died instantly or shortly thereafter. The decision was made after consulting with top US military advisors, in order to save perhaps a million US military lives, given the recalcitrance of the Japanese. On the 7th of August, Japan still refused to surrender. The next day, Russia declared war on Japan. On the 9th, a second atomic bomb was dropped on Nagasaki, and on the 10th, Japan surrendered, asking for peace. On V-J Day, 14 August, Truman announced to the nation that Japan had accepted the Allied peace terms, and the surrender was signed on 2 September, 1945. The war was officially over. The immense destruction was to haunt the world for many decades, and result in an arms race of enormous magnitude, but that is getting far ahead of the story.

Truman, a WWI veteran, was faced with many postwar problems, and at the very simple swearing in ceremony to assume the Presidency, he had pledged humbly to continue Roosevelt's policies, both domestic and foreign. In demobilization, American military and navy leaders were faced with the problem of stationing thousands of occupation troops in Germany, Italy and Japan, and were quick to warn the President of the danger of hasty demobilization. However, pressure from the American population to bring all the sons, daughters, husbands, brothers, sisters and friends home led to severe and immediate reduction of military might. The air assets shrank from 85,000 air frames to only 9,000; the navy withdrew hundreds of ships from active service, and the Army was reduced from 89 to 12 divisions. I'm not exactly sure of the numbers any more, but these are close. The teeth of the tiger were being pulled from both domestic and economic pressure, and it was indeed dangerous. Even Omar Bradley made a statement about not wreaking havoc on the US economy by trying to maintain a large standing force, which he much later retracted, but it gave credence to an apparent approval by military leaders for slashing the forces. However, some programs put into place, were better than in previous post war eras, for the returning veterans. The program was called the "GI Bill of Rights," and it did help many return and adjust to civilian life. However, for those of us who would have to carry on, it meant a paucity of personnel and resources to accomplish what was left to be done in a world ravaged by the most savage war ever conducted, and the USSR was flexing its muscles.

But demobilization at the end of World War II, according to General George C. Marshall, "It was not demobilization, it was a rout." Bradley later admitted that he had been sadly mistaken, and that the combat effectiveness had been so severe that we couldn't "fight our way out of a paper bag." On top of that, after a brief surge of success, there were labor difficulties, with strikes, and inflationary spikes that nullified the initial good wages enjoyed by returning soldiers, sailors and airmen. That was the status as I took up my new occupation duties in Bremen. American Occupation Forces had also been cut, so we had fewer men to cover larger areas, plus I was often tasked with using my cameras, to include a Bell & Howell movie camera to record some of the atrocities of the war. Much of what I saw and recorded was so horrific that I will not describe it here. And life in my small family, transplanted to this new neighborhood, #5 Elsa Bronstrom Strasse, was not peaceful, either. My wife had taken to her bed, and I will forever be thankful for the second housekeeper I hired, who treated Julie like a daughter, and my children like her own. Her spouse had never returned from the Eastern Front (Russia), and she was a godsend. When I had to go out of town, she and her daughter and son stayed at our house, so I didn't worry about my family. Also, I decided to have my oldest daughter attend the German school instead of the school for Military Dependents, which worked out well because Peter, Wilma's son, told his school mates that I was the twin of his sister, who was in the same grade as Dorothy, who became Dorothea to everyone. I will always believe that the children of a land are the best diplomats we can ever have. Dorothea already spoke German, due to lessons from her maternal grandmother, and did well both at school and at the local Catholic Church, and Peter was a determined protector. Wilma dressed the girls alike, and they rode their bicycles to school, just like everyone else.

    I was to learn that my injuries, which included blindness in my right eye, and a blown kneecap were going to be troublesome, but I did my best to hide them. I didn't want to be cashiered out. I wanted to finish my 20 years. The knee would often swell up enormously, and try as I might to avoid it, I would sometimes limp. The eyesight was easier, because I spent as much time at the firing range to perfect shooting with the eye I had left, and accomplished that easily. The thing that was becoming more debilitating was the repetitive nightmares, where I would be back in battle until I could wrest myself loose from sleep. Back then, there was very little done to treat battle fatigue, and I simply could not risk seeking help, especially since any sleep aid might lock me into those episodes so tightly that I wouldn't be able to escape. And I was worried, because my grandmother was writing to me about what was going on in Post War USA. My two youngest uncles, Clifford and Paul, were doing well with their electroplating business. Paul had been discharged from the USAAF, because with so many fewer planes, they didn't need as many pilots, so Clifford had taken him into the business as a chemist. She was complimentary about Truman, but disappointed that he was having to deal with a Republican Congress, and with unruly labor unions. She was also frightened that the military had been so drastically cut, and wanted some reassurance that my family and I were OK. I didn't tell her about any troubles I had, because it was clear that she had worries of her own. Her ability at governmental analysis hadn't suffered any over the years, and I got more accurate news from her than from any other source. She was particularly concerned over the implementation and effects of the Taft-Hartley Act of 1947, and felt that institution of government control over labor was the beginning of governmental insertion into areas where it should not be. It did reduce the power of unions and prevented them from automatically deducting dues from paychecks of the workers, but the power was now in other hands, and not in the hands of the workers in either case. Other news from home wasn't very reassuring, though, because Julie's father was continuing to go downhill. He actually died while we were in Germany, and since we didn't know in time, I couldn't get her back to the states for his funeral. I don't think she ever forgave me, but there just wasn't any way I could do it within 24 hours of the call we received.

What was going to be known as the Cold War had begun, because the USSR was trying to gain more control over areas that didn't fall exactly into its assigned quadrant. When the occupation was set up, the US had its sector in Germany proper, and a large portion of Austria. As a supervisory body over the occupation, a Control Council was set, and the objective was to insure that ultimately control would be released to the local inhabitants when denazification and demilitarization was complete in each quadrant. There was too little cooperation or communication among the occupiers of the quadrants, which resulted in significant friction, both between the nations in charge, and the natives of each region. Berlin was also divided into four quadrants, which was shortly to be challenged when the Soviets continued to bring satellite nations into its orbit through the spread of Communism. They were also seeking complete dominance over Berlin, the capitol of Germany, as well as absorbing what were later to be called "satellite" countries as it pushed westward. There would be new markers in history, like the Berlin Airlift, and the wall between East and West Germany…Once again peace had clearly not been established, and Truman would do all within his power to contain the spread of the USSR and its acolytes as best he could. But that is another chapter.

Again, there were food shortages in Germany, and that resulted in the rise of a Black Market. No surprise there. People will do what they have to in order to survive, but slowly and surely the industrious German population set about salvaging what could be salvaged of building materials, particularly in the cities, and farmers worked from dawn to late at night to put their fields in order, repair their farm buildings, and nurse the livestock from paucity to proliferation. They were not only industrious, but determined. Again the postwar reparations were severe, and as my grandmother had said after WWI, engendered resentment from the local populations toward the occupiers. At least the terms weren't as harsh, but they were not easy to bear when it was hard to get enough food for their families, and jobs in the cities wouldn't be coming back until the factories were repaired and resupplied with the necessary raw materials. I have to smile at the memory of the Army's creation of the Civil Affairs branch. We all called them "Snivel Affairs," and were convinced that they were there to baffle the people and their military comrades with bullshit. My opinion has not changed, but in certain situation, they are very useful. They did help soothe the interactions of each set of occupiers with the Control agency.

What Price Honor, Memoir of Eugene Adams

Chapter Thirty – The Bug Out War

And from the spindle of Time, which must its schedule keep, and where the earth ran red with blood, there is little time to weep. The rubble must rise to the sky again as new buildings tall and grand, before the another war erupts to knock them down again.

In Eisenhower's determination that the hideous atrocities be recorded of the Nazis against an entire segment of the German population, now known as the holocaust be recorded so that some politically motivated organizations could not later deny it. made my life there in Bremen even more complex. Armed with cameras I went on TDY (Temporary Duty) assignments to some of the camps, where I recorded the gas chambers, their results, and the faces of some of the survivors, which were only shadows of dazed, disheveled, skeletonized human beings. I had to forcefully show no emotion, and isolate my over weaning horror at what my eyes through the lenses were seeing, and what my mind could not completely reconcile. Then I would reflect on those carrion creatures who would take out the gold in people's teeth, their hair, anything of value from those sacrificed inhumanely, then cast the cadavers into mass graves. The stench would sometimes cause me to have to swallow back a retch, but the job had to be done. I was not the only photographer, nor the only one affected by the wretchedness to which inhumanity to man can be inflicted on others. On the journeys I had to take, I would reflect on the fact that Stalin hated the Jews, Christians, and any dissenters he came across, and had camps of forced labor, privation, and decimation also set up in Siberia and elsewhere. That ate away at my mind, because I felt certain that yet another series of events would lead to further global bloodshed. Somehow, I prayed, for God allow containment of the evil so that it would never again gobble up the world with slavering jaws of cruelty and destruction. Selfishly, I prayed that I would never again have to take a life, or see battles take the lives of my soldiers, and that my family would be safe from harm.

The gathering of the data began long before Eisenhower became President and declared openly that such documentation was to be taken. He neglected to mention that much of it had already been gathered, at his direction, before the formalized announcement to the American public. There were other things going on in the background of the late 1940s which would impact the geopolitical environment for decades. One of those was the formalization of a charter for the United Nations, which had begun in January of 1942 at the behest of Churchill and FDR to enhance the cooperation among combatants against the Axis powers. Formalization and a charter including the membership of 29 nations was ratified in October of 1945. The stated purpose was to prevent the occurrence of another cataclysmic war, like the one which had just concluded, at the cost of millions of lives, massive destruction of structures both new and old, and devastation beyond comprehension to the struggle of mankind to move forward instead of backward in its development. I will think more on this subject later in this manuscript.

Back in Bremen, in early 1949, my wife had discovered the Black Market, and I had to forbid her to trade in it, or have any association with it. She complained that she had only traded a few things because, according to her, I didn't make enough money for our family. I wondered why she didn't see that I had been very lucky to even have been able to remain in the Army, which was, after all, a job. She remained disconsolate over what she perceived as a reduction in her social class due to my demotion, as she saw it, from the Officer Corps. She was extremely moody, and remained in the bedroom most of the time, brooding or reading, claiming to be recovering from the birth of our fourth child, whom she would allow to nurse, but showing little interest in the infant. When my mother, who was a nurse, wanted to come visit us in Germany, I thought it might help Julie to have some help with the little ones, although Wilma, our housekeeper, treated her like a daughter and was an excellent care giver to the whole family. Julie flew into a rage, and in her spew of bitter invective, she claimed that she despised my mother, and didn't want her anywhere near her or our children. It hurt, because I loved my mother, but to keep the peace, I told my mother that she could not come. Later, I was to decide that my wife simply didn't want anyone as knowledgeable as my mother to interrupt her ruse of being ill as a result of child bearing, because she could simply refuse to emerge from her emotional cocoon.

In the interim, my little daughter had been saving tobacco from cigarette butts, whenever she got a chance, and when I asked about it, she said that the lady with the flowered scarf had told her that if she got enough, she could get a bicycle like Peter's. Signal lights flashed and I realized that my little girl was getting ready to trade on the Black Market, and that could not be permitted. After I explained things to her, she looked at me with great, wounded eyes, and apologized. The next day, I bought her a new bicycle, and told her that the price she would have to pay was to never talk to the lady with the headscarf, and never trade anything with anyone while we were in Germany. The next day, she asked me if it was OK if she and Peter continued their toy repair business. I didn't know what she was talking about, and she explained that they would repair other children's toys for a few pfenigs or a candy in trade. A few days later, I got a picture of Peter sitting up on a post next to where my daughter, screwdriver in hand, was working on a toy truck. I had to laugh, and decided that it wasn't the Black Market, it was the kid market, and the two of them had a thriving business. They would save the coins and then go buy some little trinket they wanted, or a treat at the candy shop, so I allowed it. She complained to me one day that she didn't know how to fix cameras, and handed me one that had been brought to them. It was a little box camera, and she and Peter listened in fascination as I explained to them how it worked. The only thing wrong with it was that the little mechanism to open and shut the shutter was badly stuck, and I fixed it. She and Peter discussed in German what the customer should be charged, but they decided that since they didn't actually fix it, they should tell the youngster to pay me. I declined a fee, and they were happily off to return the camera.

There were some pleasant memories from Bremen, but I had begun to wonder if my marriage would ultimately survive WWII. I loved my wife, and still do, at the time of this writing, but there was always a distance between us after that tour of duty. It ended with my transfer back to the US, where she pressured me to get out of the Army and buy us a farm, or join with my uncle in the plating business. I finally "mustered out" of the Active Army, but stayed in the Reserves and began looking for a job. They were not plentiful for returning veterans, but I did have skills. That period of time was worse in many ways than the service in the Occupation Forces. I got a job as a machinist, but that was not satisfactory to her. She wanted me to practice law, and correctly and repeatedly reminded me that I had passed the Bar Exam in Illinois, but when we went to Chicago, where I functioned briefly as an Assistant DA, she was not happy with that. She hated the "dirty" buildings, and the "rude" people, but I think she was mostly homesick. We weren't there long, though my grandmother had hoped that we would stay, because it was closer to her in Indiana. She tried to get Julie, who had a degree with a dual major in chemistry and mathematics, to consider working with General Plating Corporation, which my two uncles had built into a thriving concern. Julie did nothing but criticize the techniques being used, the payments made to Clifford's wife for bookkeeping and contracting, and it became clear that there was not going to be any way that we would be able to join that effort. We had left the children in Texas with their maternal grandmother while we were searching for our next home, and Julie landed a job with a chemical company in Indiana. She then took off in the car, went to Texas, and brought our second daughter, Mary Jane, back with her, leaving the other three with her mother. Her rationalization was that Janie, as we called her, looked just like me, and was the only one of the children for which I was present at the birth. It didn't seem reasonable to me, and shortly thereafter, since she was going to work, Julie got my mother, who was retired, to agree to look after Janie during the day...Things started to go downhill even faster after that.

    Perhaps it would be best to go back to thinking about the UN for a while, for the sadness of those years, up to and following the Korean Conflict sometimes is so profound that I sometimes lose the will to live. But I know well that I must go on, for I had already committed a mortal sin, and didn't think that second one would in any way make things better when I stood before the Judgement Seat. So, my original thoughts on the UN as a peacetime organization were very altruistic at first. My grandmother disagreed, but it began a series of very interesting discussions with her. Initially, I looked upon the UN as a potential panacea of cooperation which would benefit all mankind and eliminate the chance of another war. I tried to reconcile the removal of competing powers and universal establishment of virtual equality in education, health, nutrition, and opportunity to all children born into the world. It could release an inestimable burst of human capacity and prosperity in the absence of competing sovereignties, with common social justice for all. There would be no need to change human quality, but just a freedom from the national shackles which perpetuate an inordinate waste of human thought and development. Talented and gifted people too often have worked against tremendous discouragement, lack of funds, and little support from the mass of human kind. The intellectual harvest of each generation in all fields of endeavor in such an environment would be greater than that of the past four or five centuries combined. Then I realized I was just dreaming. Although the concept of one world order with universal law and justice would, indeed, spur on human adventure to maximize our existence on earth, I realized that in my peregrinations, I had left out greed, jealousy, and avariciousness for power, are at least equal in the human spirit with the altruism, generosity and kindness that resides there, too. My grandmother was to remind me of the impracticality of my dreams, as well.

I watched the ineffectiveness of the UN, and of mankind's desire for peace and tranquility, erode as the world again heated up, this time in Korea. It wasn't called a war. It was simply called a conflict, and arose out of dissatisfaction over the division of Korea following WWII. By June of 1950, North Korea had begun invasion of South Korea, and I waited anxiously for orders calling me back to Active Duty. I had no idea how difficult that would be, both for my home life, or for my conscience. I am a warrior, and did not want be derelict in my duty to my nation in time of crisis. I did get orders, both from the Army and from my wife. I reported in, and as an activated Reservist, I was to receive my officer rank back, but I realized that I also might be single shortly thereafter. The question was resolved when I could not pass the physical examination, because this time, I made no effort to hide the disabilities I had suffered from WWII. Actually, it wasn't possible to hide the shattered, poorly repaired knee cap or the blindness in one eye. What happened was that I was put into the hospital, and the remainder of the shattered knee cap, plus the wiring that had been placed there to hold it together was removed. It was remarkable that the swelling, which had been quite significant as well as perpetual, and the pain were vastly reduced, but so were my chances to go back onto active duty. They forgot about the eye, and started on the paperwork to put me on the disabled list, for which I would receive some compensation, but would not be allowed to serve. I felt like I had received a gut punch, because I had heard from some of my soldiers, who were looking forward to my presence in uniform, and/or in battle. I watched my brother in law, Scott Patterson, go off to serve. He was a navigator/bombardier, and would serve for the whole Korean campaign, and later retire from the USAF. I was jealous, but tried not to show it. My feelings of guilt about my inability to be there for my nation were somewhat assuaged by the fact that my wife was no longer threatening to divorce me, because she had said that she would if I went to war.

What Price Honor, Memoir of Eugene Adams

Ever May, my wife's aunt, understood my sorrow, my anguish. She had remained in the service after the end of WWII, and would move to the USAF when it became a separate entity. She actually came to see me, having taken a short leave to do so. She understood my state of mind, and did a pretty good job of soothing me, and giving me hope that things would get better, and if "push came to shove," and they really needed combat vets, I might eventually be called back up. But she encouraged me to both encourage those who would be going forward from my reserve unit, and try to be a resource for those who would be in battle for the first time in their lives. In other words, I could serve by being the "old man" who knew things, and I would be in the right place at the right time. She would go on to retire after 20 years, and Scott would retire from the USAF after a distinguished career, too. But she knew that I needed at that critical time something to bolster my sense of self-worth when the Fates seemed to be determined to cast me out like last week's garbage. My Dorothea, who now that we were in the United States had to be called "Dorothy Ann," comforted me, too, just by still following at my heels, and helping with any home project I was working on. She even learned to whistle and sing with me, and I started to pose some legal questions to her, which she would try to answer. Then, she would read the sections in the law books I still had, and gave pretty good analysis of where her answer to the questions had been right or wrong, in accordance with existing law. I started to call her "DA" and kidded her about becoming a District Attorney. My grandmother also kept up her letters, and her support, even from a distance and Mrs. LaGrone would engage me in lively conversations about what was going on both politically and in the evolving of the war which was only designated as a conflict. Another 2.5 million lives would be lost in that conflict, and the world couldn't afford that sacrifice, but Truman was keeping the spread of communism contained and avoiding the entrance of China into the conflict by limiting the crossing of a particular geographic line. We all agreed that crossing of the Yalu River would catapult the conflict into a full blown war. Korea was then divided, and is still, into North and South Korea. It was the first war the United States did not win, and escape through the ports to the south wasn't a victory. It was a retreat that would continue to fester over time.

My life was emotionally on a downward spiral, and eventually the divorce would come in any case. The dreams of the past still came, and the shame of not being able to push past that did not abate. I withdrew in many ways, though God was not yet ready for me to leave this world. I would see two of my children later involved in another conflict that we would not win, but one good thing happened at the end of the Korean Conflict. When Eisenhower was elected to the Presidency, he stopped the invasion by illegal aliens over our borders, and deported about eight to ten million of them, so that jobs would be available for returning veterans. Security at the borders was increased. He may have played some golf, but he was definitely on the job for Americans, and that was a very good thing. I had been critical of him during WWII, but came to understand some of the obstacles he was up against during that time, and I was fearful of the spread of Communism in Eurasia. The world was still at what I thought of as an uneasy peace.

Chapter Thirty – One – Dire Predictions

Though my feet will not touch another foreign shore, I shall be a warrior forevermore. There are things a man can always do, but to himself he must always stay true.

I read voraciously about the new conflict, and did my best to encourage all my fellow warriors in their trials either at home or abroad. I also saw familiar names among the leadership in what became a containment instead of a victory. One of my favorite quotations to come out of that ill-conceived operation came from one of my least favorite generals, Douglas Mac Arthur:

> *"We win here or lose everywhere; if we win here, we improve the chances of winning everywhere."*

He was busy quarreling with the President over the boundaries of that war, and I have always thought that he was more concerned with his political aspirations that with trying to understand the importance of not dragging China or the USSR into the war in support of the North Koreans. It is my understanding that the final outcome of the Korean Conflict has never been completely settled, and it will erupt again. My prediction is that the next World War will erupt when the North Koreans rise up, start a war, and the dominoes will fall quickly to involve the Middle East. I pray that I am wrong, but I was not wrong in my prediction about the fall of the wall in Germany and the end of the Cold War. That prediction was accurate right down to the year in which the event would occur.

Another of my favorite quotations from the Korean Conflict was from General Matthew Ridgeway, instructions to his troops, Korean War, 1950:

> *"Your job is to point that rifle into the other guy's face and shoot him dead."*

He embodied my concept of a true military leader, and will always be a tough act to follow by any subsequent commanding general. I couldn't find any recorded words he had to say after our troops were pushed down to the Pusan Corridor and scooped up to avoid their annihilation. I'm sure it wasn't in language for the more genteel of the general public, but perfectly accurate in its analysis. He was aware of the terrible, post war demilitarization, but was still expected to win in battle with diminished numbers, and a ROK (Republic of Korea) force understrength, poorly equipped, and poorly trained, against a North Korean army backed and equipped by the Soviets. The division of Korea at Yalta in 1945 had the Americans oblivious to the possibility that the North Korean Army would attack, but the undercurrent to me simply indicated that if the ROK could not hold them back, Korea would fall. In 1949, American troops had been almost completely withdrawn from the ROK, and the South Koreans weren't paying much attention, either, to the dire circumstances in which they were militarily.

The military status of the United States in June of 1950, due to the massive dismantling of the most powerful military in the world, was probably equivalent to the status in 1941, as WWII erupted. It seems to be a predominant repetitive pattern with the US, and is deadly. Between 1945 and 1950, the Americans didn't grasp the concept that the USSR considered the recent global war and subsequent peace as merely a pause in the ultimate conquest of the world into worldwide Socialism. A Soviet-style Democratic People's Republic had been installed in North Korea, and the Russian newspaper *Izvestia* published a manifesto in Pyongyang on 7 June, declaring war on South Korea. Atlee, the American Secretary of State, was evidently unaware of this, or that a joint election was to be held in Seoul in August between North and South Korea. So, when the elected leader of the South, Syngman Rhee, rejected this proposal, on June 10th, the North Korean Army began to move. All that was left of the American presence was a small advisory group under a BG Roberts, who had been assuring the UN that though there had been frequent incidents along the 38th parallel, the ROK had been capable of handling them. So on the 25th of June, during a heavy downpour, the North Korean Army crossed the border, where they had been building up force for at least two months. They went with air cover, and their mortars broke loose in the Onjin Peninsula on the west coast above Seoul, with the infantry moving swiftly behind them. The North Koreans had 89,000 combat troops and 150 T-34 tanks, mortars, support weaponry and logistics. The South Koreans had virtually nothing, and only 50,000 combat troops who actually had any weapons at all. They had a few Howitzers, not all of which were functional, and their small number of antitank guns were virtually useless. In short, the ROK didn't stand a chance. On that first day, they lost an entire battalion, which was ¼ of their strength, as the North Koreans came down, firing and moving rapidly down the Oijongbu corridor with infantry, tanks and artillery.

My grandmother wrote frequently, asking what I thought, and encouraging my efforts with the Reservists. She clearly drew the parallels between 1941 and 1950, and was not at all surprised when the North Koreans began their drive south. I have often thought that she would have been an outstanding Secretary of State, or perhaps a very astute military chief of staff. Mostly, she was a very insightful American citizen, who kept track of world political geography throughout her life. She wasn't well educated, but well-read and gifted in her perspective on the rise, fall, and interactions among nation states, and human beings in general. Mrs. LaGrone was equally astute, and was well educated, so her input was always welcome, too. They had both lived productive lives, seen many things, and understood many more through the prism of their avid pursuit of knowledge about world events. Neither of them was in favor of the UN, which they both thought of as similar to the failed League of Nations. I heard from them both on the subject of Korea, and the containment of the Soviet Union. It has always puzzled me how two aging women could be so wise about events so distant from their daily existence, but they both emphasized that Fate is fickle, and politics is worse. Both saw the rising conflict as just another saber rattling obsession for dominance, on one hand for global socialism (communism), and on the other for survival of nation states. Both admired Harry Truman, and understood what he was trying to do in order to contain the cancerous metastasis of socialism throughout the world, which they viewed as another kind of slavery for the common man, and woman.

There had been a debate in the US over Rhee's request for support, both financially, militarily, and logistically, where Congress and others believed that if Rhee could raise a large army, he would start WWIII. It is surprising that Clement Atlee, who was an avid supporter of preventing the spread of communism, didn't understand that a strong ROK would be a deterrent for that very eventuality. Rhee didn't understand that many of his senior officers were not well disciplined, and at the time of the attack by the North, were not at their posts, but on leave. One leader, however, had denied leaves, was on duty, and was concerned over the border build up by the North Koreans, and the danger it posed. While there was inadequate resistance along the corridor to Seoul, he was successful in defending his mountainous position to the east near the 38th parallel, preventing the North Koreans to advance down that corridor. Two regiments of North Koreans attacked. Their tanks were useless in that terrain, and the ROK forces were well positioned to put up a stout resistance and halt that advance. This was the first time the North Koreans had met any significant resistance. They then sent an armed steamer with 600 troops south to attack Pusan, but the ROK had one modern navy patrol boat, which challenged and attacked the steamer, sinking it with all on board lost. That saved the port of Pusan, which was the only portal for supplies and reinforcements for the South Koreans. Though their assets were limited, the only branch of the South Korean military which held a slight advantage over the North Koreans was the navy, and it was by a single thread that this most important naval action for the South Koreans was successful.

While this one disastrous week wore on, the US Advisory Group and the ROK leadership were busy putting together a plan to withdraw troops to the south toward Pusan. Eventually, what was called the Pusan Perimeter would be formed. There was little intelligence information, and very little understanding of the vast difference in the materiel or manpower deficits of the ROK. They had no fighter planes, and essentially no Air Force, no tanks, no antitank capability, no adequate artillery, poor training, but they did have the will to defend their country. During the first attack to the west, they even adapted some of the Japanese kamikaze spirit, throwing themselves under the tracks of the tanks, or trying to shoot into the tanks by climbing up on them, and being killed doing so. It was increasingly clear that the US, who was responsible for the security of the ROK must take action or see it gobbled up by the militarily superior North Korean aggressors. Given the degree of US disarmament under an austerity program, that would prove to be difficult. By 1949, the Army was reduced to ten active divisions and eleven separate regiments, which was a reduction by 79 divisions in four years. At the outbreak of the Korean War, four of the infantry divisions under 8th Army were assigned to occupation duty in Japan, two infantry divisions and two infantry regiments were the European force, and one regiment was station in Hawaii, one in Okinawa, and one in the Caribbean. The remainder were in the United States. On paper, the Army maintained its ten division authorized structure, but all of these divisions were understrength, and a reduction of one battalion per division was made, as well as one of three firing batteries in each of the four divisional artillery battalions. Cuts were made in support units, and the result was massively decreased combat effectiveness. The same type of cuts were made in the Marines, and the Navy was hit even more severely and scattered over the world more widely. The USAF, which had broken away from the Army went its own way, and being jealous of its new found identity, tried to distance itself from the other branches, but suffered shortages in air frames and materiel, and qualified personnel. Worse than that, the US upper echelons were confused about our role.

Dorothy A Adams

Douglas MacArthur was summoned by President Truman to take command of the situation, and luckily, the Soviet Union had been absent on the day a vote was held at the UN to participate in stopping the invasion of the ROK by the North Koreans. The UN approved participation to protect any nation threatened by aggression, which pertained to the ROK. By the time MacArthur arrived in Korea, the North Koreans had taken Seoul, the ROK capital, and as the commander of operations in Korea, he ordered immediate deployment of both US and UN troops to the region. Within a few days, US and UN troops had retaken Seoul, and pushed the North Koreans back to the 38th parallel, but Truman didn't want any further advance that might encourage the Chinese to enter the conflict on the side of the North Koreans. A disagreement between the President and MacArthur erupted, but clearly when the Chinese under Mao sent about 100,000 combat troops to the aid of North Korea, what the President had hoped to avoid became reality. Mac Arthur countered by demanding nuclear bombing of Chinese cities, blockade of their ports and extension of that threat to the Chinese government sufficient to make them cease and desist support of the North Koreans. Truman accurately assessed the possibility that such action might well escalate the war from a limited action to a global one, and his strategy was to conduct a limited war of containment and prevention of the spread of communism. The Soviets were experimenting with their own nuclear capability, had a standing army and military, and might be drawn into the war in support of the Chinese, which would be a global conflagration in the end. Unfortunately, Seoul was retaken by the North Koreans with their Chinese support, and the ROK, which had lost half of its fighting capability within the first weeks of the conflict, the US, UN, and allied forces were pushed ever southward. The battles were bloody, and the losses were mounting up, as was the conflict between the US President and his commander in the field.

Mac Arthur believed that his recommendations on winning the conflict, which were tactically sound in many respects, would stop the blood-letting, so he began to issue press releases without consulting the President. The conflict between the two of them grew to a fever pitch, and resulted in President Truman having to fire MacArthur, and replace him with someone who could understand the overall strategy of avoiding WWIII. Mrs. LaGrone was fairly vocal about the fact that the President is the Commander in Chief under the Constitution, and a graduate of West Point, a Medal of Honor winner, and career officer should obey his chain of command. She personally sent me a copy of von Clausewitz's classic book *On War* as an exclamation point for her statement. And it also was more logical to avoid another World War, and it was insubordinate of MacArthur to send out his press releases in American media, which were clearly diametrically opposed to the President's directives. At that time, in particular, the US was in no state of combat readiness or economic security to conduct another all-out war due to the tremendous cuts to the military, massive decentralization of our military power over the globe, in conjunction with economic downturns. The status made me even more miserable that I could not be on the ground with my troops, and that the youngsters we were sending into that fray were ill trained and not combat experienced. The Congress had cut basic training from 14 to 8 weeks, to save money, there were cuts to procurement of weapons and research on new weapons, because Congress was relying on utilization of assets left over from WWII instead of preparing for any future conflict. The War College had been shut down for several years (1945-1950) as an economic measure. Although the War College was reopened in 1950, because the barn door is usually closed after the horses have escaped, the new graduates generally had no combat experience. In other words, we were in a state of gross unreadiness, and even the officer corps was limited in combat knowledge and readiness, which limited their life expectancy in the field, as well as that of their soldiers. We didn't learn after WWI, WWII, and were embarking on the shores of the Korean peninsula to learn the lesson once more the hard way, in what became known as Task Force Smith. This was a small force arriving prior to the main contingent, under the command of a Colonel Smith.

Prior to the arrival of the Task Force, two battalions had been pieced together from the remnants of the ROK army, but were only barely capable of slowing the continued advance of the North Koreans, so MacArthur had gotten permission to utilize some existing assets from the US advisory force. This was granted, and by 30 June, the President had ordered naval blockade of North Korea. The British also provided forces, both naval and ground assets, to MacArthur's command. The war was on, even though the extent of it hadn't yet been realized. It is still, to this day, referred to as a "conflict" and not a war, but the "Cold War" had also begun. The "conflict" would last another three years, and the division of Korea into North and South Korea would remain an indefinite, uneasy situation until this very day. Prior to the arrival of Task Force Smith, BG Church, who had been originally sent over from Japan by MacArthur for an on ground assessment of the situation, became a commanding officer of the advisory force. Evacuation of Americans civilians from South Korea was going on, both by sea in troop ships, augmented by one Norwegian vessel, and by air in C-54s escorted by small contingent of F-80 or F-84 fighters. The fighters were initially instructed not to engage the North Korean Yaks unless fired upon. What Church found was a completely inadequate ROK army with very poor equipment and materiel support, and troops that were absolutely terrified of tanks, of which they had none of their own, and virtually no materiel support. At one point, failing to recognize them as friendlies, the US troops fired upon them, inflicting many casualties and destroying many of their vehicles. MacArthur then ordered that all ROK vehicles be marked with the US white star to avoid future disasters. Also, the US mortar rounds, even when they hit the North Korean T-34 tanks, would bounce off without doing significant damage. The only thing that seemed to even minimally work was firing Bazookas at the rear end of the tanks, which required troops to be within close range of the tanks, which were carrying infantry all over the tops of them. The North Koreans kept moving south, and the ROK and US/UN forces kept retreating southward. Finally, the US began to understand the magnitude of the undertaking, and Lieutenant General Dean was made the commander of forces in Korea. I was surprised by that choice, but hopeful that the carnage could be lessened, minimized, and stopped before our troops suffered ignominious defeat, for the first time in the history of the United States of America.

Dorothy A Adams

Chapter Thirty – Two – The War we Never Won

When going into a distant battle, it is best to have something to rattle, and above the armament, the dedication and temperament of those you seek to fight beside or face, in an alien, far-flung foreign place.

In July 1950, it looked like the American troops might be completely ejected from Korea, which had far reaching and severely deleterious consequences, weakening American alliances and strengthening proliferation of both Soviet and Chinese influence around the world. America would be completely discredited in belief in her military capability as well as worldwide foreign policy status. US leadership status in the UN would be destroyed. In early July, Generals Collins and Vandenberg, Chief of Staff of the AF, representing the Joint Chiefs of Staff, met with Gen MacArthur in Tokyo for an assessment of the status in Korea. The Joint Intelligence Committee energetically waved the possibility that the US troops would be pushed out of Korea as the North Koreans overran Pusan within the next two weeks. Though the Joint Chiefs had had horrific predictions waved in their faces before, this was nightmarish. It was truly unfortunate that the intelligence community had simply provided intel on a less threatening situation prior to engagement in what seemed only a small blip on the screen, requiring limited support of the US assets which were primarily for occupation in Korea. The capability, strength, armament and readiness of the ROK forces had been vastly overestimated, and restrictions on the occupation/advisory forces to enter into direct conflict had slowed the reaction time too greatly. When enemies perceive weakness and chaos, they will naturally intensify their efforts. Though MacArthur seemed calm during the meeting, he was adamant that he need immediate reinforcements, and he had already relaxed the combat restrictions on the occupation (advisory) forces. The question was what were the military and logistics requirements necessary if the US was to stay in Korea to fight the interlopers, and MacArthur specified that the North Koreans would have to be driven all the way back up and across the 38th parallel. To put it mildly, the Joint Chiefs were not pleased with that answer, but as one old side railed combat troop named Adams (me) said, it was what it was.

    In answer to the resistance from the Joint Chiefs, I learned from a grizzly old fellow veteran that MacArthur proposed a thought problem to them, on the spot. He was not angry. He was just going to force them to think clearly on the problem at hand. He asked them that if they lived in a city divided into four quadrants, and the first quadrant had excellent fire-fighting capability, two others had adequate capabilities under normal circumstances, but the fourth had almost nothing. If the #4 quadrant were to catch on fire, and be virtually engulfed, would you fail to bring the assets and manpower from the first one first, and the other two if needed, to quench the fire? Or would you simply let it burn until it had consumed the entire city? My informant had been a CSM, quietly sitting through the meeting, but he said that even he, without all the education, knowledge and rank, instantly knew what the answer had to be. Clearly if they let Korea go, the rest of the world would fall with it, and the analogy wasn't lost on them. MacArthur went on to tell the Joint Chiefs what his estimates were, and if honored, he could not only drive the North Koreans to the 38th parallel, but all the way to their northern border, whereupon all Korea could be occupied. Geopolitically, I understood why that was not entirely a good idea, but certainly to drive them to and across the 38th parallel was both a worthwhile and essential goal for overall world peace. But with specific stipulations, the wise old CSM agreed. Evidently, so would President Truman, but a very specific directive would come later. The immediate necessity had to be met, and quickly. The generals pledged their support, immediately went to meet with both General Walker and General Dean and recognizing the immediate need, they quickly took action to meet it.

In the heat of the moment, the Joint Chiefs hadn't analyzed exactly what MacArthur really had in mind, which was to eradicate the Soviet interest and government in North Korea in order to unify Korea as the Republic of Korea, then occupy it. That would have made Syngman Rhee's dream come true, but potentially igniting WWIII, but the Joint Chiefs were busy trying to make order out of chaos which had plagued the US military following WWII due to unrelenting cuts to it in all branches. They quickly ripped half of the soldiers from the reserve forces, and put them on short fuse orders for Korea. The 82nd Airborne and 3rd Cav were left intact, as were a few smaller, operationally essential units, but the need to rapidly increase the manpower in the Army was met for the moment. It required a Presidential Order, and Truman issued it. Elements of the National Guard were also called in. Congress cooperated. By the 22nd day after North Korea had invaded the ROK, the readily apparent disorganization and chaotic disarray of the American forces was history, and it was more of a deterrent for other ambitions from the USSR or China to further increase their direct intervention. From 10-12 July, an entire US Regiment moved in, with three battalions, followed by the 35th Infantry. On the 9th, Gen Walker had established 8th Army HQ at Taegu. The North Koreans could not have been oblivious to the change in the nature of warfare, their advance on the ground was slow, and air cover plus naval support for the Americans further impeded it. I watched and still harbored a hope that I would be recalled to Active Duty, because I could clearly see this would not be the last step in the conflict. I intensified my training of the green troops assigned to my unit, aided and assisted by other vets, principally NCOs. We were determined to do all within our power to make sure that as many as possible would survive in battle and come home to their families. Unfortunately, a green troop is a green troop, and this included the young officers, who as company commanders, were unprepared for the intense and immediate requirements of combat. This was to be exacerbated by the fact that the weapons these troops would have on hand were left over from WWII, and had been rusting in both the former Pacific area of operation and in the US. The worst shortfall was in the deterioration of the communication equipment, which had likewise been languishing, and in widely disseparate locations. Immediate deployment of a Regiment was made, so by 10 July there were 18,000 US troops present in Korea, equipped largely with old M-1s which were often both old and useless, and supply lines which had not been completely established. I'm told that one LT used an old Springfield to hold off the enemy as his unit was being overrun near the Kum River, so his men could retreat with fewer casualties. There were approximately 55,000 ROK troops, but they also suffered from the lack of weaponry, ammunition, and training, especially against the Soviet provided T-34 tanks and the air assets of North Korea. In the US, there was rapid movement to modify the old tanks from WWII with better, newer guns, upgrade mortars and artillery, and prepare to stay and fight. However, time was short and many would die as the North Koreans continued their southward assault. I felt a frustration that cut at the very fabric of my soul, because though I had tried very hard to prepare all the young troops with whom I had contact for combat, I knew that those of us who were already seasoned in that environment should be there beside them as they went into that hell called war.

The immediate US mobilization for the threat was impressive, and what the North Koreans and their allies had perceived as an insurmountable chaos in the US, much as the Japanese had miss assessed it in 1941, soon became a coherent, orderly organization for war. However, on the ground there were ignominious shortfalls. By the 13th of July, it was apparent that reinforcement with troops, armament, materiel, communications assets, and air support were absolutely immediately essential, but it was not yet to come. General Dean, reeling from the loss of the entire 63rd Field Artillery ordered an airstrike for the next morning, which though effective, was insufficient. He stayed in Taejon at his provisional Division HQ because of the pathetically poor communication assets. Loss of the infantry positions along the Kum River and destruction of the 63rd Field Artillery was largely a result of the lack of communication. Gen Dean was faced with having to do his best to defend the Pusan Perimeter with inadequate forces. He pieced together what he had left, and put any remaining artillery on the Taejon Air Strip to defend it. In the middle of the mix, Gen Walker came in, took over, and didn't tell Gen Dean what his plans were. Evidently, face to face communication isn't always good, either, even with generals. Gen Walker wanted Dean to hold in Taejon for at least two days, because reinforcements had arrived, and that was the amount of time needed to move them up. The North Koreans, in the meantime, were flanking and surrounding the remaining defensive forces, and with uncanny efficiency. Later in life, I was to receive confirmation of my suspicion that there were multiple betrayals by the South Koreans, aiding the North, which was highlighted in the fate of General Dean. Finally, after holding out as long as they could, they were given permission by Gen Walker to withdraw to the south, but the extent of envelopment by the North Koreans was not understood. The withdrawal was another bloodbath, and Gen Dean, who had gone to get water for the many wounded along that ordeal, had been severely injured, and then was betrayed by a couple of South Koreans, who handed him over to the North Koreans. He was shot. Taejon had fallen, and so had a brave and capable general.

    The Theater had quite a multiplicity of things occurring simultaneously. To the east, the ROK, with support from American and British ships along the coastal road, were fighting hard, but steadily retreating southward. Battle was going on at

Yongdok, which to Gen Walker's chagrin was ultimately lost. In the midst of the furor, the 1st Cav needed to disembark to reinforce the fighting force, but the port of Pusan was vastly overworked, therefore, the port of Pohang had to be taken from the North Koreans to relieve the pressure. The Cav successfully executed the first amphibious landing and took Pohang. By that time, there were nearly 40,000 US troops on the ground in Korea. However, the situation was more than tenuous and deteriorating steadily. Espionage was suspected to have risen significantly. One option might have been to withdraw US forces completely until the total force strength was large enough to accomplish re-entry through a beachhead. But given MacArthur's previous experience with that scenario in the Philippines, he was unwilling to consider it. Continued effort was mounted at great battle loss to both sides, but it was maintained by the US and ROK to hold back the North Koreans to a virtual crawl. In the NK camp, there was extreme dissatisfaction, because their initial battle plan had been essentially destroyed and their advance significantly slowed. They had not anticipated that the US presence would quickly expand from a handful of advisors to a credible American force, fighting hard for the ROK. Espionage and lack of sufficient trained and armed ROK soldiers had hampered the US, but it had not stopped them. Though the NK learned of fighting positions, logistic lines, and locations where ROK and US air cover might strike, another very important thing was a better understanding of the determination of the defenders of South Korea. Eventually Yongdok was retaken by the US and ROK, but at the loss to the NK of approximately ½ of a division (roughly 10,000 troops). There was a reshuffling of the senior NK military leadership by Kim Il-Sung because the victory had not been stupendous or rapid.

I found it fascinating that the news media treated Gen Walker much like they had treated Gen Clark in WWII, so I tended to take criticisms of him with more of a grain of salt than I might otherwise have. Also, the media treatment of MacArthur was absolutely glowing, and it raised my hackles, remembering Corrigidor and seeing some of the unauthorized press releases he was giving out to the public about how well things were going. I knew from the soldiers I visited in the hospitals, whenever I had a chance, that many of the press releases would have vied with the internal gas pressure of the Hindenburg, because it was often composed of hot air. Additionally, my grandmother was of the opinion that he (MacArthur) was actually preparing for a run for the Presidency of the United States at the next election cycle, and that most of his antics were simply to promote that political ambition. It was obvious to me, though, that he simply didn't really respect President Truman as the Commander in Chief, and there were some very real issues with that. The chain of command is the chain of command, and obedience to it can sometimes be difficult, but it is obligatory, and even includes generals. The presence of the Cav made a big difference, as did the addition of US tanks, mortars, and artillery, but the NK still steadily pushed southward. Details were sparse, but Gen Walker must have been at the end of his tether. From what I could gather from my reliable sources, returning wounded soldiers, there was one successful battle where the NK lost both tanks and troops at a rate of 10-1 near someplace called Hwanggan, and had to pull back, but that didn't last. The NK hierarchy knew perfectly well that they dared not retreat very far, or suffer the consequences from their own leadership. And MacArthur visited Walker and told him he had to hold the 8th Army HQ in situ, and there would be no further retreat. Walker had asked to move the HQ to Pusan. A great deal more blood would be shed. The 27th Infantry kept being mentioned by my contacts, and it was definitely taking a beating on a daily basis. By the 30th of July 1950, reinforcement by Marines was a couple of days away, and the situation was so urgent that Gen Walker knew full well that there was no further room to prevent driving the American forces first into Pusan and then into the sea. He put out a very strong, inspiring message to his downtrace. In some places, his words fell upon deaf or disbelieving ears and resulted in resentment. At this point, I stopped really tracking the action, because it was too depressing, and I grew resentful of MacArthur's constant releases claiming great success in the American efforts. The body bags were an enormous monument to the deceit. Those captured or MIA were not even counted in that blood soaked massive destruction of the 2nd Div, to which the 27th belonged. The soldiers of the ROK were fleeing and disappearing into the countryside, often leaving behind the equipment and supplies they had been given by the US. It was later to be cited as one of the great operations of the Korean Conflict, but it would not be joined by many more.

The GIs, as GIs will, nicknamed the Korean Conflict the "bug out" war, and it was a pretty apt description. It would be the first war in the history of our nation that we actually lost, and the soldiers weren't fooled by phrases like "temporary withdrawal to regroup," or "readjustment of the lines." It became harder and harder for me to track it, because newspaper accounts were misleading at best, and some of the returning injured soldiers were even confused about what had happened in their own area of operation. The Marines, when they landed, were better equipped and better trained than the units transferred over from Japan, or the war weary remnants on the ground. I essentially stopped cataloguing the action when the locations were referred to as various Hills which had to be either defended or taken like 125, 303, 284, and so on. At Hill 284, there was a victory of UN and US forces, where they had to destroy a village, and in that village stockpiles of US ammo and weapons were found, which sent a message. If the NK forces were taking and prizing these supplies, it told a tale about the status of their logistics, which was very important to the US forces. The ultimate effect was to invigorate our leadership, but it wouldn't be the last battle, and it was only

September of 1950. Taegu and Naktong held, so the Pusan Perimeter was still in place, but the state of unpreparedness of the US military to enter into a major conflict was apparent. Some blamed President Truman, but the true culprits were in Congress, because the old habit of constantly disassembling and underfunding the military had struck again, as it would in the future at any post-war point. The Pusan Perimeter held, but there would be more fighting, and an Armistice would finally be negotiated beginning on July 10, 1951, as the war continued. A new demarcation line was established for the exchange of prisoners, but nothing truly occurred until after Stalin died. The Soviet Union participated in setting the conditions of the armistice, and although Syngman Rhee opposed the conditions of the armistice and the continuation of the division of Korea, an agreement was reached in July of 1953. He finally agreed to abide by it, and it allowed both the establishment of a Demilitarized Zone bisected by the 38th parallel in places, and a formal cease fire was agreed upon. The "peace" there will be forever very tenuous, and in my considered opinion, will be the flash point for WWIII. The spark will ignite a flame that will spread, like dominoes falling, all the way into the Middle East, another uneasy place.

I have grown weary in the preparation of this recapitulation of the history of the military in times of conflict, and am watching the unfolding of yet another episode. This time, it is involving two of my children in a place called Viet Nam, where the footprint of the United States should never have been set among the rice paddies, villages, or elements of civil unrest. This is another sink hole the politicians have designed to suck us into further loss of life resulting from economic termites eating the timbers that hold the edifices, ships, and air assets together to make a credible force on the world stage. Will my nation, whose flag I hold dearer than life, ever learn? Perhaps not in my lifetime. This old soldier will rest now, but in this tome, perhaps some have understood what the price of honor exacts from those of us who serve Lady Liberty, to the last breath we draw, to the last drop of blood we can shed. Honor is what lies at the very source of the human soul, given by the Living God.

Made in the USA
Columbia, SC
22 July 2022